Releasing Children
to Literature

A TEACHER'S GUIDE TO YEARLING BOOKS

Releasing Children to Literature

BY

CHARLES F. REASONER

Associate Professor, New York University

A YEARLING BOOK

RELEASING CHILDREN TO LITERATURE:
A Teacher's Guide To Yearling Books
Charles F. Reasoner
Yearling
August 1968
Copyright Page

Dedicated to my three R's:
Kathy, Derath, and Howard

Published by
DELL PUBLISHING CO., INC.
750 Third Avenue
New York, N.Y. 10017

CONTENTS

17726

FOREWORD

Traditionally, teachers' guides seem to presume that teachers need to be shown how to teach, usually the same things to all children in the same way. Instead of "guiding," they usually bind, tying teachers and their students to static and inflexible methods as well as to predetermined goals. To be sure, writers have no control over the use of their material in the classroom; but often they prepare their guides or manuals for exact use, then fail to present their methods clearly. Further, guides for teaching literature generally are based on the premise that readers must be "checked" to see if they have comprehended the "right" or "correct" meanings from their readings, as though the guidewriter or the teacher had a direct line to the content and intent authors write into their books!

A teacher's guide for literature, I feel, must offer the classroom teacher enough breadth and width to enable her to draw upon it as a source for ideas in her creative role as a teacher of literature. Further, fine literature has always been open to many interpretations by those who read it, so a literature guide, therefore, must be *releasing* rather than restricting. It must present numerous ways in which individual readers can be freed to select their own reading material and, as they read their way into new experiences, to interact with authors in their own individual ways, from their own backgrounds of real and vicarious experiences. An effective guide for literature must show, too, how such "liberated" readers can be guided to reveal those unique meanings which they have gleaned from their reading experiences. Many of us who learned to love literature probably "caught" our love for books *in spite of* the "taught" literature lessons we received. However, if users of this guide can accept a somewhat ancient meaning of the verb "to educate"—*to lead out*—then I believe "teaching" literature is possible. No one can learn for his students; they must be released to go their own ways with what they experience. However, as with any arresting moment a child has, he will want to share it with someone he trusts, with someone who is interested in *his* ideas.

It is my hope that this guide will provide sufficient ways and means for achieving these goals.

Charles F. Reasoner
Manhasset, New York
July 1968

AN IMPORTANT WORD TO TEACHERS

ABOUT READING MATERIALS

The statement "We want children who not only know *how* to read, but who *do* read!" has become a cliche. Nevertheless, it remains an accurate statement of reading goals and, in some instances, an indictment of some current practices in the teaching of reading.

Many teachers have discovered that a child's motivation for reading depends heavily on having the appropriate materials available—materials that appeal to his interests, curiosity, reading level and mood—at the right time. Many have discovered, too, that those children who have found literature to be enjoyable often turn to books on their own in their leisure hours.

The public library has always been the reading teacher's staunch ally because inherent in its service is the idea that reading material should be available for all areas of interest and for all levels of ability. Free selection of reading materials is encouraged in the public-library system. Easy access to and free loans from these institutions have provided millions of readers with reading fare suited to their own individual interests and needs.

Today there is another great ally—the paperback. Quality literature is now published in inexpensive paperbound editions which are readily available for classroom use. Paperbacks are certainly within the means of most school budgets; a classroom library, consisting of a variety of titles dealing with a variety of interests and reading levels, with copies for 40 or 50 children, costs about $35. Of no less significance is the probably unexpected by-product resulting from this "paperback revolution": a rebirth and renurturing of feelings about *owning* books, once a privilege of only the advantaged that is now becoming known to the most ordinary elementary-school child.

ABOUT MOTIVATION

Apparently, practices which are supposed to "motivate" children to engage in literature experiences are, at least in part, a result of attempting to make classroom teaching neat and tidy—that is, having all children in the group doing the same thing at the same time. Such arrangements may indeed allow for *neat* teaching; however, learning is never so tidy that it can always be regulated precisely by clock hours and group-instruction methods.

It seems an insidious waste of time for teachers to spend time thinking up ways, devices, gimmicks, and gadgets to make children enjoy books—as if reading were something they are not supposed to want to do. Instead of preparing this "motivational stimuli," a more judicious use of professional knowledge and energy would be that of *releasing* children *to* reading material—which they would elect to read if only they knew it existed!

Even with the cleverest of motivational devices and conditions, creative classroom activities in which elementary-school children engage resist the inflexible, computer-like tactics which try to fit whole groups of children into predetermined time-and-subject-matter slots for mass-learning experiences. The experiences one has through reading literature should be just as creative as, for example, creative-writing experiences. And they are just as individual. When literature experiences are significant, individuals create meanings, with their own language symbols, right along with book authors.

To urge children into literature situations in which they abruptly must adjust their moods and interests to conform to teacher, group, and/or clock demands is to display a kind of teaching tidiness that could sweep some children under the reading carpet—perhaps for a lifetime. If creative experiences with literature are not to become sacrificial lambs on the altar of orderly arrangements, then one has to recognize that extrinsic motivation is not a panacea that makes literature—even great literature—desirable and enjoyable to children.

Regardless of how learners are organized for teaching—as individuals or in groups—each one must learn for himself, experience for himself, take himself *to* a book and receive *from* it, alone, what an author has said.

ABOUT COMPLEMENTATION

At the theoretical base of most school reading programs are fine purposes and noble goals. *Reading-skill* teaching, however—so necessary to the achievement of these ends—frequently is regarded as an *end* in and of itself instead of a *means* for accomplishing reading goals. In some instances, one finds reading programs and basic reading materials designed solely for *skill* achievement, while on other occasions, one finds appendages tacked onto existing programs and called *Outside Reading, Free Reading, Independent Reading, Recreational Reading,* or *Supplementary Reading.* Generally these "appendages" or "extras" refer to trade books, to literature.

The requisite attitude which the teacher of reading must bring to his work with children is that good literature is a necessary and complementary (not supplementary!) facet of *all* children's reading at all stages and levels, in all types of programs, and with all types of methodology. This guide does not negate the use of other kinds of classroom organizational patterns and ways which many teachers (such as those who support individualized programs) have found successful. While it is possible to teach reading skills at any level solely with trade books of fine literature, this guide does not suggest that other instructional materials for teaching reading skills to children be discarded.

There would be few who would disagree with the point that teachers' often tedious efforts to teach children how to read and children's equally frustrating attempts to learn to read are expended so that, ultimately, America's children—all of them—will be able to derive satisfaction from literature of their choice, whether for pleasure, work, or need. This guide has been prepared with that rather simple and single purpose in mind: *to make literature complementary to that part of children's lives spent in classrooms.*

ABOUT COMPREHENSION

Each reader brings his own feelings, ideas, knowledge, and experiences *to* that which he reads. In doing so, he takes something *from* book encounters which is uniquely his own: comprehension, if you will; interpretations which are distinctly different, even though sometimes only by degree, from those gleaned by other readers of the same material. Such differences cannot be judged "right" or "wrong" because they do or do not align themselves with the standard responses of a majority. Indoctrinating young readers with the idea of "correct responses" can make literary mendicants of them, dependent upon someone to tell them whether or not they were "right" about that which they read. It can also leave a child vulnerable to anything in print—with an unquestioning acceptance of everything from books to beer ads. Neither should readers be expected to try to second-guess a teacher or test maker for "proper" comprehension. Such practices deny literature its chance at greatness and readers the opportunities to read creatively and critically.

I also happen to believe that reading and comprehension are synonymous. That is to say, without comprehension, there is no reading. Therefore, since comprehension is reading and reading is comprehension, comprehension is not considered a reading skill; rather it is the end result of the application of all those reading skills we know about and teach children, especially in the early elementary-school years.

This does not deny the fact that there are kinds of comprehension, determined by the type of reading material selected and the purposes the reader has for reading (i.e., pass a test, produce a book report, personal enjoyment, get a good mark, etc.); neither does it fail to recognize the point that there are also degrees of comprehension, determined by maturity, sophistication, language proficiency, and past experiences—including those with reading books. If a reader is not able to comprehend certain predetermined meanings, it is not because he cannot comprehend. Rather, it is most likely due to the fact that his purposes for reading—and the material—are different from those expected of him.

The function of this guide has been narrowed to exclude suggestions for teaching reading skills of, for example, the phonics and structural-analysis variety. Instead, the focus is on comprehension and the ever-increasing concern of teachers, as expressed in questions such as these:

"How do I learn about each child's comprehension in a reading program which allows absolute freedom in selection of trade books?"

"Since, unlike textbooks, trade books are not written to teach, and since vocabulary is not 'controlled,' what do I do about vocabulary development when 'new' words are not always 'new' to all children?"

"I've run out of ideas to substitute for the hated book report! What can I do?"

"If my role in teaching literature is not one of simply listening and accepting; not one of checking up to make sure students are reading; not one of telling them how to appreciate; not one of 'helping' them to make 'proper' choices; and not one of inculcating and directing 'correct' comprehension responses—then what is my role?"

"What if a student chooses to read a book which I haven't read? What if more than half the class chooses to read different books, some of which I've never read before? What can I do about comprehension then?"

"What about matters of taste and appreciation? Can these be taught? Or are they 'caught'?"

"What kinds of classroom plans are there involving literature that will really 'turn kids on'?"

I hope to answer questions like these in this Teacher's Guide.

Clearly, whatever a reader comprehends or takes away from his reading is very closely linked with his *reasons* for reading, upon the degree of satisfaction he derives from the reading task. If one has never found reading satisfying; if one goes through six, twelve, twenty years unaware that books can be as alluring and fulfilling as any television program, movie, or baseball game, then he has been deprived of a significant part of his cultural heritage.

ABOUT SELF-SELECTION

No matter how well a teacher knows each of his students, the fact remains that the one person who best knows what a child's reading interests are is the reader himself! And if the child is free to choose a book, sample it, put it back and try another, then he, too, is the one in the best position to know whether or not a book is worth the effort he is putting into it.

The reading interests of many children skip about unpredictably; horse stories one week, science fiction the next. Others prefer to read their fill of fantasy before trying anything else. The freedom to have such preferences and to make such choices needs to be preserved in the classroom. Prescribed reading at any grade level alienates many children from the satisfactions that self-selection, based on individual interests, can bring. Prescribed reading material also fails to allow children to develop discriminating tastes.

When individual readers are permitted to select that which they want to read—that which they feel will bring them the most enjoyment—"motivation-to-read" problems are vastly reduced, if not eliminated.

With so much fine literature available to children today, it is indeed unfortunate that so many external pressures—extrinsic motivation and rewards—are used with children in much the same way as the mechanical rabbit is used to get greyhounds to run about a circular track. In such instances, neither the greyhounds nor the children ever seem to get close enough to the "bait" to get an opportunity really to sink their teeth into it. Even if they did, perhaps the artificiality of the lure would be enough to cause them to avoid rabbits or reading for a lifetime.

The artificial reading "rabbit" probably has more children chasing it than any other kind of academic hare that has been found for "motivational" purposes. Most children tend to slow down in reading when they lack the zest to read that which brings personal satisfaction to them. This lack of zest is often due to the fact that school- or teacher-selected reading matter is not what some children feel important or interesting to them. Or perhaps there is little or no opportunity for them to sample a book, return it, and choose another if it doesn't suit their liking or ability. Or perhaps some children who get on mystery, biography, picture-book, or informational reading "kicks," become discouraged because they find it increasingly difficult to resist a teacher's efforts to have everyone take in a "well-balanced" diet of literature in *all* categories. Or perhaps some children slow down in reading because they just don't fit neatly into the age-and-grade-level reading classifications into which some schools so tidily (and frequently with stern inflexibility) have placed all of their reading materials. Whatever the reason, the fact still remains that many teachers feel that children will not read without "literature-reading assignments."

A rich and varied collection of paperbacks in the classroom greatly enhances the scope of all children's reading choices. When two or three children have similar interests and indicate their wish to read the same book, multiple copies of certain titles can meet this need as well.

When a child reads to please himself and not others, he will not choose a book **too easy** for him, or reread one he's already read, just to fulfill an assignment. Neither will he make such a choice if his interest is genuine (and not what he thinks others feel it should be) and if his only reward is the pleasure reading brings him (and not recognition for being the leader in the class for having read the most books).

When a child reads for enjoyment and has the freedom to select the books that are right for him, the teacher will not have to be concerned about the child who may choose a book too difficult for him, one which requires more skill and ability than he has at a particular time. And, if he's free to return it and find another which he can read, there is no need to be concerned about the child who simply turns pages but doesn't comprehend. All through life we select tasks that are sometimes too difficult for ourselves. When this happens, we usually pause, step back a little, practice a little more, and try again. In this instance, the teacher's role might be that of helping such a reader to locate a similar book which he *can* read. Or, in some instances, the teacher or another child can read to the child who refuses to be satisfied enough to make another choice until he knows what a particular book has to say.

When children are "stuck" either with their own or with other's choices of reading fare, many become reading "dropouts" at a very early age. On the other hand, when children are released to make their own choices, there will be readers who find literature satisfying and enjoyable, and there is every reason to believe that, for far more children, reading will become a lifetime habit.

Regardless of *what* a child selects to read, when he has already discovered that it is well worth his effort to wrestle with the excitement and ideas found on the printed page, the coast is always clear for a teacher to help him gain more discriminating tastes, new skills, fuller appreciation, deeper understandings, greater stimulation, and wider variety in his reading.

USING THIS GUIDE

It is my fondest hope that you will use this Teacher's Guide as it is intended; as a source, a starting place, to release the resources within *you*, the teacher, just as the tiny trickle of water that begins in Itasco State Park, Minnesota, is the source of the mighty Mississippi.

If this book encourages you to capitalize on and develop your own best talents, leaving you freer, less inhibited and dependent; if it stimulates thinking and creative, individualized teaching rather than a fixed practice; if it offers ideas and suggestions upon which you can draw and then go on and turn them into original, innovative classroom experiences, I will feel that I have done my job well, because you will turn to this book not because you *have* to, but because you would have it so, and because you will know the personal satisfaction of the *creative* teacher.

ABOUT PREREADING DISCUSSION QUESTIONS (SECTION II)

Since every reader brings different ideas and experiences to the books he reads and since, as a result, no two readers ever receive precisely the same meanings from the same book, teachers are concerned about how to assess comprehension in ways that are different from (and do not depend on) "right-answer" tests, essays, and/or reports.

Prereading discussions are sparked by open-ended questions designed to elicit from a child his "stand" on certain big ideas and analogous situations *before* interacting with an author's point of view on these same issues. In using these, you are seeking children's *opinions*—opinions which are *relative to but not identical with* those in the story. This "connection" should not be revealed to the participants.

Questions are formed in such a way as to make simple "yes-no" responses impossible. Similarly, they do not allow respondents a "multiple-choice" guess at what he believes to be the correct answer. (For example: *Do you think the hero was courageous, fearful, or superhuman?)*

Whether you conduct a discussion with one child, a small group, or with a whole class, the *atmosphere* should be relaxed, uninhibited, and informal. No child is likely to reveal his deep-down beliefs to anyone he doesn't trust or in a situation where his opinions aren't respected.

Frequent discussions of book ideas are vital to any successful literature-reading program. Some children, however, may prefer to "discuss" some of their ideas *on paper,* instead of orally. Since the major purpose of such questions is *not* to teach oral or written communication skills, but rather to free children to reveal the personal feelings which they bring to and take away from their reading, those who choose to discuss their opinions *in writing* should be allowed to do so.

You may find it helpful to compare some of these responses with *postreading* responses to learn of the interesting and varied ways in which children can and do comprehend an author's words.

ABOUT PREREADING ACTIVITIES
(SECTION III)

With objectives not unlike those described for using open-end discussion questions, this section offers *other* suggestions for eliciting personal reactions and responses allied to the larger meanings and ideas contained in the book *before* it is read. These activities draw heavily upon everyday things which children know about and have experienced. These activities do not duplicate; neither are they identical to those book experiences which readers will discover for themselves. Rather, they provide *additional* means for you to discern readers' understanding, growth, and/or change of ideas as a result of their reading. Comparing these prereading activities with postreading ideas and responses can be informative and helpful.

ABOUT POSTREADING DISCUSSION QUESTIONS
(SECTION IV)

Open-ended discussion questions of this kind, as stated earlier, release children from the traditional notion that every reader is expected to obtain the same meanings and have the same ideas and feelings about a piece of literature. As with the Prereading Discussion Questions, there are no "yes-no," "right-wrong" responses expected; however, these questions are somewhat different, in that they focus on ideas in each book. By comparing prereading responses and activities with those ideas they are now contemplating, children can learn to become critical readers—learning to weigh their own understanding of themselves and others by becoming aware of their own values and the values of others.

Postreading Discussion Questions may be "discussed" in writing by those children who prefer that form. You may use them in discussions with a large group, a small group, or with individual children. You may also find it valuable to permit groups of students to select one or two questions and engage in a child-led discussion of the issues and ideas.

Your attention is directed to the related ideas in the Prereading and Postreading Discussion Questions, as well as to the complementary suggestions in Helping Children to Reveal Their Comprehension and Other Prereading Activities. While these four sections can be used interchangeably in order to compare pre- and postreading thinking and ideas, they may be used separately, for other than comparative purposes, as well. It is important to point out that *no child should be expected to* engage in *all* of the suggested activities *for any section, or in all of the activities suggested under one title.*

The abundance and variety of ideas included in the Guide were intentional and necessary to reach as many individual teachers and students as possible. Ultimately, the decision for using any of the suggestions rests with teachers and students in their school situations. In my many years of work with children's reading, I have found children's choices of one or two of the activities quite sufficient since most children are anxious to get on with their next book!

ABOUT HELPING CHILDREN TO REVEAL
THEIR COMPREHENSION
(SECTION V)

How much a reader takes away from a book he has read—always a matter of great concern to teachers of reading—depends, of course, on many things: the child's own skills and abilities, his attitude toward and purpose for reading, the availability and variety of reading material, the freedom to select books that appeal to him, and his own measures of experience. How much he receives from an encounter with literature depends also on what he believes you expect of him—or hold him responsible for—when he finishes a book. Perhaps the question should not be "How much did the child get from his reading?" but "How can I learn what the child's reading meant to *him*?" Literature experiences are *sensory* experiences. Can anyone, really, convince another that he didn't feel, see, hear, smell, or taste that which he did? To expect a child to read for someone else's meanings is to ask that he be clairvoyant.

The most persistent request from teachers, I have found, is "What ideas do you have to get rid of the *book report*?" In defense of the book report, it must be pointed out that there is nothing inherently "evil" or distasteful in it. It has become a thing dreaded and feared by students and teachers alike due to misuse, abuse, and overuse. Some students, for example, select books with only a single criterion in mind: "Will it be easy to do if I choose this book?" In other instances, book reports are used as ways to force children to read, to check to see if they have read, to see if they have comprehended the "right" meanings, to give students grades at the end of a marking period, or to "teach" them oral and written communication skills in an integrated language-arts curriculum. The point is, book reports should remain as one of many options open to readers. In this section, as well as in sections IV and VI, I have attempted to show you several alternatives.

Just as children need to be *released* to literature, i.e., to choose the books they want to read, so it is that they also need to be released so that they will feel free and secure enough to reveal to others *their* comprehension resulting from book experiences.

The activities suggested are designed to appeal to a great variety of children and provide numerous possibilities for helping children to reveal their comprehension. Some of the suggestions will ask children to reflect upon a particular character while others will call for their interpretation of setting, time, circumstance, plot, and the like. Still other activities suggest that readers respond with *their opinions* about moral or religious issues as they found them presented in the book; on other occasions, readers are invited to make comparisons between modern and historical times, real and make-believe situations, or, between the similarities and differences they perceive in their environment and that found in the book.

In helping children to reveal their comprehension, be concerned with *how* and *what* children identify with in their reading; with what they feel to be synonymous and analogous to their own lives; with their abilities to see relationships; and with the ways in which book encounters add to their experience, change attitudes, and modify behavior.

When you do not prescribe "correct" comprehension, there is likely to be an occasional reader who reveals a rather *off-beat interpretation* of a book experience. Such a child, for example, might be one who believes that Johnny Tremain is a foolish and impractical *"Pollyanna."* For those of us who love Forbes' historical Johnny, with all his faults and strengths, fears and courage, this is hard to take. It is even more difficult to resist the urge to "set such a reader straight." In other instances, a reader may simply misinterpret factual data. For example, a child who maintains that the "Boston Tea Party" occurred in a New York harbor is factually inaccurate.

In both examples, though admittedly extreme, you may be concerned about what to do. Before "doing anything about it," one might do well to think through the question: *Can one, indeed, disallow such interpretations?* There are, of course, many ways to evoke the responses you want from a learner, but, as most teachers know, it is also true that outward compliance sometimes carries with it an inward defiance on the part of a child. He may answer a question or fill in a blank correctly, but he might well be thinking, "That's not the way I see it even though Mrs. Smith says it's so."

Perhaps the important thing to be done with "off-beat" interpretations is to provide opportunities for the reader to realize that other *child* readers of the same book have found *different* ideas and understandings in it—and why! You might also ponder *why* this particular child would get such an idea from this book: what it could be in his background that has led him to this point of view, or what it is he needs, wants, or is escaping from? If you believe that it is important to *know* children beyond the comments and scores on permanent record cards, then finding ways for them to share their ideas with others becomes a vital part of this knowing.

ABOUT RELATED-TO-READING EXPERIENCES (SECTION VI)

Sometimes, as a result of a book experience, certain readers are moved to engage in activities which are related (perhaps very slightly) to the characters or events in the story. Such extensions *beyond* the covers of books are valuable and provide worthy and exciting opportunities for classroom teaching and learning. Some readers, for example, have been motivated to compose music, poems, additional chapters or sequels to the story, paintings, murals, and the like. Others have been stimulated to write to authors, to replicate a condition in the story, or to imagine the hero or heroine as a relative or next-door neighbor. Still other readers have found it hard to resist doing some further research into the time or place of the story. Whatever the degree to which the activity is related to the book, ideas—such as those mentioned above—which excite children to new experiences should be encouraged.

Many of these activities I have learned from children with whom I have worked over a period of years. Most children need little more than the freedom to try out their ideas, although sometimes in the "trying out" stage they learn that their ideas are more "kooky" than creative—but this is an important discovery, too. Other children respond enthusiastically to the slightest suggestion offered them by someone else and are able to take the idea and make it their own, while others are perhaps more cautious, less ambitious, dependent, the type of learners who prefer to put a "period" at the end of every experience and who would feel uncomfortable about taking part in these activities, even though they could be the very ones who most could profit from such experiences.

The activities listed in this section, then, are suggestions for those who *do* want to go on, but require a "nudge" or help of some kind or other. They are not to replace children's ideas; neither are they intended to "integrate" literature-reading with other curriculum areas. They are examples of how literature reading can "turn children on."

ABOUT VOCABULARY THAT MAY NEED DEVELOPING (SECTION VII)

Most people have at least four vocabularies: reading, writing, listening, and speaking. Vocabulary development in literature reading is concerned with helping readers toward independent use of a variety of methods, clues, and cues to acquire understanding of *(a) unfamiliar words* or *(b) familiar words used in new and different ways.*

Lee C. Deighton in his study[1] makes the point that a "reader never gets all the meanings of a word at any one encounter; ... meaning comes from experience, not from a dictionary; that as experience broadens, meaning becomes richer; that he [a reader] is never to seek *the* meaning of a word." The same study revealed that traditional and still current methods of word study—dictionary surveys of word parts, dealing with roots, prefixes, and suffixes—"are not only inadequate but downright misleading."

In a speech delivered at the American Educational Research Association a few years ago, Henry D. Rinsland made the following point:

Meanings are not printed; they are in people's minds. A word or a picture is only a mark on paper. Two things marks cannot do—they cannot make sounds and they cannot impart meanings alone. Whenever we write, we impart meanings;

[1]From *Vocabulary Development in the Classroom* by Lee C. Deighton. Teachers College Bureau of Publications, Columbia University, (New York: 1959).

whenever we read, we should obtain the meanings imparted by the writer. . . . Meaning is a mental function and operation.

Elihu Root makes the following observation:

> Words are like those insects that take color from their surroundings. Half the misunderstanding in this world comes from the fact that the words that are spoken or written are conditioned in the mind that gives them forth by one set of thoughts and ideas, and they are conditioned in the mind of the hearer or reader by another set of thoughts and ideas, and even the simplest forms of expression are frequently quite open to mistake, unless the hearer or reader can get some idea of what were the conditions in the brain from which the words came.[2]

Leland B. Jacobs states a similar point of view in pointing out that reading is more than words:

> For, though the words are the pegs upon which the literary production is hung, all the words written by the author cannot be held exactly in the reader's memory. The writer, in order to develop his mood and meaning, necessarily employs many more words than the reader can immediately recall. What the reader considers the big ideas, the pivotal meanings, constitutes what he keeps in mind as he continues to read. He does not even try to hold onto all the words that the writer has employed. Instead, the reader makes of the words such sequences or series of meanings as seem urgent and sensible for him to move ahead with the writer, comprehending meaningfully. The reader lets words construct time, place, scene, or situation—or whatever it is that the writer is developing—and it is these vivid constructs that the reader clings to so that he may go ahead with the author with confidence. To the extent that time, place, situation, mood, or character are made

[2]Quoted in *Elementary English,* January, 1952, published by the National Council of Teachers of English, Champaign, Illinois.

arresting through words, they can serve to aid the reader. By their precision and fitness, they help the reader to hold in the foreground of his mind the ingredients of the prose or poetry that are essential to the central thought—the total meaning—of the author's work.[3]

For each of the literature titles found in this Guide, there is a section that attempts to deal with vocabulary development. In some instances, words and phrases used by the authors have been listed and suggestions for meaningful research and study have been described. In other instances, words have been listed which do not actually appear in the text of the books. They are words, however, ith meanings and ideas closely associated with those encountered the book. Experiences such as these can serve to broaden and deepen a reader's vocabulary by extending his experiences to greater dimensions.

Some vocabulary *activities* have been included which can provide r some children experiences with some of the "big ideas and otal meanings" and thus make them more independent in all of eir reading encounters. In this way, then, you are urged to go eyond the traditional practice of "introducing" *new* words to readers. It also discourages the handicapping practice of teaching "one word, one meaning" to children. The activities are based upon the premise that "reading is more than words" and that "as experience broadens, word meanings become richer."

SOME CLASSROOM IDEAS FOR FURTHER
LITERATURE ADVENTURES

When you plan to make literature reading an important, *complementary* facet of every classroom day, some of the following ideas will further children's excitement in book adventure:

[3]From "More Than Words" by Leland B. Jacobs, published in *Childhood Education*, December 1960.

1. Plan a "Book Party" with children; each can come in masquerade, disguised as a book character.
2. Help children to learn about library procedures by setting up a free-loan library arrangement in their own classroom. One way to begin a Card Catalogue is to request the first reader of a title to fill out a 3 x 5 card with information about the contents of the book (synopsis, author, publisher, etc.).
3. Encourage "Book of the Month" recommendations, "Hall of Fame" nominations, projects which result in he publishing of a helpful list of recommendations of "musts" for summer or vacation reading: *Six Summer Selections Too Good to Miss— for Camp/Travel/Escapesville!*
4. Permit children to organize book clubs, : ɔ., a Lenski Clu Spy Club, or a Space-Fiction Read°r: C ɔup.
5. Suggest that children open and examine a box of paperbacks when it arrives. As they skim through the titles, there will be opportunity as well as need to teach them how to classif books, for record keeping and distribution purposes. One cl wanted to do the job as quickly and as accurately as possib They decided to divide the books up among the volunteers the class and listed the following criteria for classifying a boo quickly (but temporarily, in case a more careful examination later reveals an ill-founded decision):

   a. Read the pictures and the words on the front and back covers.
   b. Think about the title.
   c. Look at the names of the chapters.
   d. Sample a paragraph or two at random.
   e. Do you know the author? Many writers tend to write the same "type" of book.
   f. Read the first paragraph or the first page.

6. Try having children skim a book they've selected as one they think they might be interested in reading, paying attention to criteria listed above or to those they may decide to follow. After five or ten minutes, have them write a brief paragraph or two on what they believe to be the plot, major character(s),

etc. This opinion then is sealed in a "Time Capsule" (an envelope) and preserved until the writer (or another reader) has completed the reading of the book. The "Time Capsule" is then opened and evaluated in terms of its accuracy, etc.

7. Permit children to play BOOKWORD, a takeoff on the television quiz PASSWORD.

SOME HELPFUL HINTS

- Children should *not* be required to engage in discussions or activities (such as those in this Guide) for *every* book they read. If a child chooses to read several titles in a given period, permit him the choice of title (or titles) on which to report.
- Do *not* use *all* the Prereading or Postreading Discussion Questions with each reader. Rather, choose the one (or more) that fits the child's interests.
- All children should *not* be asked to respond to the same question or participate in the same activity. There are numerous and varied ideas and suggestions for each title, so that different readers will respond according to their different feelings and interests.
- The questions in this Guide should *not* be used as "guided-reading" checks for children to refer to as they read.
- Activities in this Guide should not be used as *assigned* "homework."
- When functioning as a discussion leader, do *not* offer your opinions or appear "more satisfied" with one response over another.
- Avoid revealing the "connection" between Prereading Discussion Questions and the related ideas to be found in the book.
- Do *not* mark or grade activities. Instead, keep them on file to refer to when it comes time to evaluate children and place a mark on their report cards.
- Make sure that everyone who wishes has an opportunity to express his opinion. Avoid "calling on" students (go to another question instead, if there is no response). Avoid the rigid practice of requiring children to raise their hands if they have something to say. Rather, teach children to respect the speaker and refrain from being rude or using ridicule.

- Encourage and permit small groups of children to engage in literature discussions and activities *on their own,* without teacher leadership. When it is important or desirable for teachers to learn about some of the ideas going on in child-led groups, you might consider the use of a tape recorder (if children have had previous opportunities to rid themselves of "microphone shyness)." With older children, one of the group members may be willing to serve as recorder and keep track of some of the main ideas discussed.

- Investigate the ways in which questions and activities listed for one book may be applicable to other titles. In order to provide as much variety as possible, a conscious effort was made to present different ideas for each book. Care was also taken to avoid redundancy by not referring to prereading questions and activitie in the ideas which suggest ways to help children reveal their comprehension. When helpful, *don't* miss the opportunity to make such comparative assessments with children.

- Search for convenient and economical ways which allow children to work independently with their choices. For example, from the Guide, Other Selections on a Similar Theme may be typed on a X 5 card and attached to the inside back cover. Prereading and Postreading Questions may also be put on cards and filed under book titles or under categories like those found in this Guide: *About Love, About Innovation, About Punishment,* etc. Ideas for written discussion, "Opinionnaires," directions for experiments or construction activities may be duplicated and filed in folders or 9 X 12 manila envelopes and labeled with the title of the book(s) and the nature of the activity.

A SELECTION
OF
IMPORTANT REFERENCES
ON CHILDREN'S READING

Fenner, Phyllis. *The Proof of the Pudding.* N.Y.: John Day, 1957.

Hazard, Paul. *Books, Children and Men.* Boston: Horn, 1948.

Holt, John. *How Children Learn.* New York: Pitman, 1967.

———. *How Children Fail.* New York: Dell, 1966.

Jennings, Frank G. *This Is Reading.* New York: Dell, 1966.

Nesbitt, Marion. *A Public School for Tomorrow.* New York: Dell, 1966.

Smith, Lillian. *The Unreluctant Years.* New York: Viking, 1953.

THE BEECH TREE
by PEARL S. BUCK

Illustrated by Kurt Werth

JOHNNY JACK AND HIS BEGINNINGS
by PEARL S. BUCK

Illustrated by Kurt Werth.

I. THE STORIES

The Beech Tree

Mary Lou got along fine with her grandfather when he came to live with her family. He always had time to talk with her and answer her questions. Then Mary Lou's mother became worried about taking care of Grandfather, and decided to send him to a nursing home. Mary Lou was surprised and even shocked to learn what was worrying her mother. How the family worked things out makes a story for every child who has a grandparent.

Johnny Jack and His Beginnings

Johnny Jack lived on a farm, where he watched baby chicks hatch and puppies being born. One day he wondered about his own beginnings, and with the help of an honest and tactful mother, the animal babies around him and the arrival of his own baby sister, his questions were answered. Johnny Jack fit his new knowledge neatly into the wonders of his everyday world.

II. PREREADING DISCUSSION QUESTIONS

The questions which follow are illustrative of the kinds which teachers can prepare for the purpose of releasing children to reveal how *they feel* about some of the same larger ideas and bigger meanings contained in the book *before* it is read.

About Aging
1. What is there about grandparents that young children seem to like so much?
2. Why is it that so many people your age hate to throw or give away old toys, dolls, games?
3. Many people feel that people who have grown old are different and that they need to be treated differently. What are some of the differences between very old people and people your age?
4. Why is it that some people say that very old people act "funny" and have "funny" ways? What behavior and habits of old people do they have in mind?
5. What would be your ideas about some of the advantages of being very, very old?

About Beginnings
6. Why is it that so many people your age love to watch and play with baby animals—kittens, puppies, colts, chicks, etc.?
7. So many things seem to have *beginnings,* but there seem to be as many *different kinds* of beginnings as there are different kinds of things: *games* have beginnings; *ideas* have beginnings; *races* have starting places; *tools, machines,* and *bicycles* have beginnings; and, of course, *human beings, plants, animals, birds, fish, insects,* etc., all have their beginnings somewhere, someplace in "history." Why is it that so many people are so curious and interested in finding out about as many *beginnings* as they can? What are some of the differences in these kinds of beginnings?

About Questions and Answers
8. What kinds of questions seem to annoy grown-ups the most?
9. Why do some people seem to hate to answer questions?

10. What kinds of questions have you asked that seemed to get you very confusing answers—if any answers at all? What kinds of questions have you asked that brought you answers that made you feel foolish and stupid?

III. PREREADING ACTIVITIES

1. Some children find it fascinating to trace their *family trees.* Others may wish to trace the family tree of a famous personage on a "chart" similar to the illustration below:

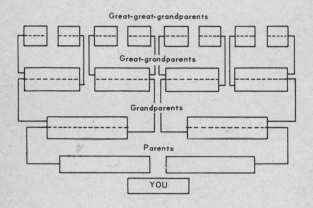

Great-great-grandparents

Great-grandparents

Grandparents

Parents

YOU

IV. POSTREADING DISCUSSION QUESTIONS

1. What makes something old? When is something old? How *old* is old?
2. What makes something new? When is something new? How *new* is new?
3. Tell why you think it was (or was not) a good idea for the publishers to put these two short stories in the same book.
4. Tell what you think the following statements mean and why you feel they might apply to *The Beech Tree* and/or *Johnny Jack and His Beginnings:*

3

a. "I'm going to *turn over a new leaf*."
b. "From a tiny acorn, the mighty oak does grow."
c. "It's as *old as the hills*."
d. "He's *a chip off the old block*."
e. "Like father, like son."
f. "As innocent as a newborn babe."
g. "The hand that rocks the cradle is the hand that rules the world."

V. HELPING CHILDREN TO REVEAL THEIR COMPREHENSION

The Beech Tree:

1. Why do you think Mary Lou's mother was unhappy and worried so much about Grandfather's living with them?
2. If Grandfather had been the father of Mary Lou's *mother*, tell why you think her father would (or would not) have been worried and unhappy about his living with them.
3. Suppose you found a letter that Grandfather had written to explain why he decided to leave. What would it say?
4. The author, Pearl S. Buck, calls this story *The Beech Tree* and yet it is a story of *people.* Suppose you were going to try to explain the *relationship* or connection between trees and people to a younger brother, like Timmie in the story. With *pictures* and *words,* show how you'd try to help him understand.

Johnny Jack and His Beginnings

5. John Jackson, or Johnny Jack as he was called, always asked "why" questions about the origin of everything. Why do you think he didn't seem to show much curiosity about the *endings* of things?
6. Suppose you had a younger brother or sister who asked you about the *beginnings* of the following things. Write down the kind of explanation you would give.

a. Where does an *idea* come from?

4

b. Where does a *turtle* come from?
c. Where does a *hamburger* come from?
d. Where does a *telephone* come from?
e. Where did *I* come from?

VI. RELATED-TO-READING EXPERIENCES

1. Observe the metamorphosis of a caterpillar; construct a simple incubator and hatch an egg; raise a family of white mice or hamsters. Prepare a report discussing the similarities and differences in *beginnings.*
2. Find out all you can about *family reunions:* Why were they held? Who attended? Why are they not so common today as they were twenty-five years ago?
3. Find out all you can about *(a) birth certificates* and *(b) social*

a. "What I'd Change About Me"
b. "A Leaf from Our Family Tree"
c. "A Page from Our Family Album"
d. "Why My Great-Great-Great-Great-Grandfather (or Grandmother) Would Be Proud of Me"

VII. VOCABULARY THAT MAY NEED DEVELOPING

1. Words related to some of the major ideas in these two stories by Pearl S. Buck are listed below. An investigation of the meanings and how they may and may not be applied to certain things will help some readers expand their vocabularies and will contribute more precision in their understanding of familiar words.

   old, antique, obsolete, aged, ancient, archaic, elderly, venerable, primitive, antiquated

5

new, modern, novel, original, fresh, start, beginning, recent, current, birth, originate, origin

VIII. OTHER SELECTIONS ON A SIMILAR THEME: A SELECTED BIBLIOGRAPHY

Burton, Virginia Lee. *The Little House.* Boston: Houghton Mifflin, 1942.

———. *Mike Mulligan and His Steam Shovel.* Boston: Houghton Mifflin, 1939.

MacDonald, Golden. *The Little Island.* Garden City, N.Y.: Doubleday, 1946.

Newberry, Claire Turlay. *April's Kittens.* N.Y.: Harper, 1940.

Taylor, Sydney. *All-of-a-Kind Family.* Chicago: Follett, 1951. (Available as a Dell Yearling book.)

White, E.B. *Charlotte's Web.* N.Y.: Harper, 1952. (Available as a Dell Yearling book.)

Poetry

"Andre" by Gwendolyn Brooks, from *Bronzeville Boys and Girls,* N.Y.: Harper, 1956.

"Everybody Says" by Dorothy Aldis, from *All Together,* N.Y. Putnam's, 1925.

"Smells (Junior)" by Christopher Morley, from *The Rocking Horse,* Philadelphia: Lippincott, 1946.

THE WATER-BUFFALO CHILDREN

by PEARL S. BUCK

Illustrated by William A. Smith

THE DRAGON FISH

by PEARL S. BUCK

Illustrated by Esther Brock Bird

I. THE STORIES

The Water-Buffalo Children

When a little girl picks up a stone and rubs it, a great, lumbering animal appears with two Chinese children on its back. The children believe the stone is magic and have a day of amusing adventures trying to discover the extent of its "powers."

The Dragon Fish

Two little girls, one American and one Chinese, tired of their brothers, decide to run away. With the help of a magic Dragon Fish, they go off to the city seeking adventure and find much more than they had hoped for.

II. PREREADING DISCUSSION QUESTIONS

The questions which follow are illustrative of the kinds which teachers can prepare for the purpose of releasing children to reveal how *they feel* about some of the same larger ideas and bigger meanings contained in the book *before* it is read.

About Similarities

1. Although children your age who live in other countries may be *different* in a lot of ways—such as in the food they like to eat, the way they dress, talk, look—because they *are* human beings, they feel and act and think the same as you do about a lot a things. Often, their problems are just like yours. Whether a boy or girl your age lives in Africa, England, China, or the United States, tell what kinds of things you think all of you have in common. Why?

2. Sometimes people living in one country hear "stories" about people in another country—stories which really are not true and, in fact, sound pretty silly. What kinds of "stories" have you heard about people from other countries, such as China, Japan, Russia, Italy, France, Spain, Africa, etc.? Have you heard such statements as:

   a. *All* Japanese people have "slant-eyes" because. . .
   b. The American Indians are called "redskins" because. . .
   c. *All* Italians always. . .
   d. *All* Mexican children like to. . .

   What others can you add?

About Sibling Differences

3. In most families, brothers and sisters get along very well with one another. However, even in the most "harmonious" situations, brothers and sisters do things that *irk* each other, cause arguments, fights, and hard feelings that last—usually very briefly—until they make up. Tell some of the reasons you know about for brothers and sisters becoming angry with one another.

4. Sometimes, in a family where there are several children, one of the children thinks he is better than, more privileged than the rest of his brothers and sisters. Very often this is the oldest or the youngest child. Can you think of any reasons that this is

8

so? Suppose you had a brother or sister who thought you were just *silly, dumb, good-for-nothing.* What do you think your life at home would be like? What would you do? How would you feel?

5. Suppose you have a brother or sister who likes to have "fun" by *teasing* you—*harmlessly*; or, who doesn't like to have you around or take you anyplace; or, who won't play any games or do anything with you that *you* enjoy doing—what would you do? How would you feel?

About Magic, Make-Believe, and Good-Luck Signs

6. Many people like to believe in magic and magic things. For example, someone might keep a *magic* coin, rabbit's foot, buckeye, pin, stone, or piece of rock with him (or her) *at all times.* Someone else might believe in the *magic powers* of stars, wells, fortune tellers, rivers, or animals. What opinions do you have about *magic*? Is there any such thing? Have you ever seen any magic or had anything "magical" happen to you?

7. "If you wish *long enough*, wish *strong enough*, then *wishing* will make it so!" A lot of people believe in wishing because they have had their *wishes "come true."* Tell about the kinds of wishes you have had that have come true.

8. What's the difference between just *wanting* something very badly and *wishing* for something?

9. Tell about a time when you pretended something so hard for so long that you actually believed it was real or true.

10. In what ways are daydreaming, pretending, and imagining the same? How are they different? Can you give examples?

III. PREREADING ACTIVITIES

1. Prepare a display of as many "good-luck" charms (or drawings of them) as you can discover.

2. Prepare a booklet called *Witchcraft, Superstition, and Bad Luck: Warnings for the Unlucky.* In it list as many *bad-luck* signs as you can discover. You might phrase your "rules" in

this way: *In order to avoid bad luck, be careful not to break a mirror. This will bring you seven year's bad luck*! If you can find any "cures" which are supposed to break the bad-luck spell, include them in your booklet, too.

3. Conduct a survey or an investigation. Interview different people and find out how they try to shut out unwanted sounds or unpleasant sights, uncomfortable thoughts or boring situations simply by pretending that they aren't there. What do they do and where do they "go" when they escape these things?

4. Suppose you were an *only child* and your parents moved to another country where no one spoke your language, looked like you, ate, dressed, or did the things you like to do. You would look and act just as "funny" to the children of this new country as they would look and act to you. Write a letter back ~ne of your friends in the United States and tell him how you ~~~. What mistakes did you make? How did you have to change? How are you treated? What new things do you find exciting? What things do you miss most?

IV. POSTREADING DISCUSSION QUESTIONS

1. What do you feel about men's and boys' attitudes about women and girls in these two stories?

2. Even in the United States, some people believe that women are not given "equal rights" with men. Describe some examples of this.

3. If you heard someone make the following statement, what do you think he would mean?

   "Oh yeah? Well, if cows could drive trucks, they would deliver your milk in person!"

4. Some people believe that *magic* is nothing more than *superstition* or trickery. Others believe that *magic* is *faith* or *believing.* How do you feel? Is magic possible? What kind of magic would you find hard to believe in? What kind of magic do you think possible to accept?

5. It is very common today to walk down the street and see a very strange-looking person—someone who really looks odd, is dressed funny, does things in strange ways. Perhaps you've seen someone like this on the street, in a bus or train or store. How does watching him (or her) make you feel? What if this person happens to see you watching? What do you feel like doing then?

6. When a wish "comes true," a lot of people will say:

"Phooey! It was going to happen anyway. You shouldn't have wasted all your time and energy wishing. If you'd look at the facts and examine the thing *logically,* you would see that I'm right. Wishes are for dopes and dummies!"

How do you feel about it? Can wishes that come true be explained? Did you waste your time wishing? Why? Why not?

V. HELPING CHILDREN TO REVEAL THEIR COMPREHENSION

The Water-Buffalo Children

1. At the end of the story, Michael asked his mother: "Was it a magic stone?" To which his mother replied: "How can I ever know? Nobody knew except Da Lobo, and she couldn't tell!" Suppose Da Lobo *did tell—YOU!* Write an answer to Michael's question about the "magic stone."

2. It could have been many things or just "something" that made Da Lobo run. What do you think? Draw a picture of what *you* believe could have been the cause; then write a brief explanation of why you think so.

3. Why do you think Big Brother was so slow in rubbing the stone and saying the magic words?

4. What kinds of strange ideas did these Chinese children seem to have about Americans? Why did they think the American girl looked funny with yellow hair and blue eyes? In what way could this have made Big Brother careful about rubbing the stone?

11

The Dragon Fish

1. Why do you think that Alice and Lan-may really did (or did not) plan to run away?
2. What kinds of feelings did you have about the pawnshop keeper? Why? Did these feelings change? Why? Why not? How? Why do you think that the girls' parents did (or did not do) the right thing by letting the pawnshop keeper keep the Dragon Fish?
3. In what ways were Lan-may and Alice alike? In what ways were they different? Which do you believe to be the more important to them—their likenesses or differences? What are your reasons for thinking so?
4. In this story, a lot of different people learned important "lessons." Tell who they are and what lessons they learned.
5. What do you think Mr. Wu meant when he said that they would have *to pay the guard to open the gate*?
6. In what ways were th   ts of Alice and Lan-may exactly alike?

VI. RELATED-   READING EXPERIENCES

1. Do some research: Gather some factual information and some pictures and compare the water-buffalo with the American bison.
2. Chinese people, for years, have used the water-buffalo for a variety of things. What are some of them? Instead of the water-buffalo, we in the United States have other "substitutes." Find out what these are.
3. Have someone bring in and discuss some of the Chinese stamps (or coins) he has in his collection.
4. Many of our modern ways of living have been influenced by inventions of the Chinese. Find out what some of these are.
5. Try to find out as much as you can about Chinese customs, foods, good-luck charms.
6. Who was *Confucius* and why (and in what ways) is he quoted so much today? Collect and bring in some of Confucius' sayings.

VII. VOCABULARY THAT MAY NEED DEVELOPING

The themes of magic and faith are common to both tales. Some readers will profit from the excitement of learning the "magical powers" contained in some of these pertinent words and their "now you see it, now you don't" kinds of meanings:

legerdemain	*sleight of hand*	*portent*	*omen*
superstition	*black magic*	*witchcraft*	*sorcery*
clairvoyance	*prestidigitation*	*trick*	*voodoo*
charm	*spell*	*sign*	*curse*

VIII. OTHER SELECTIONS ON A SIMILAR THEME: A SELECTED BIBLIOGRAPHY

Coatsworth, Elizabeth. *The Cat Who Went to Heaven.* N.Y.:

Ha

Lew

19

Yashima, Taro. *Crow Boy.* N.Y.: Viking, 1955.

Poetry

"Behind the Waterfall" by Winifred Welles, from *Skipping Along Alone*, N.Y.: Macmillan, 1931.

"Could It Have Been a Shadow?" by Monica Shannon, from *Goose Grass Rhymes*, Garden City, N.Y.: Doubleday, 1930.

"I Keep Three Wishes Ready" by Annette Wynne, from *Piping Down the Valleys Wild*, selected by Nancy Larrick, N.Y. Delacorte, 1968.

SAILING THE SEVEN SEAS

by MARY ELLEN CHASE

A North Star Book in the Yearling Series (Nonfiction)

I. THE STORY

Sailing the Seven Seas is the fascinating true story of seagoing New England families and the packets, East Indiamen, and swift clipper ships on which they journeyed to distant ports. The children who were lucky enough to sail with their parents had the ocean for their homes and the whole world for their geography books. Their mothers taught them to read and write, the first mates taught them navigation, and the sea itself, with its storms and icebergs and dangerous shoals, taught them courage and endurance. As fresh and salty as an ocean breeze, as spicy as the ginger, cloves, and fragrant sandalwood which sometimes constituted part of the cargo, the true adventure found between the covers of this book captures some of America's proudest moments.

II. PREREADING DISCUSSION QUESTIONS

The questions which follow are illustrative of the kinds which teachers can prepare for the purpose of releasing children to reveal how *they feel* about some of the same larger ideas and bigger meanings contained in the book *before* it is read.

About Teaching and Learning
1. Many people feel that there are some things that just *can't* be learned from books or, even, in school. What do you think some of these things might be?
2. If someone said to you, *"Experience is the best teacher!,"* what do you think he would mean?

14

ost every person, every animal, every thing we come into
ct with teaches us something. In this sense, therefore, our
s and brothers and sisters are our teachers. So, too, are
like automobiles, streets, trees, rainstorms, fish, mos-
dogs, milk, etc. Tell about one of your most unusual
" and what you learned.

a river, mountain, lake, ocean, storm, desert, city,
your teacher? What would they teach you? How
ossible for them to teach but impossible for you
em?

"Pioneers"

daring, courageous men and women
in places or regions little known to
These "new pioneers" risk dangers for
it's the challenge; for others it's the
the will to be *first*. For others, it's a
uncharted jungles and caves; they
space, and ocean bottoms; they
es, and so forth. Tell why

III. PREREADING ACTIVITIES

1. Obtain sea and air maps and compare the inform
   give.
2. List and locate the oceans of the world. Tell whic
   to be used most by ships? Tell which you be
   most dangerous.
3. Find out all you can about the meaning of *in*
   and why such a term is necessary.
4. Find out all you can about *superstition*
   you think it might have been easier
   believe in superstitions than people
5. Find out all you can about the
   they located? What kind of In
   Chinooks compare with other
   Why is it we seem to hear m
   Iroquois, Apache, Wyandot, et

IV. POSTREADIN

3. Almost every person, every animal, every thing we come into contact with teaches us something. In this sense, therefore, our parents and brothers and sisters are our teachers. So, too, are quilts like automobiles, streets, trees, rainstorms, fish, mos- "teach dogs, milk, etc. Tell about one of your most unusual

4. How cos" and what you learned.
or fire be a river, mountain, lake, ocean, storm, desert, city, might it be your teacher? What would they teach you? How to learn from possible for them to teach but impossible for you em?

About Land, Sea, and Air

5. Even today, there are "Pioneers" daring, courageous men and women trying to conquer certain places or regions little known to people like you and me. These "new pioneers" risk dangers for many reasons: for some it's the challenge; for others it's the sport or competition and the will to be *first*. For others, it's a necessity. Explorers go into uncharted jungles and caves; they explore mountain tops, outer space, and ocean bottoms; they swim channels, climb into volcanoes, and so forth. Tell why you think this kind of adventurer chooses to live so danger- ously—and often so uncomfortably?

6. Traveling by ship or sending freight by ship has certain advan- tages *and* disadvantages over traveling or shipping things by air. What are these advantages and disadvantages? On what does it "all depend?"

7. The captain of a ship acts as a policeman, judge, and even preacher on certain occasions. Why do you think he has so much "power?"

8. Whether one lives on land or sea, *the wind* can be both helpful and destructive, faithful and treacherous, valuable and mur- derous. It can do man's work for him and it can enslave man and work him. How many examples can you give of *the wind's* Jekyll-Hyde character?

III. PREREADING ACTIVITIES

1. Obtain sea and air maps and compare the inform... ...y give.
2. List and locate the oceans of the world. Tell wh... you believe to be used most by ships? Tell which you b... ...ieve to be the most dangerous.
3. Find out all you can about the meaning of i... *ternational waters* and why such a term is necessary.
4. Find out all you can about *superstiti*... *us of the sea.* Why do you think it might have been easier... for sailors to accept or believe in superstitions than peopl... living on land?
5. Find out all you can about the C... Chinook Indians. Where were they located? What kind of In... dians were they? How did the Chinooks compare with other I... Indian tribes you know about? Why is it we seem to hear m... ore about the Sioux, Mohawk, Iroquois, Apache, Wyandot, et... ...c.?

IV. POSTREADING DISCUSSION QUESTIONS

1. On page 2, the author asks a question: "How many seas are there?" And then she answers it with a quote from an early geography book. Tell why you think that answer is or is not still a "correct" one.
2. Throughout the adventure, the author keeps referring to many kinds of *teachers*. In some places she even suggests that schools and books are not so good as some of the other kinds of teachers:

   "...and the stories of sailors were far more exciting and real than any of those contained in any schoolroom or within the covers of books." (p. 14)

   "He might not have the book-learning of the clergyman, the college professor, the lawyer, or the doctor; but he possessed other qualities quite as valuable for his country's prestige and welfare." (p. 39)

Discuss whether or not you feel the author is for or against schooling of the kind you now attend. What do you think she is trying to point out? Why?

Later on, on page 98, she says: "... By the time they were thirteen or fourteen and ready for an academy or high school, their parents were likely to leave them at home for studies usually not available on board a ship." Is this contradictory? Why? Why not?

3. Tell why you think more education would or would not have saved the two ships (the *Sarah E. Snow* and the *Bride*) which sunk to the bottom of the sea.

4. Tell why you think it would be a good idea for your mother to be your schoolteacher. (Or, why you feel it would *not* be such a good idea.)

V. HELPING CHILDREN TO REVEAL THEIR COMPREHENSION

1. Suppose you had been to sea for several months with Captain Chase and had experienced *(a)* the Westerlies, *(b)* the Trades, and *(c)* the Doldrums. Write a letter home telling of these three experiences.

2. Suppose you had been to sea for two years with your parents, aboard a ship much like Captain Melatiah K. Chase's. Write a letter back to your former classmates (those in your class now) and tell them about your many teachers—including the Old Woman, Chips, Sails, the supercargo, first mate, and the sea itself.

3. Before it was customary for women to go to sea with their captain-husbands, some aspects of sea life may have been different. Write a B-W and A-W description (Before-Women, After-Women) of what changes you think there might have been.

4. Suppose you are on a ship like Captain Chase's and you will be stopping at the places listed below. The cargo in the hold of your ship is divided into four groups of items as you leave the East Coast. Tell how it changes as you stop at each foreign

port: What's unloaded? What's taken aboard? When you return to Cape Hatteras, what's your cargo likely to be? You leave with: *(a)* 1/4 cargo raw cotton; *(b)* 1/4 cargo trinkets; *(c)* 1/4 cargo ice; *(d)* 1/4 cargo lumber. Your *ports of call* are: (1) Rio de Janeiro; (2) Valparaiso; (3) San Francisco; (4) Nootka Sound; (5) Honolulu; (6) Sydney; (7) Canton; (8) Singapore; (9) the Cape of Good Hope; (10) Cadiz.

5. Tell about the winds you would use on a trip such as the one above. Tell about the changes in food, clothing, books.

VI. RELATED-TO-READING EXPERIENCES

1. Learn about the time-telling system of bells aboard ships.
2. Learn about the stars and constellations and those which are most useful and necessary to sailors.
3. Learn about the Morse code and how it became important to ships at sea.
4. Learn about the meanings of flags and flag signals used aboard ships.
5. Find out about how ships are named—both merchant ships and U. S. Naval ships.
6. Find out about present-day customs of women traveling on merchant cargo or naval ships.
7. Find out about present-day ranks and how they are earned aboard merchant and naval ships.
8. Find out about present-day import and export needs of some of the major countries of the world.
9. Find out how much shipping today is done by air as compared with ocean shipping.

VII. VOCABULARY THAT MAY NEED DEVELOPING

Weighing anchor and hoisting sail with Mary Ellen Chase, the reader visits unusual ports of call via style and vocabulary. While the author takes care to define and illustrate nautical language, other interesting and colorful words could provide some readers—"landlubbers" and sailors alike—with a more memorable sea adventure if they become familiar with meanings for some of the following:

1. *dregs* (p. 140)   *tempestuous* (p. 75)
   tirades (p. 123)   *raucous* (p. 100)
   taut (p. 102)   *derision* (p. 109)
   lithe (p. 61)   *sumptuous* (p. 65)
   alacrity (p. 101)   *aversions* (p. 137)
   traffic (p. 47)   *wrought havoc* (p. 125)
   irony (p. 75)   *tinned variety* (p. 116)
   a purveyor of good luck (p. 113)
   insubordination (p. 94)
   capricious (p. 77)
   dignitary (p. 146)
   insolent (p. 65)
   tutelage (p. 93)
   derelict vessel (p. 90)
   a considerable gulf (p. 121)

2. Some readers may profit by keeping a "captain's log" of the many seafaring terms. They may even want to devise a "test" and score the takers with rank assignments from cabin boy to captain, or master (see Chapter 6). A few suggestions might be:

scuttlebutts (p. 113)   *supercargo* (p. 152)
beam ends (p. 79)   *holystoned* (p. 66)
Old Man (p. 88)   *Old Woman* (p. 88)
capstan (p. 99)   *deck boards* (p. 101)
boatswain (bo'sun) (p. 101)   *aft* (p. 103)
the pilot (p. 102)   *port* (p. 103)
starboard (p. 103)   *mess* (p. 108)
companionway (p. 107)   *mate* (p. 121)
stern (p. 110)   *seaman* (p. 129)
sails (p. 124)   *young salt* (p. 139)
jetsam (p. 128)   *quarterdeck* (p. 88)
rigging (p. 68)   *galley* (p. 88)
forecastle (fo'c'sle) (p. 101)   *ensign halyards* (p. 103)

dunnage (p. 103)   *hold* (p. 113)
chips (p. 124)   *flotsam* (p. 128)
country's ensign (p. 147)

VIII. OTHER SELECTIONS ON A SIMILAR THEME:
A SELECTED BIBLIOGRAPHY

Clarke, Arthur C. *The Challenge of the Sea.* N.Y.: Holt, 1960.
(Available as a Dell Mayflower book.)

Fon Eisen, Anthony. *Bond of the Fire.* N.Y.: World, 1965. (Available as a Dell Yearling book.)

Moody, Ralph. *Riders of the Pony Express.* Boston: Houghton Mifflin, 1958. (Available as a Dell Yearling book.)

Silverberg, Robert. *Time of the Great Freeze.* N.Y.: Holt, 1964. (Available as a Dell Mayflower book.)

Wibberley, Leonard. *The Epics of Everest.* N.Y.: Farrar, Straus, 1954. (Available as a Dell Mayflower book.)

Poetry

"A V   t and a Flowing Sea" by Allan Cunningham, from
T   or Poetry by May H¹¹ Arbuthnot, Chicago: Scott,
F   .nan, 1952.

"C   oes" by John Masefield,   *Story of a Round House,*
N.Y.: Macmillan, 1940.

"Maps" by Dorothy Brown Thompson, from *Bridled with Rainbows,* N.Y.: Macmillan, 1949

"Sea-Fever" by John Masefiel   n *Piping Down the Valleys Wild,* selected by Nancy Larr   Y.: Delacorte, 1968.

"Travel" by Robert Louis Ste   ., from *A Child's Garden of Verses,* available in many edit

"Wander-Thirst" by Gerald Gou   , from *Time for Poetry* by May Hill Arbuthnot, Chicago: Scott, Foresman, 1952.

LANDSLIDE

by VERONIQUE DAY

Illustrated by Margot Tomes

I. THE STORY

A gay vacation in the mountains turns into tragedy when five children are trapped inside a lonely cottage by a landslide. While they sleep through their first night, not noticing the strange rumblings around them, earth covers the roof and windows of the house, cutting them off from the outside world. Days and nights of darkness go by as the children, buried alive, struggle to devise a plan for escape before it is too late.

II. PREREADING DISCUSSION QUESTIONS

The questions which follow are illustrative of the kinds which teachers can prepare for the purposes of releasing children to reveal how they feel about some of the same larger ideas and bigger meanings contained in the book *before* it is read.

About Ingenuity

1. Tell about a time when you found yourself *cornered*—
   "trapped like a rat in a trap." How did you manage to escape?
   How were you "saved" or rescued?
   *(In a free discussion, it is almost certain that ideas will come
   out about being trapped "mentally"—as in a lie or fib or not
   being able to remember answers to test questions—as well as
   being trapped "physically"—as in games of "Hide and Seek" or
   in the "Fun House" at a carnival. Allowing children to compare the similarities and differences between these two ideas
   not only is appropriate but valuable as well.)*

21

2. Almost everyone, at one time or another, has been lost (at a circus or fair, for example, or in a department store, ball park, forest or woods, strange neighborhood or city, museum, large house, etc.). Usually there are friendly people around who can help. Sometimes, however, they cannot help even if they are willing to do so. Describe an experience you've had "on being lost" and tell what you did to find your way out of the situation.

3. If you lost your way in a strange place where no one spoke your language, what things would you try to do in order to find your way back to the place where you are staying and to the people you know?

About Improvisation

4. When a person finds he needs *something* in order to finish a particular job but *cannot find what he needs*, he usually quits or else he "improvises," or "invents," or "innovates." That is, he uses his brain and those materials *which he does have on hand* and makes something else work in place of what he needed originally. For example, if you're out fishing and a fish takes your last hook, you might "invent" a hook by using a bent pin or nail. And what person hasn't folded a piece of paper to use for a drinking cup, made a "ball" out of a stuffed paper bag, or used a coin as a screwdriver? Such improvisations are the kind that people such as you and I make—or innovate—almost every day in order to repair something, or when camping, traveling, on the beach, or alone with nothing to do. Describe the situation and tell of the kinds of "inventions" you've made that seem unusual to you.

About Heroes and Courage

5. What kinds of people are heroes? What makes them heroes? Who decides whether or not a person is a hero? Can a notorious "bad man" be a hero? Describe what you would call an "heroic act."

6. Frequently a hero turns out to be just an ordinary person such as you and I—a friend who sits next to you in school or a neighbor who lives next to you. Even though such a person

22

may not think he's very brave, something unexpected could happen to bring out the "hero in him." As you think about the ordinary things you do, the places you go, and the people you see or speak to each day, describe how you (or one of these people) could become a hero in situations such as those suggested below, or others that you may think of:

a. fire
b. an earthquake
c. a blackout (power failure with no electricity, TV, radio, or telephone)

d. an accident
e. a loss or theft
f. a flood, tornado, or hurricane
g. a blizzard
h. a lost small child

7. Everyone has a certain amount of *courage*—usually more than he knows he has. Courage is not reserved only for heroes, soldiers, athletes, or important politicians, like governors, mayors, presidents, or kings and queens. Very often, courage comes out of a person when he's most afraid. What would be an example of a time when you've found you needed to be very courageous?

About Fear and Danger

8. Why do you think so many people are afraid of the dark?
9. Tell why you'd agree or disagree with the idea that the greatest *fear* that man has to learn to conquer is *fear of the unknown*.

III. PREREADING ACTIVITIES

1. Some people keep telling others about how "silly" their fears are—even though they may be afraid of things that seem just as silly. How "silly" do you think it is for a person to be afraid of some of the things listed below?

a. bugs, mice, snakes, spiders
b. dogs or cats or horses
c. death

23

d. strangers
e. a school subject (e.g., math)
f. hurting oneself
g. being disappointed
h. giving a talk or speech
i. falling while skating or riding a bicycle
j. heights
k. the water
l. being locked in a room
m. tasting new foods
n. taking part in a contest
o. your dreams
p. storms
q. flying in an airplane

If you were writing a newspaper column under the pen name of Dr. Heeza Okay, and your job was to give advice to people who wrote in to you about their fears, which ones would you choose to write about and what advice would you give?

> Dear Dr. Okay:
>
> I have a very serious prob-
> lem and I need your help
> very badly. Everyone says
> I'm silly, but I know I am
> not. I'm *really* terribly
> afraid of*
>
> Won't you please help
> me? Thank you.
>
> Sincerely yours,
>
> I. M. Knutz

*Fill in from the preceding list.

2. There are many kinds of signs and signals which man has invented and used for centuries in order to communicate to somebody else—miles away—who knows what the signs or signals mean, *someone who knows the code.* Such signals as *Hello!, Help!, Come!, Danger!, Go Back!, Warning!* are some examples. Ships at sea use *flags* to send some of these communications. What are some other ways you can think of that you might use to signal a message to someone—miles away—if there were no electricity, telephone, telegraph?

3. Sometimes a person finds it very hard to obey the instructions of a leader who is put in charge of the things he is doing— especially if the person is about your same age or younger. Sometimes you feel the leader isn't qualified or you feel he's too bossy or you feel he has no right to be the leader because he's too young or because he's a "pet." This happens, for example, at home when parents have to go away and put one of their children in charge of his or her brothers and sisters; it happens in school when a teacher puts a classmate in charge of your group; it happens when a coach of a team makes one of the players captain; it happens in Scout's ... Explain how you feel about such leaders ... you to do something you think is wrong, stupid, and/or unfair.

IV. POSTREADING DISCUSSION QUESTIONS

1. If you were the leader of a small group of people about your age and one person refused to do anything you asked or to follow any of the rules that the rest had agreed upon as necessary and right, what would you do? Some possible situations might be:

   a. a three-day hike   c. a trip to a fair
   b. a bus trip across country   d. putting on a play

2. If a fortune teller told you in advance that you were going to be shipwrecked on a deserted island—alone—and there was *no way* you could avoid it, what would you take along for survival and rescue if you were allowed only one small suitcase?

3. Tell how you feel about the following ideas:

   a. "Some people are brave because they don't know what fear is."
   b. "Some people are brave because they know what fear is, but they are able to hide it."
   c. "Courage is simply fear that has said its prayers."
   d. "There is nothing to fear but fear itself."
   e. "He's afraid of his shadow!"
   f. "Don't cry over spilled milk."

4. On page 110, Véronique describes herself, Bertille, and Laurent. Read the description aloud, then discuss how accurate you think she is.

V. HELPING CHILDREN TO REVEAL THEIR COMPREHENSION

1. As you know, Véronique kept a diary of their twelve-day adventure under the landslide. Suppose Véronique is your best friend and she let you read two weeks in her diary (from December 27th through January 9th). What would you find there? Put yourself in Véronique's place. What would she have written?
2. What might Bertille's postcards have said if she had written one each day *after* the landslide (with the intention of sending them home after the rescue)?
3. Suppose there were *not* five but *six* children trapped by the landslide and *you* were the sixth person. Tell about *your* feelings, experiences, and contributions in this adventure. How would things have been different if you had been there?
4. Draw a map of the children's journey from the time they left their home in Paris to the hotel where they were taken (except for Laurent, who was taken to the hospital) after their rescue.
5. Suppose Laurent had taken a flash camera, eight flashbulbs, and a twelve-exposure roll of film with him. What pictures do you think he would have selected to take as a record of their

"vacation"? Sketch and caption the pictures as they might have appeared after they'd been developed and put into Laurent's photo album.

6. Such an event as this would probably gain worldwide coverage in newspapers, magazines, and on radio and television. As a reporter, feature writer for a magazine, or radio/TV newsman, you are first on the scene for an exclusive interview. Write a newspaper account or feature article for your magazine of the near-tragic experiences of these five children. Or conduct a radio or TV interview with these five children (or with one of them). What were the major incidents? Who were the heroes? How did *luck* enter into the situation? What deaths occurred?

7. The three columns below are headed with the names of the three oldest children trapped by the landslide. Put an "X" opposite as many of the words and phrases (add any you don't find!) which best tell what your opinion now is of each of these people:

LAURENT	VÉRONIQUE	BERTILLE
bossy	weak	spoiled
mean	lazy	brave
stupid	unreasonable	a good leader
a good leader	foolish	a troublemaker
wise	brave	unselfish
selfish	a poor leader	thoughtful
spoiled	fearful	strong
misunderstood	compassionate	independent
fearful	fair	intelligent
courageous	loving and kind	cruel
shy	irresponsible	dishonest
creative	selfish	childish

VI. RELATED-TO-READING EXPERIENCES

1. Houdini was a magician and "escape artist" *extraordinaire*! Certain detective or mystery stories and stories of adventure as well as many television programs are popular because their heroes get into *impossible-to-escape-from* situations. Yet, they always manage to escape. Most people seem to like those stories in which escape is *believable* because it's managed by careful planning or by being clever, tricky, and a little lucky instead of having Superman come to the rescue at the last moment. Try your hand at being a "literature (or TV) detective" on the trail of believable solutions to plots which writers have written for their heroes. You might want to use a "research form" like the one below:

Date	Title (Book or TV program)	Character(s) Involved	The Problem Situation	The Outcome	Your Rating

2. Choose one or two of the television programs you watch regularly and make a list of the *improvisations* or "inventions" the characters in the program make in order to help themselves in some way to get out of a jam or to play a joke, etc.
3. Have a mock trial—"The People of the State *vs.* Bertille" (or Laurent)—with judge, jury, defense and prosecuting attorneys attempting to find and punish the person to blame for the near-death of the five children.
4. Compare the situations, the problems, and the people in *Landslide!* with those in *Robinson Crusoe* and/or *Swiss Family Robinson.*
5. The author, Véronique Day, does not give the reader very many clues about the personalities of the two youngest

children trapped by the landslide: Alexis and Daniel. Write a biographical sketch of these two boys so that the reader will feel he knows them as well as he does Laurent, Bertille, and Véronique.

6. Laurent's father said (p. 8): "But the world needs boys who can take responsibility. The world, Laurent, doesn't need snails."

Monsieur Nortier said (p. 18): "The ravine is a bad neighbor whom I make use of since I can't get rid of him. In life one should try to reap some benefit even from the troubles that can't be avoided."

Discuss what you feel these two men meant; give some other examples of situations you know about; tell whether you agree or disagree with their ideas and why.

7. Investigate the uses and meanings for the words *pessimistic* and *optimistic*. Make a list of all the people in the story and tell why you feel they were pessimistic or optimistic (or a little of both).

8. In the story, the author presents you with some ideas about suffering from pain, filth, hunger, cold, flood (p. 77); about obedience (p. 67); about fears of insects and rodents (p. 82); about fears of darkness and the unknown (p. 29); about birth (p. 85) and death (pp. 21, 87–88, 89). Since most of these are unpleasant things to think about, tell why you think the writer should (or should not) have put them in the book.

9. Go to the library and get a copy of the *Boy Scout Handbook* and/or the *Girl Scout Handbook* as well as some of the merit-badge books such as those on *Camping, Handicrafts, Signaling, Pioneering, Cooking, Forestry,* and *Electricity.* From this research, make a display of some of the things that anyone could improvise with common, ordinary materials he finds free in his surroundings—cooking utensils, a compass, etc.

10. Find out all you can about Samuel Morse and the famous Morse Code. Prepare a *This Is Your Life* report and find someone (a Scout or local telegrapher, perhaps) to come in and demonstrate message-sending via Morse Code.

VII. VOCABULARY THAT MAY NEED DEVELOPING

1. Some readers may enjoy the values gained from an investigation of meanings and origins of foreign words that have achieved common usage in written and spoken American English. Such a study might be called "Word Imports from France" (or Germany, England, etc.). Motivation for this kind of research may stem from a discussion of such words as: *rucksack (pack, knapsack), plague, au revoir, madame, mademoiselle, monsieur,* etc.

2. Words such as *crippled, spoiled, trapped,* and *lost* have multiple meanings. Some students may enjoy creating as many different sentences as they can to show different meanings for such words. For example:

   "You *lost* me way back at the beginning of your story!"
   "I nearly *lost* my mind when. . ."

VIII. OTHER SELECTIONS ON A SIMILAR THEME: A SELECTIVE BIBLIOGRAPHY

Chase, Mary Ellen. *Sailing the Seven Seas.* Boston: Houghton Mifflin, 1958. (Available as a Dell Yearling book.)

Defoe, Daniel. *Robinson Crusoe,* available in many editions.

George, Jean. *My Side of the Mountain.* N.Y.: Dutton, 1959.

Hoff, Carol. *Johnny Texas.* Chicago: Follett, 1950. (Available as Dell Yearling book.)

Sperry, A   ng. *Call It Courage.* N.Y.: Macmillan.

Wyss, Jc   d. *Swiss Family Robinson,* available in many editions.

Poetry

"Cold Winter Is Now in the Wood" by Elizabeth Coatsworth, from *Away Goes Sally,* N.Y.: Macmillan, 1934.

"Hope Is the Thing with Feathers" by Emily Dickinson, from *Emily Dickinson,* N.Y.: Dell, 1960.

"Stopping by Woods on a Snowy Evening" by Robert Frost, from *Piping Down the Valleys Wild*, selected by Nancy Larrick, N.Y.: Delacorte, 1968.

"Winter Night" by Mary Frances Butts, from *Time for Poetry* edited by May Hill Arbuthnot, Chicago: Scott, Foresman, 1952.

THE SATURDAYS

by ELIZABETH ENRIGHT

Illustrated by the Author

I. THE STORY

The four Melendy children—Mona, Rush, Randy, and Oliver—live in an old brownstone house in New York with their widowed father, who is a writer, and their old housekeeper and nurse, Cuffy. Tired of wasting good Saturdays doing nothing but wishing for bigger allowances, the Melendys jump at Randy's idea for the Independent Saturday Afternoon Adventure Club, in which they agree to pool their resources so that each of them can have at least one really good spree.

II. PREREADING DISCUSSION QUESTIONS

The questions which follow are illustrative of the kinds which teachers can prepare for the purpose of releasing children to reveal how *they feel* about some of the same larger ideas and bigger meanings contained in the book *before* it is read.

About Using Leisure Time

1. Almost everyone at one time or another has found, perhaps due to illness or because of the weather or some punishment, that he has had to stay in all day. List the kinds of things you have done on such a day. Now, look at the list. What if, on a certain day when you were forced to stay inside, *none of these things had any interest for you*? What if you were just bored, *bored,* BORED? This, too, has happened to most people your age. Tell of a time when you felt this way and how you came up with something *new* and *different* to do in order to get over your boredom.

About Cooperative Enterprises

2. In order to help out in a "common cause," many people "pitch in" and donate their efforts or their time or their money. All together, they are able to do things that one or two of them alone would find very difficult, if not impossible, to do. Sometimes this is called *teamwork* or *national effort, community drives, school spirit, family enterprises, esprit de corps, cooperative ventures, club projects, fund campaigns,* and so on. What are some examples of team projects of which you have been a part?

3. Suppose a group of people got together and decided to pool their money so that one of their members could benefit by having a terrific vacation. What do you think about such an idea? What kinds of problems do you feel it might present? What kinds of advantages?

4. What cooperative enterprises do you know about (cooperative markets, apartments, Social Security, etc.)?

About Clubs and Organizations

5. What kinds of clubs or organizations have you belonged to? What were their names? Their purpose? What did you do?

6. What kinds of clubs or organizations do you know about to which adults belong? What are their names? Their purposes? What do the members do?

7. How many reasons can you think of that people form clubs?

8. How many reasons can you think of that people want to join clubs that are already organized?

9. There are some people who think that clubs or organizations are unfair, un-American, prejudiced because not everyone wants to can join them. What are your feelings about such clubs?

About Atypical Families

10. It is not so unusual anymore to find "incomplete" families. Some children are raised by grandparents; others are raised by aunts and uncles or other relatives; some are raised by a stepmother or stepfather or by a nurse, housekeeper, or "nanny." Other families—through some kind of misfortune or other—have to grow up with only one of their two parents in which

33

case the father, for example, has to assume the role of both mother and father for his children. Why do you think it's possible for such children to grow up happy and successful under such circumstances?

III. PREREADING ACTIVITIES

1. Many clubs and organizations, government agencies and the like use the *initials* of the name of their organization as a "nickname." Do some research. Using a newspaper, make a list of all those you can find in addition to those you know about and hear frequently. USO; NAACP; SPCA; AAA; UN; NBC; GM; USAF; FBI; and so forth. In your search, organize your findings into such categories as: *(a)* Children's Organizations, *(b)* Unions, *(c)* Federal Agencies, *(d)* Business Firms, Companies, or Corporations, *(e)* Professional Organizations (teachers, doctors, etc.), *(f)* Military Branches, *(g)* Social Organizations, etc.

2. Suppose you and a few of your very best friends decided to form a special, secret club around some secret purpose or interest all of you have agreed upon (such as weight watching, body building, reading, writing, game playing, dancing, etc.). Think of an unusual name for it which can be formed by the first letter of each word in the name.

3. Most people, in one way or another, are hoarders—collectors of all kinds of "precious" things—things they've made, been given, found or bought while on a trip, and so on. Look through your precious souvenir collections and make a list of twelve of your most prized possessions. Also, make a list of twelve articles which you easily "could part with" now—although at one time they were so valuable to you that you decided to save them. If you don't mind others knowing, tell where you "store" your collections. Find out where others keep theirs.

4. Suppose, in your house or apartment, there were a room given to you—*with absolutely no strings attached*—to arrange, decorate, and use in anyway you desired. The size of the room is

13-1/2 feet by 48 feet. It has one door, three windows, two electric lights in the ceiling, and three electric wall sockets. Tell what you'd put in this room. How would you arrange it? How would you decorate it? What would you do in it? Who else, besides yourself, would be permitted to enter? What name would you give to this room?

5. Note Elizabeth Enright's illustration on the title page of this book. Write a brief paragraph telling what you think it means.

IV. POSTREADING DISCUSSION QUESTIONS

1. In what way(s) was the *Independent Saturday Afternoon Adventure Club* the same as clubs you have helped form? In what way(s) was it different?

2. On page 12, the author, Elizabeth Enright, gives us a pretty big clue about how the Melendy children were able to get along so well without a mother; she also gives a clue about Cuffy's personality when she writes: "Cuffy ruled the house. And it was an extensive domain." What incidents do you recall (or, can you locate) that would support that statement?

3. On Saturdays Two, Three, Four, and Five, each of the four Melendy children has *his Saturday*. Which one of th: spent his Saturday (and his or her money) in the queerest, most ridiculous way? Why do you think so?

4. On page 62, Rush meets a rather grumpy, gloomy old man when he stops to watch a snow-removal machine at work. How do you explain this man's feelings? How are they the same as those of some people today who don't like change or who are afraid of it?

5. After Mona left the beauty shop, she felt gloriously happy (page 96): "It's something to discover that you're going to grow up beautiful instead of ugly." Suppose Mona had said this to you, her best friend. What would you have said in answer to Mona's new feeling about herself?

6. Along with Mr. Melendy's approval of the I.S.A.A. Club went his conditions or rules. As serious and important as they are, one *might* think that the children didn't think so since, on

several occasions, they *seemed* to be poking fun at them. How can you explain this? What do you think? Are Mr. Melendy's rules similar to any you've heard before (page 23)?

V. HELPING CHILDREN TO REVEAL THEIR COMPREHENSION

1. Suppose that, instead of four Melendy children, there were five and *you* are the fifth—the twin brother or sister of any one of the four: Mona, Rush, Randy, or Oliver. What woul your name be? What unusual trait or talent would you ha that would make you a part of this unusual family? Wh would your interests be? What would you want to be whe you grow up? What kinds of "good habits" and "bad habits" would you have? Write an additional chapter called "Saturday 5-1/2," answering these questions as well as the most important one of all: What would you do with your $1.60?

2. You have been asked by *Look* magazine to do a feature article on this most unusual Melendy family. Select what you feel to be the twelve to fifteen most interesting, human-interest situations in the book and sketch them. (Or, if you're a photography "bug," you may want to get some of your friend together and "stage the scenes" for your *Look* article.) Examine some issues of *Look* (or *Life*) magazine. Notice that most feature picture articles have a paragraph or two as an introduction and one or two as a conclusion. A brief paragraph then, in addition, about each of your pictures should make most interesting article to read. You might want to call you article "The Miraculous Melendys."

3. As you know, the Melendy children's father, Mr. Martin Melendy, was a writer and lecturer. Suppose one of his favorite "games" to help pass the time while he was away from his family was that of keeping a "running account" of words and phrases that best described the characteristics of each person in his house in New York City: Mona, Rush, Randy, Oliver, Willy, Cuffy, and even Isaac (who came along later). What would his list look like?

4. A $100 Shopping Spree! Using one or more mail-order cata-
logues, make a list of the things (and their prices!) that you
would buy if you had an old room like the Melendys'
OFFICE. Stretch your money to make it go as far as you can.
Make or build everything possible. The only thing that is in
this room is an old piano.

5. Suppose you lived across the street from the Melendys and
that you were the very best friend of Mona, Rush, Randy, *or*
Oliver. Since they had no money to spend for three out of
four Saturdays, you spent those days with the one who is your
best friend. Describe what you did on those *three* Saturdays
with your Melendy pal.

VI. RELATED-TO-READING EXPERIENCES

1. Write for a free "Visitor's Map of New York City." On it,
attempt to locate the Melendys' house; the places visited by
Mona, Rush, Randy, and Oliver on each of their Saturdays; the
tea party with Mrs. Oliphant on Saturday Seven; Randy's mis-
hap on Saturday Six; and the various places suggested on pages
120–121.

2. Throughout the story, numerous references are made to a war
which later became World War II. Find out as much as you can
about World War II. Trace it from its earliest beginnings. What
countries became involved? What leaders were in power?
Cuffy's brief, descriptive statement on war to Mona on page
101 sounds authoritative yet comforting. Locate as many
references to World War II as you can. Compare this information with that you turned up in your research. How would you
decide whether or not the feelings of the characters in this
story were typical of the feelings held by most Americans at
that time in history?

VII. VOCABULARY THAT MAY NEED DEVELOPING

1. Willy Sloper's language is as revealing as it is different. Some children may find it fun, as well as beneficial, to examine Willy's level of language not as "poor" or "bad grammar" but as a level of language used in effective communication. Some may want to view it as a "foreign language" and translate such words as *opry, Eyetalian, dang, minna, bronickal,* etc.

2. Prepare a full-page magazine advertisement (or television commercial) for one's favorite food, sport, or celebrated personality, book, etc. The following words must be used in the "ad": *virtuous* (p. 99), *lugubrious* (p. 10), *disheveled* (p. 140), *inexorably* (p. 28), *wheedlingly* (p. 65), and *vanity* (p. 103).

3. *Antique Collectors:* Many children like to begin notebooks or card files of words which are becoming extinct through disuse although they still appear in the more "permanent" language of talk written down via literature. Words like *icebox* and *salt cellars* are two examples.

VIII. OTHER SELECTIONS ON A SIMILAR THEME: A SELECTIVE BIBLIOGRAPHY

Enright, Eli   .. *The Four-Story Mistake.* N.Y.: Holt, 1942. (Available   . Dell Yearling book.)

_____ . *Then   here Were Five.* N.Y.: Holt, 1944. (Available as a Dell Yearling book.)

_____ . *Thimble Summer.* N.Y.: Holt, 1938.

Taylor, Sydney. *All-of-a-Kind Family.* Chicago: Follett, 1951. (Available as a Dell Yearling book.)

_____ . *All-of-a-Kind Family Uptown.* Chicago: Follett, 1959. (Available as a Dell Yearling book.)

_____ . *More All-of-a-Kind Family.* Chicago: Follett, 1954. (Available as a Dell Yearling book.)

Poetry

"I Meant To Do My Work Today" by Richard Le Gallienne, from *Piping Down the Valleys Wild,* selected by Nancy Larrick, N.Y.: Delacorte, 1968.

"The Little Land" by Robert Louis Stevenson, from *A Child's Garden of Verses*, available in many editions.

THE FOUR-STORY MISTAKE

by ELIZABETH ENRIGHT

Illustrated by the Author

I. THE STORY

The Four-Story Mistake is a house—a very odd-looking house because the architect mistakenly built only three stories when the owner had ordered four, and the unimaginative owner added a fourth story in the shape of a cupola when he really should have left well enough alone. Into it moved the Melendy family—Rush, Mona, Oliver, Randy, Father, Cuffy, their long-suffering housekeeper, and Willy Sloper, furnace man, handyman and, now, farmhand. There they soon forgot their dejection at having to leave their old brownstone house in New York City, and become busily absorbed in the exciting adventures of life in the country and all sorts of attractions discovered in the Four-Story Mistake.

II. PREREADING DISCUSSION QUESTIONS

The questions which follow are illustrative of the kinds which teachers can prepare for the purpose of releasing children to reveal how *they feel* about some of the same larger ideas and bigger meanings contained in the book *before* it is read.

About Moving

1. When people pack up and move from one house or apartment to another, from one town, city, state, or country to another, usually they have mixed feelings: a little bit *sad* about the place they are leaving, a little bit *glad* about the place they are going to. Sometimes these feelings are mixtures of *fear* about the unknown that's ahead and the *excitement* of discovering

unexpected pleasures. Sometimes these feelings are mixtures of *anger*—because such a change brings an interruption to one's comfort and conveniences, disrupts one's routines, and leaves good friends and familiar places behind—and *happiness* about the possibility of new people and new places being "better than ever."

Most people your age can remember such a move and the feelings they had. Tell one of the most *pleasant* and one of the most *unpleasant* feelings you have had about moving.

2. For what reasons do families move? What things do parents think about before they decide to move? What things do children think about when they are told that they must move? What kinds of problems frequently occur when people move into a new place? What kinds of adjustments do people have to make?

About Exploring New Places

3. Almost everyone has had the experience of inves g place on his own, exploring and discovering thi u himself. It could be a friend's or neighbor's hou e attic of your own house; a cabin in the woods r cot e at a lake or seashore which your parents rented for a few eeks; it could be a new fishing spot on a river or a place in the woods where you've stopped to rest or camp; it could be a relative's house or a room in it, or a garage or barn; it could be a vacant lot, deserted house, boat, trailer, etc. Tell about a time when you've been in a *completely new* place—one absolutely foreign to you. Describe how you felt, what you did, how you went about it, what expected *and unexpected* things you uncovered, etc.

4. Some people seem to be able to find things more easily than others. How many parents have said, "Good grief, Sara Lou! Here's your arithmetic book—right where you left it! If it were a snake, it would bite you!"? Others seem always to be the ones who find lost balls, a coin in the street, a ring or watch nobody claims, etc. These people seem to have their eyes wide open—always looking, thinking, noticing, "never missing a thing." Tell about something you've always been looking for

41

but never found. Tell about something valuable you found accidentally that you could claim for your own and keep.

5. What do the following statements mean and how do you feel about them?

"Finders keepers, losers weepers!"
"Possession is nine-tenths of the law."

About Learning New Skills

6. As you remember your problems, hardships (and, perhaps your aches and pains, too!) when you first tried to learn to roller-skate, ski, ice-skate, ride a bike, swim, jump rope, climb a tree, and so forth, what "best advice" would you offer a good friend (or brother or sister) who is just about to learn for the first time? What "most important thing to remember" would you mention? What other kind of help might you give?

About the Hardships of War

7. When a country is at war, what kinds of hardships do the people (who are not on the battlefield) suffer? What kinds of sacrifices do the people at home have to make? What kinds of things can they do on the "home front" to help win a war being fought thousands of miles away by their own relatives, friends, and fellow countrymen? What things could people your age do? If, for example, something like *rubber* or *soap* were needed badly by the military men doing the actual fighting, and it became very, very scarce, how would you decide who should have first choice? Our soldiers or the people at home?

III. PREREADING ACTIVITIES

1. Not everyone is *gifted*, but all people have *gifts*—unusual talents to do something particularly well or better than average. One person's gift may be cooking, while another's might be sewing. Still others may have unusual skills in music, art, mechanics, wood or metal craft, nature, storytelling, acting,

singing, speaking, electricity, chemistry, or athletic feats, and so on. Since these are *talents* which are distinct and "better than average," they are valuable. They are worth something to those who don't have equal ability. Such *gifts* usually develop through a lot of practice and experience because a person *enjoys* and *likes* the task, and *not* because he has to or is made to do it.

Think about your unique skill or gift. What would you consider to be your *most "salable"* one? If there were some emergency and you had to help earn some money, present an example of what you would do that others would pay for.

2. Suppose your class needed $100 to take an all-day trip at the end of the school year. Write a detailed plan to present to the class on the best, fastest, most enjoyable way to earn money. Be sure to list all the details. Will anything have to be purchased? When would the best time for "selling" be? What would be a fair price? Who will probably be your best "customers," etc.?

3. Plan a concert, art show, fun 'n' game night, play, magazine, auction, cookie or candy sale, etc., in order to raise some money for a worthy cause. What would be involved in terms of time, place and space, money, adult help, number of people needed, etc.?

IV. POSTREADING DISCUSSION QUESTIONS

1. As you know, Mona's greatest hope and constant dream is that of becoming a famous actress—then, she was offered a radio contract to act; Randy found a precious diamond, which she sold; and Mrs. Oliphant, it seems, always has the habit of appearing out of nowhere (like a good fairy) with solutions, special treats, and surprise gifts. What do you think: Is this story just pure fiction—a long "fairy tale"—or do things like this really happen? Could they happen to ordinary, real people like us?

2. One thing you may have noticed which doesn't make Mona, Rush, Randy, and Oliver very "believable" as a family is that

they never seem to fight or argue very much. If they do get angry with one another, it seems to be only for a brief moment. If Elizabeth Enright were visiting you today, what suggestions would you make to her?

V. HELPING CHILDREN TO REVEAL THEIR COMPREHENSION

1. Both Oliver and Randy discovered secret rooms in the Four Story Mistake. Choose either one of these incidents (or both if you wish) and write a radio script. Then, with a cast you select, dramatize the situation. Remember: background music, sound effects, and natural dialogue can turn this into a spine-chilling "thriller."
2. "Clarinda—1869." What famous person might she have been? Write her biography. The author, Elizabeth Enright, gives you only a few clues and facts. Using these, make her turn out to be a well-known personage of recent times.
3. Sketch a picture of the Melendys' "OFFICE."
4. Sketch a picture (or make a model, two inches equaling one foot) of Rush's tree house.
5. Following the program (p. 94) of *The Melendys' Christmas Show,* make a series of "Shoebox Theatres"—still-life scenes from the show.
6. Suppose you are a wealthy aunt or uncle of the Melendy children, and you know each of them very well—their likes, interests, etc. Tell what you'd buy for each one of them for their birthdays. What would be *the most appropriate* gift for each of them? What would you buy for Cuffy? Willy? Mr. Melendy (who is your "brother")? What would you buy for:
   a. John Doe
   b. Phony
   c. King Cole, King Kong, and Licorice
   d. Crusty
   e. Lorna Doone
7. If Mona, Rush, Randy, and Oliver all were your very best

44

friends, and if you were theirs, what do you think you would
find underneath your Christmas tree this year? What would be
in each of the four packages *for you* from each one of the
Melendy children?

8. Write a story about Willy Sloper's childhood and life before he
was hired by Martin Melendy. (You may want to read *The
Saturdays* and *Then There Were Five* to get more information.)

VI. RELATED-TO-READING EXPERIENCES

1. Do some research and write a guide booklet entitled *How To
Raise an Alligator.* Or you may want to try the same title with
a humorous slant: *How To Raise an Alligator—Single-
handedly!*
2. Go on an Architectural Hunt. Find the oldest houses and/or
buildings in your community. Look for houses with dormer
windows, buildings with cupolas, etc. Take photographs of
them (or sketch them) to share with other readers of this
book.
3. Find out how the streets, houses and buildings, businesses and
airports in your community got their names.
4. If you live near a shallow stream, creek, or river (fresh-flowing
water), search for some caddis fly cocoons (or, caddis houses,
as Randy calls them) and bring them to school. Learn all about
them. What time of the year, usually, are they found? How
long does it take them to hatch? How do they reproduce?
What is their life-span, food preferences, etc.?

VII. VOCABULARY THAT MAY NEED DEVELOPING

From the *naturalness* of time, place, and circumstance as well as
from the author's vast and varied experiences, most readers will
come away from their interaction with *The Four-Story Mistake* with
a deeper appreciation of literature resulting from their contacts with
the rich vocabulary so necessary to the telling of this tale.

It would be valuable and interesting for children to pool their special "technical" vocabularies—and add to them throughout the year—by creating a dictionary of technical terms and their meanings. For some readers, *The Four-Story Mistake* could be a starting place:

Music words: *sonata, opus;* Dance words: *pirouetting, cakewalk;* Theatre words: *audition, Duse;* Nature words: *caddis fly, jack-in-the-pulpit, Dutchman's-breeches;* Architectural words: *cupola, dormer window;* Words of another time: *gramaphone, antimacassars, melodeon;* Words of war and freedom: *the duration, Victory garden, War Bonds, Savings Stamps, U-boats, rationing, to hoard;* and so on.

VIII. OTHER SELECTIONS ON A SIMILAR THEME: A SELECTED BIBLIOGRAPHY

Coatsworth, Elizabeth. *Away Goes Sally.* N.Y.: Macmillan, 1934.
_____. *The Fair American.* N.Y.: Macmillan, 1940.
_____. *Five-Bushel Farm.* N.Y.: Macmillan, 1939.
Enright, Elizabeth. *The Saturdays.* N.Y.: Holt, 1941. (Available as a Dell Yearling book.)
_____. *Then There Were Five.* N.Y.: Holt, 1944. (Available as a Dell Yearling book.)
_____. *Thimble Summer.* N.Y.: Holt, 1938.
Sawyer, Ruth. *Roller Skates.* N.Y.: Viking, 1936.
_____. *Year of Jubilo.* N.Y.: Viking, 1940.

Poetry
"Our Circus" by Laura Lee Randall, from *Child Life,* September 1924.
"Sneezles" by A.A. Milne, from *The World of Christopher Robin,* N.Y.: Dutton, 1958.

THEN THERE WERE FIVE

by ELIZABETH ENRIGHT

Illustrated by the Author

I. THE STORY

With Father in Washington and Cuffy away visiting a sick cousin, the Melendy children—Mona, Rush, Randy, and Oliver—have to take care of themselves and the farm with just Willy, the hired man, to help. Things begin to happen right from the moment when Rush starts out in the buggy to collect scrap, and discovers a mysterious house and a boy who needs a friend desperately.

II. PREREADING DISCUSSION QUESTIONS

The questions which follow are illustrative of the kinds which teachers can prepare for the purpose of releasing children to reveal how *they feel* about some of the same larger ideas and bigger meanings contained in the book *before* it is read.

About Patriotism
1. What kinds of qualities would you expect to find in a person who really is a *patriotic citizen* of his country?
2. In what ways would a United States *patriot* differ from a *patriot* who is a citizen of another country—Russia, England, Turkey, etc.?
3. In the history of the world, there have been many celebrated *patriots*. What are the names of some of them? Do you recall any facts that may have led to their being distinguished as *patriots*?

4. What kinds of qualities would you expect to find in a United States citizen who is considered *unpatriotic*? Can you remember the names of any famous people who became celebrated because of their *unpatriotic* ideas, beliefs, or deeds?

About Causes and Campaigns

5. What is the difference between a *cause* and a *campaign*?
6. How many *causes* can you list?
7. How many different kinds of *campaigns* can you list? (E.g., political; religious; fund; service; donations of blood, food, clothing; "support-the-idea" campaigns such as signing a petition, voting; etc.)
8. Disasters, emergencies, tragedies of all kinds (fires, floods, wars, diseases, assassinations, power failures, transportation accidents, epidemics, and so forth) tend to unite human beings for a common purpose or cause, namely survival. People make sacrifices in order to "fight" the emergency. Sometimes this means helping less fortunate people even though you may have many problems of your own. Most people give this kind of aid willingly because they know they are helping themselves by helping others. Thus, in such times, one might say that the "cause" becomes more important to an individual than his own personal interests, needs, and wants. In some situations, however, the crisis somes so quickly and is so grave that a person doesn't have much of a choice (if any) about sacrificing something "for the good of the cause."

   Suppose the hospital or jail in your community burned to the ground and your parents—along with everyone in the town—*were ordered* to donate *the use of one room* in your house or apartment for a patient or prisoner until the rebuilding was completed. What are your ideas about making such a sacrifice? Would you feel differently if your parents had been *asked* instead of ordered? Why? If people in your community were *asked* to do such a thing (it might be for as long as two years!), do you believe there would be enough volunteers? Why? Why not?
9. Happy, pleasant, enjoyable occasions also cause large numbers of people to rally together for a common cause: a spectacular

48

science experiment in space, the World Series, a sandy beach on a hot summer's day, Bob Hope's Christmas shows, the coronation of a king or queen, an eclipse of the sun, parties, donating food and clothing to the needy, giving gifts to poor children at Christmastime, etc. During such situations, people also contribute time, money, effort, interest, oral or written support, their physical presence, etc. Although such contributions probably are not "sacrifices" in the usual sense, they are investments in one's own pleasure and frequently require an individual to make choices and sacrifices in order to participate—such as saving one's money for a World's Series ticket or using his time to deliver food packages to orphanages.

Suppose a wealthy man in your community died and left the town enough money to buy the land and all of the materials for a community recreation center and swimming pool—*but not enough money for the labor to have it built*! Since the terms of his will said that everything must be completed on or before September 1st (or else the money would be used for something else), all the children aged ten to sixteen—girls as well as boys—have been asked to contribute their *entire summer vacations* this year (6 days a week, 9 to 5) digging, hauling dirt, mixing concrete, building, sawing, sewing, painting, etc., under the direction of several adults who are donating their time to teach you what to do. What are your ideas about your having to give up your summer plans for this project?

10. There have been other wars since World War II (1941—45) and the United States has been involved in some of them. For example, the Korean war and the Vietnamese war. What are your opinions about the involvement of the United States in these wars.

III. PREREADING ACTIVITIES

1. Go to the library and find several of Shakespeare's plays, for example, *Midsummer Night's Dream, Macbeth, Hamlet, The Taming of the Shrew, The Merchant of Venice.* Open them

randomly, skim through them, and search for a dozen or so brief quotations that you understand which you think are especially beautiful and wise. List them and read them to the class.

2. Consult a reference book of quotations. Make a collection of a dozen or so Shakespearean quotations which you feel would describe perfectly your ideas or feelings about *(a)* evildoers; *(b)* beautiful or lovely people, places, or things; *(c)* foolishness and folly; *(d)* sadness and/or *(e)* happiness, and so on.

3. By using newspapers, magazines, circulars mailed to your house and by asking parents and friends, how many *causes* and *campaigns* can you uncover? (Also note the "public service" commercials on radio, television as well as the ads on billboards and in trains and buses.) Categorize these in some way, e.g.:

> *International:* Foster Parents Plan, UNESCO, CARE
> *National:* Forest conservation (Smokey the Bear), civil rights, water and air pollution
> *State:* Aid to education, parks, campsites, lotteries
> *Local Community:* Fluoridation of water, traffic lights
> *Neighborhood:* Clean-up, fix-up, paint-up
> *School:* Band uniforms, books, movie projector, trips

Or such causes and campaigns may be organized under such headings as: *(a)* Freedom, *(b)* War-Peace, *(c)* Charity, *(d)* Conservation, *(e)* Prevention-Protection, *(f)* Money-raising, *(g)* Political, *(h)* Time-Skill-Service donations, *(i)* Material collections, etc.

4. Find the *Federal Laws*—and as many reasons for them as you can—which prohibit individuals like us from making medicine from drugs, making our own liquor, printing money. Why do you think such laws are necessary? States have similar laws about guns, cigarettes and tobacco, swimming and camping places, fireworks, times and places for hunting and fishing, etc. What are your opinions about the necessity for these laws?

5. Suppose today you wake up and find yourself living *fifteen years in the future*! You are fifteen years older; you are not in

school (unless you're a teacher!) but, instead, you are busy at your work—as a housewife, ball player, writer, television actress, taxi driver, waiter in a restaurant, etc.

Next door to you there is a ten-year-old boy (or girl) who lives with his (or her) *only* relative, an uncle. You have known this boy for more than seven years; you've played with him, taken him many places with you, invited him to spend his vacations with you, etc. He seems like a member of your family and you've become very, very fond of him. Thus, when you learn that his uncle has gone away and left him, you feel that the *most natural thing in the world* to do would be *to adopt* him to keep him from being sent to an orphanage. What things would you need to consider? What things would you have to do? Where (and from whom) would you go to get advice and help?

[NOTE: It might prove extremely valuable to have a social worker, a representative of a local adoption agency, and/or a lawyer or judge come for a visit to answer questions and provide accurate information.]

IV. POSTREADING DISCUSSION QUESTIONS

1. Discuss the relevancy of the author's use of the following:

   a. "Coals to Newcastle" (p. 146)
   b. "Johnstown Flood" (p. 14)
   c. "Great Wall of China" (p. 8)

2. Which one of the Melendys might be considered "accident prone?" Give reasons that you think so. (NOTE: Enright seems to have had her ideas, too. See page 5.)

3. Among their other creations, the Melendy children seem to have talent for inventing games to play. One might be called "The Vegetable-People" game (see page 181). Try playing this game using well-known athletes, movie or television stars. The other game in this story is one Rush just "happened to invent"

after he sat on a bunch of sandburs. It might have been called "The Troublesome Things I Can Do Without" game (see pages 63-64). Try playing this game with a few of your friends.

4. Suppose your class wanted to start a national campaign to guarantee help and equal rights for all *left-handed* people (or, to make the peacock the National Bird, or poison ivy your state flower, or to lower the prices on all candy, ice cream, and movie tickets for children under age eighteen). How would you begin? What would you do? Whose help would you need? Why? What kinds of other help would be needed? Why?

5. Discuss the meanings you believe are in the following quotations:

   a. After Father patted Lorna Doone and had given her a lump of sugar, he said, *"Don't let Washington hear about this."* (p. 11)

   b. After Father had told his children that he was "unfortunately too old and too decidedly a father" to be a soldier, Rush said, *"If we keep somebody* [his father] *from going to war by being dependents, then it seems as if we ought to do extra things about helping generally."* (p. 17)

   c. *"Under his* [Mark's] *ribs the hard, cold, fist-shaped thing that had hidden there for years became smaller, less and less, as if it were melting away, and in its place something grew and opened like the expanding leaves of a plant. Something warm and comfortable that tickled his ribs as it grew, and made him want to laugh a lot and be happy, and to see other people laugh."* (p. 143)

V. HELPING CHILDREN TO REVEAL THEIR COMPREHENSION

1. Write an *epilogue* to the story called: "Ten Years Later." What would the Four-Story Mistake look like? Who would be living there? How many more additions and subtractions would there be? How old would Mona, Rush, Randy, Oliver, and Mark be? Where would they be? What would they be doing? What of Willy and Cuffy?

2. Suppose Martin Melendy, the children's widowed father, during his long absences due to his work in Washington, had met, fallen in love with, and married a wonderful woman to bring home to Braxton to live with them in the Four-Story Mistake. Write Elizabeth Enright's next book for her: *Then There Were Six*. What would their stepmother be like? How would they get along with her? How would she get along with them? What of Cuffy and Willy?

3. Using any reference material you can find (seed, bulb, flower, and grass catalogues are helpful), make a collection of pictures (sketched, cut out, or photographed) of all the plant and vegetable life found growing around the Four-Story Mistake. Using "word pictures," make a floral arrangement which you feel would look beautiful as a centerpiece on a large banquet table.

4. Using the school's public-address system (or tape recorder) hold "Man on the Street" interviews with eyewitnesses to these incidents: (1) The Citronella Caper; (2) The Mysterious Death of Oren Meeker; and (3) Oliver's Ordeal (in the well).

VI. RELATED-TO-READING EXPERIENCES

1. What kinds of "drives" have you noticed recently? What drives would you support if you could? What kinds of drives have you worked on (church, school, Scout, community, etc.)?

2. Some organizations collect scrap (paper, cloth, iron) and sell it. Find out how much is paid per pound for these materials.

3. During World War II, there were drives to collect metal, paper, and fat. Try to find out why. Also, during World War II, people were asked to "help win the war" by *conserving* all kinds of things: gasoline, rubber, food, fuel, certain medicines, sugar, coffee, and so forth. Why were they asked to do this? How could this help win a war? When people won't conserve things voluntarily, what can be done about it? Would you call them unpatriotic?

4. During World War II, people—out of necessity—learned to improvise, invent, substitute, much the same as one would "make do" if he were lost in a forest, marooned on a deserted

island, or trapped miles from anywhere
lanche. Prepare a *Recipe Book for Deserte*
include not only things to eat (sassafras t
but also *recipes* for making soap, fire, can

5. Make a variety of items (pictures, original m
   original books, toys, games, etc.), then
   auction. Invite a professional auctioneer to
   to teach you about auctions. A few may
   attend a local auction and report to the
   observed.

6. Newspaper Headline Research: Go to the l
   see the back copies of newspapers (man
   are on "film strips") from about 1939-40
   notebook with you and write down the hea
   think reveal or reflect people's feeling about
   time. Others may wish to do the same with
   Vietnam wars. What similarities and differe
   During this research, it also would be interestin
   of *prices* of food, clothing, cars, etc., and comp
   present—as well as to prices mentioned in *The*
   The Four-Story Mistake.

7. Prepare a simple guidebook called *Canning and*
   Young Cooks (jellies, jams, pickles, tomatoes, et

8. Prepare a report for the F.B.I. called "The T
   and Traitors"—people like Aaron Burr, Lee l
   and "The Man Without a Country" are exam
   who might be included.

9. Find out what is meant by *subversive* and *subve*
   tions.

10. Go on a musical scavenger hunt. Find the titles a
    the music, too, if possible—perhaps some old
    records are still in storage) of America's war son
    those of World War II). What do these tell you a
    and the people during these times? Below are a
    help you begin your search:

    God Bless America
    Any Bonds Today?

2. Suppose Martin Melendy, the children's widowed father, during his long absences due to his work in Washington, had met, fallen in love with, and married a wonderful woman to bring home to Braxton to live with them in the Four-Story Mistake. Write Elizabeth Enright's next book for her: *Then There Were Six*. What would their stepmother be like? How would they get along with her? How would she get along with them? What of Cuffy and Willy?

3. Using any reference material you can find (seed, bulb, flower, and grass catalogues are helpful), make a collection of pictures (sketched, cut out, or photographed) of all the plant and vege-table life found growing around the Four-Story Mistake. Using "word pictures," make a floral arrangement which you feel would look beautiful as a centerpiece on a large banquet table.

4. Using the school's public-address system for tape recording, hold "Man on the Street" interviews with eyewitnesses to these incidents: (1) The Citronella Caper; (2) The Mysterious Death of Oren Meeker; and (3) Oliver's Ordeal (in the hall).

VI. RELATED-TO-READING EXPERIENCES

1. What kinds of "drives" have you noticed recently? What drives would you support if you could? What kinds of drives have you worked on (church, school, Scout, community, etc.)?

2. Some organizations collect scrap (paper, cloth, iron) and sell it. Find out how much is paid per pound for these materials.

3. During World War II, there were drives to collect metal, paper, and fat. Try to find out why. Also, during World War II, people were asked to "help win the war" by *conserving* all kinds of things: gasoline, rubber, food, fuel, certain medicines, sugar, coffee, and so forth. Why were they asked to do this? How could this help win a war? When people won't conserve things voluntarily, what can be done about it? Would you call them unpatriotic?

4. During World War II, people—out of necessity—learned to improvise, invent, substitute, much the same as one would "make do" if he were lost in a forest, marooned on a deserted

island, or trapped miles from anywhere by a flood or avalanche. Prepare a *Recipe Book for Deserted People*. It should include not only things to eat (sassafras tea, bee balm, etc.), but also *recipes* for making soap, fire, candles, ink, rope, etc.

5. Make a variety of items (pictures, original music compositions, original books, toys, games, etc.), then plan to have an auction. Invite a professional auctioneer to come to your class to teach you about auctions. A few may want to plan to attend a local auction ⌐rt to the class what they observed.

6. Newspaper Headline Research: Go ⌐ ⌐ library and ask to see the back copies of newspapers (many of these now are on "film strips") from about 1939-40 to 1945. Take a notebook with you and write down the headlines which you think reveal or reflect people's feeling about war during that time. Others may wish to do the same with the Korean and Vietnam wars. What similarities and differences are noted? During this research, it also would be interesting to make notes of *prices* of food, clothing, cars, etc., and compare them to the present—as well as to prices mentioned in *The Saturdays* and *The Four-Story Mistake*.

7. Prepare a simple guidebook called *Canning and Preserving for Young Cooks* (jellies, jams, pickles, tomatoes, etc.).

8. Prepare a report for the F.B.I. called "The Ten Worst Spies and Traitors"—people like Aaron Burr, Lee Harvey Oswald, and "The Man Without a Country" are examples of people who might be included.

9. Find out what is meant by *subversive* and *subversive organizations.*

10. Go on a musical scavenger hunt. Find the titles and lyrics (and the music, too, if possible—perhaps some old phonograph records are still in storage) of America's war songs (especially those of World War II). What do these tell you about the war and the people during these times? Below are a few titles to help you begin your search:

God Bless America
Any Bonds Today?

This Is the Army, Mr. Jones
American Patrol
This Is My Country
I'll Be Home for Christmas
I'm Getting Tired So I Can Sleep
Praise the Lord and Pass the Ammunition
I Left My Heart at the Stagedoor Canteen
When the Lights Come on Again All Over the World

World War I and earlier:
You're a Grand Old Flag
Over There
Battle Hymn of the Republic
How're You Gonna Keep 'Em Down on the Farm
Oh, How I Hate to Get Up in the Morning
The Star-spangled Banner
When Johnny Comes Marching Home

What can you find out about composers of songs like these?

11. Find out about *causes* such as the *Women's Suffrage Movement, Prohibition,* etc. Who were the major leaders on both sides—pro and con?

12. Collect circulars, advertisements, and other information on all of the *foundations, societies,* and *associations* you can. A convenient but large listing can be found in most paperback copies of *world almanacs* such as *Information Please* and *World Almanac and Book of Facts.* Select some of these and write to their headquarters asking for information about their organizations.

13. What can people do to protect themselves from being "conned" by fraudulent *causes, campaigns,* and *fund-raising drives* that seem good because they have been disguised?

VII. VOCABULARY THAT MAY NEED DEVELOPING

1. Some readers will enjoy beginning a collection of words no longer in popular usage, such as *dry goods* (store), *confectionery* (p. 102), *surrey* (p. 11), and World War II words, *flak* (p.

150), *Zeroes* (p. 17), a *Sherman tank* (p. 73), a *blockbuster* (p. 9), *ration ticket* (p. 146); and so on. Such a collection might be called "Attic Antiques."

2. In addition to the veritable "jungle" of names of plant and animal life, some children will find it interesting to find different ways and situations in which to use *dilapidated* (p. 205) and *pandemonium* (p. 195). Two other words hold exciting information about natural phenomena: *obsidian* (p. 67) and *Perseids* (p. 89).

3. Probably it would prove most valuable to suggest that children search out as many different meanings of the word *still* as they can find. (Oren Meeker's *still*, of the "moonshine" variety, in an indirect but most significant way, affects the lives of everyone in the story, from Chapter II on.)

VIII. OTHER SELECTIONS ON A SIMILAR THEME: A SELECTED BIBLIOGRAPHY

Cleary, Beverly. *Ellen Tebbits*. N.Y.: Morrow, 1951.

_____. *Henry and Beezus*. N.Y.: Morrow, 1952.

_____. *Henry and Ribsy*. N.Y.: Morrow, 1954.

_____. *Henry and the Club House*. N.Y.: Morrow, 1962.

_____. *Henry and the Paper Route*. N.Y.: Morrow, 1957.

_____. *Henry Huggins*. N.Y.: Morrow, 1950.

Enright, Elizabeth. *Gone-Away Lake*. N.Y.: Harcourt, 1957.

_____. *Return to Gone-Away Lake*. N.Y.: Harcourt, 1961.

Estes, Eleanor. *The Middle Moffat*. N.Y.: Harcourt, 1942.

_____. *The Moffats*. N.Y.: Harcourt, 1941.

_____. *Rufus M*. N.Y.: Harcourt, 1943.

McCloskey, Robert. *Centerburg Tales*. N.Y.: Viking, 1951.

_____. *Homer Price*. N.Y.: Viking, 1943.

Spykman, E.C. *A Lemon and a Star*. N.Y.: Harcourt, 1955.

_____. *Terrible, Horrible Edie*. N.Y.: Harcourt, 1960.

_____. *The Wild Angel*. N.Y.: Harcourt, 1957.

Van Stockum, Hilda. *The Cottage at Bantry Bay.* N.Y.: Viking, 1938.

_____. *Francie on the Run.* N.Y.: Viking, 1939.

_____. *Pegeen.* N.Y.: Viking, 1941.

Poetry

"Disobedience" by A.A. Milne, from *The World of Christopher Robin,* N.Y.: Dutton, 1958.

"Pretending" by Harry Behn, from *Windy Morning,* N.Y.: Harcourt, 1953.

"The Sounds in the Morning" by Eleanor Farjeon, from *Over the Garden Wall,* Philadelphia: Lippincott.

HARRIET THE SPY

by LOUISE FITZHUGH

Illustrated by the Author

I. THE STORY

Harriet the Spy has a secret notebook which she fills with utterly honest jottings about her parents, her classmates, and her neighbors. Everyday on her spy route, she "observes" and notes down anything of interest to her:

> I BET THAT LADY WITH THE CROSS-EYE LOOKS IN THE MIRROR AND JUST FEELS TERRIBLE.

> PINKY WHITEHEAD WILL NEVER CHANGE. DOES HIS MOTHER HATE HIM? IF I HAD HIM I'D HATE HIM.

> IF MARION HAWTHORNE DOESN'T WATCH OUT SHE'S GOING TO GROW UP INTO A LADY HITLER.

But when Harriet's notebook is found by her schoolmates, their anger and retaliation and Harriet's unexpected responses explode in a hilarious and often touching way.

II. PREREADING DISCUSSION QUESTIONS

The questions which follow are illustrative of the kinds which teachers can prepare for the purpose of releasing children to reveal how *they feel* about some of the same larger ideas and bigger meanings contained in the book *before* it is read.

58

About Privacy

1. Tell why you think most people don't like to have someone "snooping around" or "spying" on them.

2. There are strict laws which prevent you from "tapping" someone's telephone, opening another's mail, "bugging" someone's home, or searching another's property—his home, car, or person—without a search warrant. What advantages and disadvantages do you see in such laws?

3. As a young person, you have probably felt that your parents, teachers, and other adults have not allowed you the kind of *privacy* you feel you're entitled to. Tell why you think children your age should (or should not) have the same kind of "freedom to privacy" as adults have guaranteed them by law.

4. Although people lawfully can't "tap" your telephone, open your mail, search your property without your permission, or hide a microphone in your room, they *can* (if you're outside your home) *follow you, watch your every move, take pictures of you, eavesdrop or listen in on your conversations,* or *write things about you*—even though you don't like it. Why are there no laws prohibiting these things? Why do you think there should (or should not) be?

5. Describe a time when you were searching someone else's property without his permission. Why were you doing it? Do you think you had the right to do it? How did you feel while you were actually doing the searching?

About Disrespect

6. Describe the kinds of things you might do if you wanted people to call you a "spoiled brat."

7. When a person has no brothers or sisters, he's called an *only child.* What advantages and disadvantages do you think there are in being an *only child*? Why do so many people think that all *only children* are alike in so many ways?

8. Describe a time when you refused to do something your parents asked you to do, even though you knew you'd be punished. Why did you refuse? What happened?

About Revenge

9. When people do unkind or nasty things to us or say mean or cruel things about us—things that hurt or make us feel guilty or embarrassed—it is difficult to hold one's temper in check; it is hard to keep from getting angry, and harder still (if not impossible) to "turn the other cheek." If one doesn't do or say anything in return, he feels cowardly. If he fights back—by word or deed—in order to "get even," people often think he's bad or evil for *seeking revenge*. Tell what you would do if somebody . . .

   a. "fixed" a school election so you'd lose.
   b. called you "a mean, rotten pig with funny knees" in fron[t] of your friends.
   c. put a snake in your desk at school.
   d. cut off a big chunk of your hair so that it left a bald spot.
   e. told your parents a lie to get you into trouble.
   f. said embarrassing things about your parents.
   g. stared at you constantly with mean, nasty looks.
   h. poked, pinched, shoved you every chance he got.

10. When somebody who dislikes you succeeds in making you feel foolish or causes you to lose your temper, it usually means that he's found one of your "weak spots"—something you find extremely distasteful or unpleasant, something you're afraid of, something you're very touchy about. How can a person guard his "weak spots" in order to protect himself against such enemies?

III. PREREADING ACTIVITIES

1. *Tough Situations and Hard Decisions*—Write an explanation of what you would do in each of the following situations. Be sure you give the *reasons* why you feel the way you do.

   a. Suddenly your brother or sister—or very best friend—starts acting very strangely: nervous and frightened. By chance, you happen to be the first one to the mailbox one day and find a very suspicious-looking letter addressed to him (or her). You are convinced that it might explain this person's strange behavior, so . . .

Tell why you think you should (or should not) open it.

b. Suppose your best friend suddenly becomes very angry with you and, without any explanation at all, says: "I never want to see or speak to you again!" Then, while you are playing one day at another friend's house, this former best friend telephones and the two of them begin to talk. You feel positive that they are talking about you, so you go upstairs to the extension telephone and . . .

Tell why you would (or would not) pick up the telephone and listen in.

c. A person who lives across the street from you uses a power-ful telescope and, from the window in his room, watches everything you do. Since he's not breaking any laws, he can't be arrested.

Tell how you would feel about such a person. Try to think of several ways to get him to stop his snooping. Why not call your list of ideas "Snooper-Stoppers."

d. Although every U.S. citizen is guaranteed freedom of speech, no freedom, however, is completely unlimited. People must be protected against those who misuse freedom of expression. Therefore, we have laws that make it a crime to utter publicly, or put into print—in words or pictures—irresponsible or false statements about another that may ruin his reputation. Suppose a person you know keeps a diary or notebook in which he writes *his honest feelings or impressions* about the people he knows—including you. Because he's not a very nice person, you feel pretty sure that a lot of things he writes about you (and others) are nothing but cruel, nasty lies. One day, as he is coming out of the school and down the steps in front of you, his notebook slips out of his arms and falls in front of you, unnoticed. You pick it up and . . .

Tell what you would do with it and why. Also, tell why you think a person should (or should not) be stopped from keeping such a diary or notebook.

2. Choose five places near your home where you are almost always certain to find the same people and the same things going on (a barber shop, the corner newstand, the school playground after school, a service station, corner drugstore, etc.) at the same time. Then, *making certain you are not trespassing on other people's property,* visit these places regularly. Make notes on the people you see—how they look, what they do and say. (See suggested form below.) After you have visited each of these five places ten times, consult your notes and write a confidential "Private Investigator's Report" for your chief (teacher), giving all the facts *and* your opinions about what you have observed and heard.

Private Investigator's Notebook

Date	Time: from—to	Place	Actual "Photo" Word Account	Investigator's Feelings —Interpretations

3. Some newspaper or magazine writers can take a purely innocent situation or common object and make it look very suspicious or unusual. People who write advertisements for magazines, radio or television also do the same thing. Usually, they do not *actually* tell lies; instead, they frequently leave out some of the facts that are uninteresting so that only the exciting or fantastic suggestions are left for you to believe.

For about ten minutes, observe the people getting drinks of water at a busy time at the drinking fountain in your school. Write this in such a way as to make it look *very suspicious* to anyone who reads it. Or choose a part of a room in your house or apartment; people shopping (or checking out) in a supermarket; a small group of people playing on the playground or in the park; someone's pet; or a common object like a telephone, chair, hair curler, bottle, box, or jar, etc.

4. One of the most wonderful and interesting things about human beings is that they are different. They are all made up of different and complex bundles of habits (good and bad)—or *idiosyncrasies.* Since habits are usually judged "good" or "bad" by the way they affect other people, a person doesn't always know whether his idiosyncrasies are helpful or harmful to him. To make matters even more complicated, the same habit may be accepted by one person and rejected as *horrible* by someone else. Listed below are some "habits." On the blank *in front,* put an "M" if you feel it's one of your habits. Put an "X" if you feel it isn't. On the blank *which follows* the habit, put a "G" if you think it's a *good* habit and a "B" if you think it's *bad.* Add any more to the list you can think of.

_____ always giggles _____
_____ imitates others _____
_____ stares _____
_____ sniffles _____
_____ tattletale _____
_____ daydreams _____
_____ volunteers for hard jobs _____
_____ doesn't talk much _____
_____ wiggles _____
_____ sassy _____
_____ dirty hands _____
_____ careful of others' feelings _____
_____ doesn't listen _____
_____ lazy _____
_____ messy hair _____
_____ polite _____
_____ talks about other people _____
_____ is friendly to everyone _____
_____ stuck-up (loves self) _____
_____ twists the truth _____
_____ studies hard _____

63

_____ has bad breath _____
_____ squints _____
_____ stutters _____
_____ cries easily _____
_____ truthful at all times _____
_____ wild imagination _____
_____ bites nails _____
_____ spits _____
_____ never smiles _____
_____ smelly clothes _____
_____ "yakks" too much _____
_____ doesn't mind his own business _____
_____ tries to be popular _____
_____ good taste in clothes _____
_____ dependable _____
_____ keeps a secret _____
_____ flirts _____
_____ swears _____
_____ never looks you in the eye _____
_____ interrupts and butts in _____
_____ cooperative _____

_____ _____ _____
_____ _____ _____
_____ _____ _____

IV. POSTREADING DISCUSSION QUESTIONS

1. Children, as well as adults, seem to like certain routines. What kinds of routines do you have and why do you like to keep them?

2. Mr. Heeza Beeg Snoop is the world's best spy. Tell why it's possible for him to be—*both at the same time*—a hero and a villain; honored and hated; hunted and respected.

3. Ole Golly used a lot of famous quotations when she talked with Harriet and they seemed to fit in and serve a purpose most of the time. What do you think about the quote on pp. 128-129 which Ole Golly and Harriet recited back and forth to one another? Was it "just for fun?" A game? Or do you think it was appropriate to the story at that point? Why?

What meanings do you receive from the way Louise Fitzhugh has punctuated the lines?

Can you find out who wrote the lines? Discuss some of the other "famous quotations" which Ole Golly used (or which Harriet used).

4. Discuss what you think the quotations below mean and whether or not you think they are good rules to live by:

a. "Revenge is so sweet."
b. "An eye for an eye, a tooth for a tooth."
c. "A dose of the same medicine."
d. "Fighting fire with fire."
e. "Turn the other cheek."
f. "Survival of the fittest."

V. HELPING CHILDREN TO REVEAL THEIR COMPREHENSION

1. You probably have no trouble in remembering how Harriet felt about *(a)* being an onion in the school play; *(b)* going to dancing school; *(c)* having her "spy notebooks" taken away from her by her parents; and *(d)* wearing her "spy clothes." Instead of being stubborn, disobedient, sassy, and unhappy about these things, suppose it would have made a difference if she had used her writing talents and written a petition— explaining how she felt—about being an onion (to Miss Elson and Miss Berry), or to her parents about dancing classes, keeping her spy notebook, or wearing her spy clothes. What would Harriet's petition have been like? What would her reasons, explanations, compromises have been?

2. There could be some *connection* in what appears to be three different, separate events in which Harriet becomes involved: (1) the visit to Dr. Wagner's office; (2) the letter from Ole Golly; and (3) Harriet's becoming Editor of the Sixth Grade Page. Suppose they didn't "just happen" through chance, but that they were planned. Who was involved? Why was it done? Why didn't Harriet "catch on?"

3. On page 266, Harriet overhears part of a conversation between her father and Dr. Wagner. The author, Louise Fitzhugh, gives us only Mr. Welsch's words and puts "..." for those words spoken by Dr. Wagner at the other end of the line. Suppose you had been listening in on an extension and could hear both conversations. In play-script form write what you believe to have been the *complete* conversation between these two men, using Mr. Welsch's words exactly as the author wrote them.

4. At one time or other, most parents say about their children: "I just don't understand her (or him)!" What kind of parents do you think Harriet has? What suggestions would you have for them?

5. Ole Golly's letter (pp. 275-76) was full of advice. Some of it was obvious and some was not:

   a. Why did Ole Golly tell Harriet to lie? Tell why you think this was (or was not) good advice.

   b. Why didn't Ole Golly just tell Harriet not to write any more notebooks? If she had, don't you think that Harriet would have stopped? Why or why not?

   c. What makes you think that Ole Golly might have been right when she told Harriet she knew Harriet wouldn't like to apologize.

   d. Ole Golly encourages Harriet to keep on writing in two different places and in two different ways in her short letter. What do you think Ole Golly was really hoping Harriet would do?

   e. Ole Golly said: "Gone is gone. If you're missing me I want you to know I'm not missing you. I never miss anything or anyone because it all becomes a lovely memory. I guard my memories and love them, but I don't get in them and lie down." What do you think this really tells you about the way Ole Golly felt toward Harriet? Can you explain why it might seem "hard-boiled" and cruel? Why do you think Ole Golly felt she had to talk to Harriet in this way?

6. Suppose Harriet, along with her notebook, also used a *camera* to record her "spy information." Choose one of the places on Harriet's Spy Route and draw or sketch a series of pictures that would show her at work and the situations she uncovered.

7. Evidently Harriet didn't understand or chose not to listen to Ole Golly's advice because, after the first edition of her Sixth Grade Page, she did what Ole Golly predicted she might do. (See "news items" on pages, 284, 285, 286, 288, 289). Ole Golly said: "Remember that writing is to put love in the world, not to use against your friends." How do you feel about Harriet's newspaper writing? Had she learned a lesson or not?

8. Probably the main reason for the Spy Catcher Club was to teach Harriet a lesson and, in some ways, it did. If you had been a member, knowing as much about Harriet as you do now, what different suggestions would you have made?

VI. RELATED-TO-READING EXPERIENCES

1. If someone hired a private detective to spy on you, what things would he be allowed to do under the law? What things would be unlawful? Make a list of specific questions. Go to your local police station and interview the Chief of Detectives. Or have the Chief of Detectives come to school to talk with those in your class who are interested.

2. From your investigation and reading of the First Amendment to the Constitution, history books, encyclopedias, and after listening to a local editor of a newspaper or magazine speak to you about *libel* and *slander*, what are your opinions about *freedom of speech* and *freedom of the press* in America?

3. By using only newspapers (try to use more than one, if possible), "spy" on a current person who is in the news. Keep a notebook on him (or her).

4. Reread all of Harriet's notebook entries. Make a list of all the adjectives and other descriptive words she uses when she talks about people. If you had to describe Harriet's personality from these words (which she uses to describe others) alone, what would you write about Harriet?

5. Choose two or three people you see very often and, with your pen or pencil, "paint" *word portraits* of them.

VII. VOCABULARY THAT MAY NEED DEVELOPING

1. *Coded Words to Break:* The following words have meanings which are difficult to "nail down" definitively. Some readers may find it exciting to become Word Sleuths and track down distinguishing meanings for the following:

    a. *spy, traitor, detective, secret agent, investigator, subversive, (an) official, plainclothesman, undercover agent, member of the underground, right-winger, left-winger, fink.*

    b. *libel, slander, invasion of privacy, public nuisance, trespass, in ˙reason.*

    ˙ve, conceited, inconspicuous, anti.*

VIII. U¬. SELECTIONS ON A SIMILAR THEME: A Sᴇᴧ ECTED BIBLIOGRAPHY

Fitzhugh, Louise. *The Long Secret.* N.Y.: Harper, 1965. (Available as a Dell Yearling book.)

Kastner, Eric. *Emil and the Detectives.* Garden City, N.Y.: Doubleday, 1930.

Lawrence, Isabelle. *A Spy in Williamsburg.* Chicago: Rand McNally, 1955.

Meader, Stephen. *Shadow in the Pines.* N.Y.: Harcourt, 1942.

Meigs, Cornelia. *Invincible Louisa.* Boston: Little, Brown, 1933.

Norton, Mary. *The Borrowers.* N.Y.: Harcourt, 1953.

Rugh, Belle Dorman. *Crystal Mountain.* Boston: Houghton Mifflin, 1955.

Stolz, Mary. *The Bully of Barkham Street.* N.Y.: Harper, 1963. (Available as a Dell Yearling book.)

Poetry

    "I Want To Know" by John Drinkwater, from *All About Me,* Boston: Houghton Mifflin.

    "Primer Lesson" by Carl Sandburg, from *Slabs of the Sunburnt West,* N.Y.: Harcourt, 1922.

"Strange Tree" by Elizabeth Madox Roberts, from *Under the Tree*, N.Y.: Viking, 1930.

"The Conjuror" by E. V. Lucas, from *Playtime and Company*, N.Y.: Doubleday, 1925.

"The Listeners" by Walter de la Mare, from *The Listeners and Other Poems*, N.Y.: Holt.

THE LONG SECRET

by LOUISE FITZHUGH

Illustrations by the Author

I. THE STORY

July 1
Who is leaving those notes all over town?
It's some kind of religious fanatic.

July 6
Watch that new family in town. That Jessie Mae is bats and her twin Norman is fat as a whale. They are up to something. Pay attention.

Harriet the Spy refuses to become ruffled when some unidentified person starts leaving uncanny and disturbing notes all over the quiet little beach town of Water Mill. Oddly dependent on Harriet's brash leadership, mousy Beth Ellen is dragged along into all kinds of odd and embarrassing situations in Harriet's determined efforts to reveal the culprit. Observing in her own special caustic way with her ever-present notebook, Harriet is, at first, undaunted by the Preacher's fierce warning: "DO YOU KNOW THE PERILS OF UNDUE CURIOSITY?"

II. PREREADING DISCUSSION QUESTIONS

The questions which follow are illustrative of the kinds which teachers can prepare for the purpose of releasing children to reveal how *they feel* about some of the same larger ideas and bigger meanings contained in the book *before* it is read.

About Summer Vacations

1. Some people spend all or part of a summer vacation—every year—in the same place. Tell why you think a person would do this year after year and not tire of the place and get bored.

2. Tell about a time when you've been away from home and, by coincidence, happened to meet someone from your class at school.

About Mysteries

3. There are many "mysteries" that are not crimes or unlawful in any way. You've probably heard a lot of different people say something like this: "It's a *mystery* to me!" Describe some of these "mysteries." What could they be? Why would anyone call them a *mystery*?

   ˑˑ about a mysteries sound you've heard or a mysterious vou've seen—something strange and out of the ordinary which, at first, you didn't understand and couldn't explain. Describe how it turned out to be something very common and ordinary.

About Homecomings

5. A *homecoming* usually is considered to be a happy time when people who haven't seen each other in a long time get together once again. Sometimes a *homecoming* means a person's return to a place after being away for quite a while. Suppose *you* used to live in a town called *Joyville* where many of your friends still live. You spent your first eleven years in Joyville and finished sixth grade before you moved away with your family. Now, five years later, at the age of sixteen, you're coming back for a visit. What are the first three things you'd do? What is one *pleasant* thing you'd expect to find? What might be one *unpleasant* thing which you'd expect to happen?

6. Suppose your parents have won a free six-month vacation in Europe. Describe how you think you would feel if arrangements have been made for your *aunt and uncle*—whom you haven't seen since you were four years old—to come and take care of you. Their names are Heeza and Ima Karefree; they are young, pretty wealthy, have no children, and—in almost

every way—they are completely opposite from your parents. Tell how you think you might feel? What things might be different for you? What things would they allow you to do? What things wouldn't they allow you to do? What kinds of things would they enjoy most?

About Curiosity

1. What makes a person curious?
2. How can you tell whether or not a person is curious? What kinds of clues would you look for? What traits or behavior? What *does* a curious person do?
3. Almost everyone is *curious,* in some way, to some degree. It seems to be a very common human trait, yet it's hard to find people who are all curious about exactly the same things in the same way. Listed below are a few of the things some people are most curious about. *Tell the ways you think they would try to satisfy their curiosities.* How might they go about it?

   a. a person who is curious about people
   b. a person who is curious about animals
   c. a person who is curious about God
   d. a person who is curious about the weather
   e. a person who is curious about sports
   f. a person who is curious about insects, rocks, racing, and so forth.

III. PREREADING ACTIVITIES

1. Make a list of the ten most interesting things you did last summer (or during your last holiday). Then, after each one, describe a way that each of these *could have been spoiled or ruined* by a good friend of yours called Yora Knutz. For example:

   I went to Howard's birthday party. *My best friend, Mike, "accidentally" spilled punch all over me because I beat him in a contest.*

2. Without anyone's seeing you, take a piece of chalk and on the sidewalk print: *"Follow these arrows."* Then, approximately every 15 feet, draw another arrow with your chalk which, in turn, will point to the next one you will draw about 15 feet away. Draw these arrows so that anyone following them will walk around the block. Find a place where you can hide but still see most of the "trail" you've drawn. Watch this place during a time when there are a lot of people around. Take notes on how many people follow your trail. Who were they? How many started, then gave up? How do you explain this?

3. Below is a list of nuisances dreamed up by that clever, cunning "criminal," *Public Annoyance #1*. On the blanks in front of each nuisance, use these abbreviations and mark your reactions to them—the way you thin____'d affect you:

     I: infuriating
     A: would make me angry
     B: doesn't bother me but I'm going to find out w__ this person is and get even
     N: pooh! just a nuisance
     C: the person's just a crackpot; best to ignore the whole thing

_____ At the beach or swimming pool you go to most often, sud_____ everyone begins to "lose" his sunglasses.

_____ Everytime you open one of your school books, you find a silly picture drawn on a piece of paper with your name below it.

_____ Whenever someone in your class is speaking before the group, a marble rolls across the room.

_____ For the past three weeks, everyday, just as you and your classmates get ready to leave for home, someone finds a strange emblem from "The Kook Society" taped to his coat or sweater.

_____ Each day, when you come to school, you find that someone has printed a lot of notes or signs and left them for everyone to see. Each day, a different person is chosen and such things as the following are found: *"Mary Lou used to suck her thumb.* " Or, *"Billy has to wash dishes, dust, and iron clothes.* " Or, *"Betsy thinks she's going to be a great actress.* "

Tell what you'd do if you could find out who this *Public Annoyance #1* is. Write a complaint.

4. Below are several "mysteries." Probably one or more of them is familiar to you. Choose one (or more, if you wish) and then *write out a plan to tell how you might go about solving the mystery.* Be sure to include the following: *(a)* a list of the questions or problems you would try to get answers for; *(b)* what proof you would need to test out your hunches; *(c)* what hunches you would have; *(d)* what kinds of things you would do to try to get evidence.

Situation 1:
The "mystery" of someone's sudden strange behavior (for example, your mother, who always did certain things in a particular way, now—with no apparent reason—does them differently).

Situation 2:
The "mystery" of something important which you can't find, such as a free ticket to the circus.

Situation 3:
The "mystery" whereby you keep finding the things that belong to you moved, used, handled by someone without your knowledge or permission.

Situation 4:
The "mystery" whereby each morning, at about the same time, you keep hearing the same sound, which you can't explain.

Situation 5:
The "mystery" of trying to explain the solution to a math problem. Such as: Why are the answers you get in the

multiplication of fractions smaller than the numbers you'd get if you were to *divide* the *same two fractions*?

5. Write a vivid description of the most *suspicious* person you've ever seen. What did he do, say; how did he act to cause you to feel this way?
6. Write a clear account of the most *frightening* moment in your life. Where was it? Who was involved? Would it have been frightening to anyone, or just to you? How did you feel when you were frightened?
7. Write a description of the most dangerous situation in which you were ever involved. What made it dangerous? How dangerous was it? How did you get out of it? Did you receive a help?

IV. POSTREADING DISCUSSION QUESTIONS

1. Why do you think the *note leaver* used Biblical quotations?
2. In many, many ways, Beth Ellen and Harriet were complete opposites. Tell why they were very much alike in their ability to observe and understand people.
3. Do you think the author, Louise Fitzhugh, wants you to believe that such a thing as *"toe medicine"* (What would it be for, anyway?) could be made out of *watermelons*? Or did she just write about Mama Jenkins in this way to be funny? Give your opinions for thinking as you do.
4. Tell why you think Harriet will (or will not ever) be a very good poet.
5. On page 40, Harriet remembers where she was and how she felt before she started writing a poem. Tell what you think is meant by:

> *"Feelings that just appeared and were not attached to anything had always fascinated her."*

6. On page 4, Harriet wonders:

"Funny about Beth Ellen. . . .I never see her in the winter the way I do Janie and Sport, even though I go to school with her; and in the summer she's my best friend, just because she lives in Water Mill too, I guess."

Tell why you think Harriet's "guess" was right or wrong.

V. HELPING CHILDREN TO REVEAL THEIR COMPREHENSION

1. Before making *The Long Secret* available to children, take a piece of construction paper (7-1/2" X 5") and glue or tape it neatly in the seam of the book between pages 264 and 265. To this "extra page" glue an envelope, address side down. The envelope would contain the following instructions:

Before you read the last chapter and find out who the note writer is, go back to page 2 and copy the contents of the first note on the reverse side of this sheet of paper ("JESUS HATES YOU"). Go through the book, listing all of the notes and the persons who received them. Punch a hole in the box opposite the name of the person below whom you believe to be the culprit. If you have a second or even a third guess, put a "2" and a "3" in those boxes. Give this to your teacher, then read Chapter 25.

☐ Harriet Welsch   ☐ Zeeney Baines
☐ Norman Jenkins   ☐ Magnolia Jenkins
☐ The Preacher   ☐ Jessie Mae Jenkins
☐ Agatha Plumber   ☐ Mama Jenkins
☐ Beth Ellen   ☐ Wallace Baines
☐ Bunny Maguire   ☐ Mrs. Hansen

---

2. Now that you know who the note leaver is, go back to the different places and situations and write a brief paragraph explaining how the guilty person was able to leave the notes without being seen or discovered.

76

3. Write titles for each of the chapters.
4. Draw and label these scenes: Mrs. Hansen's house, the Shark's Tooth Inn, Jessie Mae's church, Mama Jenkins' "laboratory."
5. In many ways, *The Long Secret* is *Beth Ellen's* story, *not* Harriet's. Beth Ellen has many fears; she's frightened easily; she's uncertain, lonely, unhappy; she feels she's unloved, a nobody; she's searching for something and someone to love; and although she's obedient, intelligent, and very sensitive, she also seems to be very plain, a bit dumb or naïve, and weak—easily led around by others. Reread some of the places where the author lets you in on the way Beth Ellen feels about herself. What *is* she searching for? What evidence can you find that she might have been a better "people watcher" than Harriet? What evidence can you find which shows she wasn't weak and dumb? The last paragraph on page 246 leads us to expect a *different* Beth Ellen from here on in. Why is this? How has she resolved her problems, feelings, and worries?
6. If you were the author of this story and wanted Beth Ellen to have parents who were "more her type," what would you change about Zeeney and Wallace Baines? Sometimes Zeeney and Wallace were cruel to Beth Ellen. For example, on page 161, when Bunny asks Zeeney if Beth Ellen were her child, Zeeney replies: "Oh, don't be ridiculous, Bunny. I got her from the orphanage for the day. I heard that you couldn't get in here without a child."
Do you think they know they were hurting Beth Ellen? Do you think they care? Explain your reasons.

VI. RELATED-TO-READING EXPERIENCES

1. Find a reference book of quotations and learn how to use it. Try to find some of the note leaver's quotations in it.
2. *A Spy Catcher's Thinking Test:*

Who Is The Vicious Note Writer?

At the beach near Water Mill, New York, there are five beach cottages of different colors, all in a row. Each one is occupied by a person with a different type of bathing suit, a different pet, and a different drink, and each is doing something different. One is secretly writing nasty, vicious notes about people.

Here Are Your Clues:

1. The person wearing the bikini is in the red beach cottage.
2. The person wearing the striped bathing suit is reading a book.
3. The person who has the turtle occupies the green cottage.
4. The person wearing the polka-dot bathing suit has a pet dog.
5. The green beach cottage is immediately to the right (*your* right) of the white beach cottage.
6. The person drinking iced coffee is listening to records.
7. The person drinking iced tea occupies the yellow beach cottage.
8. The person who has the pet cat is in the middle cottage.
9. The person wearing the plaid bathing suit occupies the fifth cottage on the left (*your* left).
10. The person drinking milkshakes is in the beach cottage next to the person who's listening to the radio.
11. The person who likes to sunbathe occupies the beach cottage next to the person who drinks iced tea.
12. The person drinking the orange juice is the one who owns the pet bird.
13. The person wearing the psychedelic bathing suit drinks sour lemonade.
14. The person wearing the plaid bathing suit is in the beach cottage which is next to the blue beach cottage.
15. The person drinking sour lemonade does not have a cat.

NOW: Who is the note writer? Who owns the monkey?

ANSWER

Yellow	Blue	Red	White	Green
Monkey	Dog		Bird	Turtle
Plaid	Polka Dot	Bikini	Striped	Psychedelic
Radio	Sunbather	Record Pl.	Reader	*Notewriter*
Iced Tea	Milkshake	Iced Coffee	Orange Juice	Lemonade

Helpful Hint: Write each of the 25 clues on a separate slip of paper (For example: bikini, lemonade, red beach cottage, cat, sun bathing). Move them around until solution is found.

3. *Superspy Test:*

This is a test to see if you qualify to be a superspy! If you follow the directions correctly, you will change the name of a famous writer of children's books into the name of one of her most famous book characters.

(*Answers*)

1. Write down the words: LOUISE FITZHUGH.

79

2. Take out all of the U's and the space between the words. — LOISEFITZHGH

3. Exchange the positions of the L and Z. — ZOISEFITLHGH

4. Wherever two consonants or two vowels come together, separate them with the letter R. — ZORISEFITRLRHRGRH

5. Replace every O with an A. — ZARISEFITRLRHRGRH

6. Take the last three letters as a group and move them so they will become the first three letters. — GRHZARISEFITRLRHR

7. Remove the first two letters. — HZARISEFITRLRHR

8. Reverse the order of the first two letters; skip the next three; reverse the order of the next two; skip the next four; then reverse the next two letters. — ZHARIESFITRRLHR

9. Add an S after each seventh letter. — ZHARIESSFITRRLHSR

10. Wherever a double consonant appears, take out both letters. — ZHARIEFITLHSR

11. Take out the fourth vowel and substitute an E in its place. — ZHARIEFETLHSR

12. Remove the middle letter and substitute a W in its place. — ZHARIEWETLHSR

13. Take away the final letter and replace it with a C. — ZHARIEWETLHSC

14. Using only the last three consonants, change the order so that the first consonant in the group occupies the last position. — ZHARIEWETLSCH

15. Move every T so that it will appear before each W; then add an R before every I. — ZHARRIETWELSCH

16. Discard the first letter and insert a space between the T and W. — HARRIET WELSCH

4. *Mini-Mystery Writers:* Write quick, baffling, A-B-C, three-clue mysteries for your friends to solve. For example, try to solve the following "mini" Whodunit:

A—This gang causes many girls to scream and faint.

B—Insects of this variety from Japan are hungry killers.

C—This English quartet captures its victims by using wax, vibrations, "wiggle-power," and harmonious sounds.

Answer: *The Beatles*

Also, see television game show *You Don't Say* for a variation on this theme. Try writing hidden homonym clues for famous personalities.

VII. VOCABULARY THAT MAY NEED DEVELOPING

Whether screamed or written, the words Harriet uses are not always the kind you and your friends use when you talk with each other. Yet, these are just exactly the words one might expect from an only child, a Harriet-the-Spy child, a person interested in words because she wants to be a great writer. It's possible to understand the story, *The Long Secret*, without knowing the meanings of some of Harriet's words. But if you really want to get in on the laughs, why not keep a *Harriet-the-Spy Dictionary*? Many readers will enjoy *breaking* Harriet's "word codes," like those which follow.

plummeted	(p. 17)	*stentorian voice*	(p. 32)
sidle	(p. 36)	*Biarritz*	(p. 43)
brazen	(p. 68)	*devastating*	(p. 71)
unperturbed	(p. 73)	*inexplicably*	(p. 80)
erupting	(p. 80)	*pungent*	(p. 80)
creosote	(p. 80)	*catapulted*	(p. 81)
chagrined	(p. 93)	*mesmerized*	(p. 100)
behemoth	(p. 110)	*aberration*	(p. 122)
pompously	(p. 128)	*unmitigated*	(p. 131)

81

inanities	(p. 151)	*incarcerated*	(p. 152)
wanly	(p. 154)	*frothing*	(p. 168)
blithely	(p. 159)	*obsessed*	(p. 169)
peignoir	(p. 176)	*imperiously*	(p. 207)
revved	(p. 185)	*paroxysm*	(p. 212)
stoically	(p. 244)	*apoplexy*	(p. 244)
daft	(p. 38)	*somnambulism*	(p. 156)

VIII. OTHER SELECTIONS ON A SIMILAR THEME:
A SELECTED BIBLIOGRAPHY

Colman, Hila. *Julie Builds Her Castle.* N.Y.: Morrow, 1959. (Available as a Dell Mayflower book.)

Fitzhugh, Louise. *Harriet the Spy.* N.Y.: Harper, 1964. (Available as a Dell Yearling book.)

Hightower, Florence. *Dark Horse of Woodfield.* Boston: Houghton Mifflin, 1962.

_____. *Mrs. Wappinger's Secret.* Boston: Houghton Mifflin, 1956.

Stolz, Mary. *In a Mirror.* N.Y.: Harper, 1953. (Available as a Dell Mayflower book.)

_____. *Rosemary.* N.Y.: Harper, 1955. (Available as a Dell Mayflower bu

_____. *Who Wants Music on Monday?* N.Y.: Harper, 1963. (Available as a Dell Mayflower book.)

Whitney, Phyllis. *Mystery of the Green Cat.* Philadelphia: Westminster, 1957.

Poetry

"Hope Is the Thing with Feathers" by Emily Dickinson, from *Emily Dickinson,* N.Y.: Dell, 1960.

"I'm Nobody" by Emily Dickinson, from *The Poems of Emily Dickinson,* Boston: Little, Brown, 1939.

"The Creation" by James Weldon Johnson, from *God's Trombones,* N.Y.: Viking, 1927.

"The Day Will Bring Some Lovely Thing" by Grace Noll Crowell, from *Silver in the Sun,* N.Y.: Harper.

JOHNNY TREMAIN

by ESTHER FORBES

Illustrated by Lynd Ward

I. THE STORY

The year is 1773; the scene is Boston. Johnny Tremain is fourteen and apprenticed to a silversmith. He is gifted and knows it. He is gay and clever and lords it over the other apprentices until the tragic day when a crucible of molten silver breaks and Johnny's right hand is so burned as to be useless. After a period of despair and humiliation, Johnny becomes a dispatch rider for the Committee of Public Safety, a job that brings him in touch with Otis, Hancock, John and Samuel Adams, and other Boston patriots, and with all the exciting currents and undercurrents that were to lead to the Tea Party and the Battle of Lexington. There, on the battlefield, he learns from Dr. Warren that his maimed hand can be cured so that he can use a musket and some day return to his trade.

II. PREREADING DISCUSSION QUESTIONS

The questions which follow are illustrative of the kinds which teachers can prepare for the purpose of releasing children to reveal how *they feel* about some of the same larger ideas and bigger meanings contained in the book *before* it is read.

About Pride

1. How would you describe the different meanings in the statements below? Tell why you believe one is more desirable than the other.

"He takes *pride* in his work. He'll go places."

"It's his *pride* that's holding him back. He needs a good lesson in humility!"

"Look at the way he struts around! He's as *proud* as a peacock."

2. Perhaps you've known or heard about a person who was too proud to ask for help, even though he (or his loved ones) was suffering great hardships. How do you feel about this kind of pride? How can *being proud* be good and evil at the same time? At what point does one come to grips with his pride, compromise, give in? Does a compromise with one's pride also mean a compromise with one's *principles*?

3. Although there are no laws to punish persons for having a "fierce pride," such people seem to be judged and punished anyway. "He's paying for his pride!" is not an uncommon statement but it's hardly an explanation. Tell of some of the ways you know about in which—rightly or wrongly—a person has been punished because of his pride.

About Freedom and Causes

4. All over the world there are different kinds of "freedom causes"; people struggling, fighting, dying for, and defending ideas, principles, property, human life, etc., under the banner of freedom. How is it possible for two countries to be at war with one another—both for the same reason: *freedom*?

5. Many causes, organizations, and campaigns are founded on the idea of people's right to be free. In some countries, these causes are permitted *only* if they happen to agree with those in power. In other countries, even the most cruel, brutal, and hateful anti-freedom organizations are allowed because those in power believe in freedom to disapprove, disagree, and to oppose. Suppose in a country such as ours, where most people are democratic, peace-loving, and free, there suddenly appears a wealthy and powerful organization called the *Society of Lawful Advocates for Victorious Enslavement* (S.L.A.V.E.), whose purpose is to do away with elections and have an emperor instead of a president. They claim they will *really*

84

make all people equal—everyone will have the same amount of money, care, property, etc. No one will be hungry or suffer because the emperor will take care of everyone, fairly, equally. How would you feel about permitting or restricting such an organization? Why do you believe as you do?

6. If you and a group of your friends were asked to make and agree upon a list of *Anti-American Behaviors*, what would be included on this list? For example, would such things as agreeing or refusing to serve in the United States Army be included? Would criticizing the President? Would sending supplies to people in Communist countries?

7. Give some examples of situations in which young people sometimes find themselves when they feel they shouldn't "go along with the gang" but find it very difficult not to do so.

8. What kinds of arguments would you use to persuade young people your age to take part in community or school activities for which they get no credit or pay? How would you deal with this type of response: *"Why should I? What's in it for me?"?*

About Holding Grudges

9. Suppose by accident, carelessness, or as a practical joke, someone caused you a severe injury that left you handicapped for life. Since the physical damage to you cannot be "undone," what can you gain by feeling hateful and revengeful? Why is it so hard to forgive in such instances? What reasons do people give for advising you to throw away your feelings of self-pity and bitterness? Suppose such a situation had caused you *the loss of one eye or your hearing; a crippled arm or the loss of a leg; an ugly, scarred face.* How would any of these impairments affect your future plans and hopes? Why would such a loss be greater and forgiveness harder than losing a tooth or having a bone broken? Why is it that some people never seem to recover from such tragedies?

About Friendship

10. What kinds of things do people look for in choosing friends?

11. Although some people prefer to be "loners," most find that close friends can help, understand, share. What makes a close

friendship different from other friendships? What kinds of things do close friends do, talk about, confide, help each other with? What's one thing you'd expect of a close friend—without fail?

12. Sometimes a person is disappointed, hurt, or wronged by someone he thought was his close friend. Why are these feelings so painful, so hard to live with?

13. Suppose in *every way,* a person proved to you he was your closest and best friend *except* for the fact that he refused ever to talk about himself or his feelings toward you. How do you think this would affect your feelings?

14. Suppose someone had done you a grave injustice, hurt, or mistreated you. While everyone else felt sorry for you, your one and only best friend refused to show any pity or sympathy. Tell how you think he might be right in behaving this way toward you.

III. PREREADING ACTIVITIES

1. Keep a record of everything you do for one day, from the time you get up until the time you retire for the night. Be sure to note the details, such as what you wear, what you eat, how you get from one place to another, the news of the day, what you hear and talk about, the places you go, the things you do, etc. Once your record is complete, pretend that you could step into a "Time Machine" and relive that day all over again—*but 200 years ago, in the eighteenth century.* You might call this unusual one-day diary, "A Day in My Life—Then and Now" and record your activities in two columns like this:

John Doe: May 5, 17–	John Doe: May 5, 19–
1.	
2.	
etc.	

2. *Freedom* in the United States of America is based on certain fundamental and natural *premises*. A premise is something that is taken for granted or assumed. Many premises—especially those beliefs and ideas about people and human rights—are difficult, if not impossible, to prove scientifically. And since they are equally difficult to disprove, we tend to accept them as facts. The first paragraph of the *Declaration of Independence* begins thus:

> "We hold these truths to be self-evident, that all men are created equal, that they are endowed by their Creator with certain unalienable Rights . . ."

What are these Rights (and why is the word capitalized?) *endowed* by our *Creator*? Are they assumed? Can it be disproved that each of us was *not* endowed with these Rights?

Have various people prepare and practice and then read aloud to the class some of the following famous statements about freedom and liberty. What "Rights to Freedom" did the authors of these doc̲ ̲ ̲ ̲ ̲ ̲ ̲ ̲ ̲ ̲ ̲ ̲ be endowed with?

a. The first paragraph of the *Declaration of Independence.*
b. The Preamble to the *Constitution of the United States.*
c. Patrick Henry's *Speech before th̲ ̲ ̲ ̲ ̲ ̲nia House of Burgesses.*
d. Thomas Paine's *The Crisis, No. I: December 19, 1776.*
e. James Otis' speech to the Boston Observers, found in *Johnny Trem̲ ̲ ̲* Chapter VIII, Section 5, pp. 175-177.

3. Your father is owner and president of a large, well-known, big profit-making business. Ever since you were born, he has been waiting anxiously for the time to come when you would take over the business. As this time now approaches, you feel his business would make you the most miserable, unhappy person alive. But how can you tell him this? You love him and he loves you. You don't want to hurt and disappoint him; yet,

you have your own future to think of. Write your father a letter (1) explaining how you feel and (2) offering him a possible solution which you feel he might agree with.

[*NOTE TO TEACHER: Items 4, 5, 6 and 7 are "Opinionnaires." Since an individual's comprehension of a piece of literature is affected by his real or vicarious past experiences (including the values, attitudes, opinions, etc., which he holds), Opinionnaires can help readers to examine their "set ideas" critically, in a new light as they interact with particular book characters. They can also help readers to reveal any changes of opinion as they progress in their reading. For each, it is suggested that a "Form A" and a "Form B" be used. Form A would show opinions held by individuals on various items before the book is read. These would be collected and stored until the book has been completed, at which time Form B would be filled out. Form B would contain the same items as Form A except that the respondent would be asked to mark it as he believes Johnny Tremain (or Cilla, Rab, Mr. Lapham, Dove, Lavinia, etc.) would have responded. A final step would be for the reader to compare his two Opinionnaires and attempt to explain any differences that may exist.—C.F.R.*]

4. Put an "X" on the blanks below opposite those words which you think best tell how *you* would describe a person who is *too* proud:

___ a wise guy	___ one who puts on airs	___ swell-headed
___ a bully	___ conceited	___ intelligent
___ a king	___ lucky	___ offensive
___ a peacock	___ ungrateful	___ humiliating
___ a snob	___ humble	___ wealthy
___ a prima donna	___ stuck-up	___ selfish
___ a beggar	___ bossy	___ revengeful
___ a hero	___ polite	___ skillful
___ a politician	___ a criminal	___ a soldier

(Add any others you may not find listed here.)

5. Put an "X" on the blanks opposite those items which best describe what you'd like to see happen to a person who thinks he is better than anyone else.

I'd like to see such a person . . .

___ lose everything he has which makes him so "big and stuck-up."

___ become as unhappy as those people he has made so unhappy.

___ learn his lesson and begin to be a good person.

___ sent far away from people where he couldn't cause any more harm or sadness.

___ locked up in prison.

___ meet someone who is even worse who could teach him a lesson.

___ left alone so he can do what he feels is right.

___ left free to do what he wants as long as he doesn't break the law.

___ left free to act the way he chooses, even though it isn't very nice.

___ left free to do what he pleases, even though people don't like him.

___ _____

___ _____

(Add any others you may not find listed here.)

6. There are many times, places, and people—as well as many ways—which teach a person *right* from *wrong*. Some of these work for some people, while some do not. Listed below are some of these ways of "teaching people to be good." Place a mark on the blank opposite those which you feel would *not* work for *you*. If you think of any others which apply, write them in at the end if you wish.

___ constant reminders whenever you make mistakes or displease someone.

___ listening to lectures or stories about people who "go bad ways."

89

___ being made to write an essay about how wrong your behavior is and how much better it is to be good.

___ writing "I will not . . ." over and over again.

___ talking your situation over with someone who wants to listen and who wants to understand how you feel.

___ being sent to talk with a law-enforcement officer or counsellor who will give you proper advice.

___ being warned "for the *last time!*"

___ being taken to see where people are living the wrong kinds of lives and are doing the wrong kinds of things.

___ being taken to see what happens to people who have had bad ideas or who have done bad things.

___ being given a second chance.

___ being made to read certain passages from a religious book.

___ being made to pray for forgiveness.

___ being forced to apologize in public or before family or friends.

___ being slapped, spanked, beaten, or threatened in some way.

___ not being allowed to be with your friends, or to telephone them.

___ being watched or supervised constantly.

___ being deprived of privileges you've always enjoyed.

___ _____

___ _____

___ _____

___ _____

7. Different people become angry for different reasons. Listed below are some types of peo**p**' who often make others angry. Put an "X" on the blank c, ite those descriptions of people who would make *you* the angriest:

___ People who act as if they were much better than you.

___ People who make you do embarrassing things.

___ People who tease you.

___ People who call you names.

___ People who talk about you behind your back.

___ People who tell lies about you.

___ People who bully or boss you.

___ People who constantly remind you of your mistakes.

___ People who never seem to forget that "one silly thing" you did a long, long time ago.

___ People who *pretend* that they are your friends.

___ People who can't stand to see you enjoying yourself.

___ People who are always bothering you or tagging along wherever you go.

___ People who "tattle" on you.

___ People who are always "chewing you out" or scolding you.

___ People who seem to like to try to hurt you—either your feelings and/or with physical pain.

___ People who are always forcing you to do things you don't enjoy because they think you should enjoy them.

___ People who are always trying to coax you to do things that you really can't do because they think you're "just plain lazy" or that you're "not trying hard enough."

___ People who only seem to see your weak points.

___ People who are old-fashioned and don't seem to know about people your age in the world today.

___ People who always agree with you.

___ People who never criticize you.

___ People who always give in to you and do things your way.

___ People who admire you and look up to you.

___ People who always ask you for help.

___ People who are always complimenting you for your excellence.

___ People who go out of their way to speak to you.

___ People who sit around and wait for your decisions.

___ _____

___ _____

___ _____

___ _____

(Add any others which may not be included on this list)

IV. POSTREADING DISCUSSION QUESTIONS

1. Discuss the following:

   a. It's better to have the guilty go free than to punish the innocent.
   b. It's better to light a single candle than to curse the darkness.
   c. Johnny Tremain is too big for his britches.
   d. A person doesn't hold opinions; they hold him.
   e. If you want music, then you'd better expect to pay the piper.
   f. And the Lord said, "Let there be light."

   In what ways are each of the above statements related to people, ~~·   ~~ents in the story?

2. Why did~~ ·   ~~.~~ ·   ~~ Lyte pursue Johnny and have him arrested a second time?
3. It seems as though everyone knew that the "raiders" involved in the Tea Party were *not* Indians. Why, then, did they go to all that trouble and even keep up the "act" by speaking "like-um Injun?"
4. How would events have been different if Johnny had gone to sea after selling his cup to Mr. Lyte?
5. Recite the lyrics to the song "Yankee Doodle." Tell why you believe this song was written about Billy Dawes. What happened to Billy Dawes? Did he contribute in any other way in the Revolutionary War?
6. Tell how you feel about the wisdom or stupidity of Johnny Tremain's pride. Should he have made any compromises?
7. What are the true issues involved in the controversy about passing a law restricting the sale of firearms to citizens?
8. Shakespeare wrote:
   "This above all, to thine own self
       be true,
   And it must follow, as the night
       the day,
   Thou canst not then be false to
       any man."

To whom would that quotation apply? What reasons can you give?

9. Look up the meanings of *sedition, espionage, subversion, disloyalty.* Compare the meanings with those you can find for the word *treason.*

10. What do you think was meant by the statement "a parody of a trial?" (p. 131)

V. HELPING CHILDREN TO REVEAL THEIR COMPREHENSION

1. Write a persuasive editorial for the *Boston Observer.* In it, try to convince all *Tories* to join the *Whigs* in their determination to be firm with England on the matter of taxation.

2. Prepare a facsimile of the *Boston Observer,* complete with advertisements, cartoons, local and international news, etc. What would the headlines and articles have been like following the incident of the Tea Party? Of the Battle of Lexington?

3. Why didn't Rab tell Johnny how he felt about him? Suppose Rab had written a letter, sealed it, and had given it to Cilla to give to Johnny "in case of his death." What would have been in Rab's letter?

4. Prepare Jonathan Lyte Tremain's "family tree." (Refer to pages 162-63, 232-35.)

5. In this story, as you know, *placards* were used to get information quickly to large numbers of people. They were also used for propaganda purposes—that is, advertising "causes." Prepare a series of *Whig* and *Tory* placards based on some of the issues, slogans, and political beliefs of the day. For example: "Disperse, Ye Rebels!"—"Salt-Water Tea"—"Taxation without Representation Is Tyranny!"—"The Piper Must Be Paid!"—"Be a Yankee Doodle!"—"Don't Ride Two Horses"—"PEACE: Time, Patience, and Respect for British Law"—"Yokels Can't Stand Up!" and so on.

6. Dramatize the *Trial Scene* in Chapter Four, Section 5, or the *"Interrogation" Scene* in Chapter Nine, Section 2, between Dove, Johnny, and Rab.

7. Suppose Governor Hutchinson and Sam Adams were holding a debate on the Boston Commons. Prepare "freedom speeches" that you believe could have been delivered by these two men.

8. On the blanks opposite the words listed below, place an "X" beside those you feel are indicative of Johnny Tremain's personality at various stages in the story. When you finish, put a circle around those you feel he "outgrew"—as a result of his experiences in these three years.

___ a bully	___ courageous	___ inconsiderate
___ skillful	___ dishonest	___ heroic
___ artistic	___ proud	___ ambitious
___ stupid	___ unappreciative	___ bossy
___ meek	___ a cheat	___ talkative
___ hostile	___ quick-tempered	___ sassy
___ sullen	___ uncreative	___ rude
___ a liar	___ a daydreamer	___ thoughtless
___ conceited	___ cowardly	___ sulky
___ intelligent	___ crude	___ arrogant
___ inventive	___ meddlesome	

9. Write a sermon for the Reverend Samuel Cooper. In it try to show the religious feelings and beliefs of the time. Cite several examples of how religion entered into the story in a significant way.

10. Write an explanation in which you try to resolve the differences in your responses on Parts "A" and "B" of the "Opinionnaires." (See *Prereading Activities*, items 4, 5, 6, and 7.)

11. After reading *Johnny Tremain*, you probably now have a pretty good mental picture of the kind of person he is. Place an "X" below on the blanks opposite those statements which *you* find closest to your way of thinking. If you have any others to add, write them in on the blanks provided at the end.

I think that Johnny Tremain is . . .

___ the kind of person I'd like to have as a close friend.

___ a poor, unfortunate orphan, mistreated by everyone.

_____ a boy who is not so well liked by grown-ups as he is by those his own age.

_____ a person with a sour personality who will never be well liked.

_____ the type of person who got exactly what he deserved.

_____ a comedian—a clown.

_____ actually, a very kind, friendly person.

_____ ashamed of his family and has disgraced them.

_____ a person who will always be in a lot of trouble.

_____ someone who likes to ridicule and pick on other people.

_____ a boy who controls his temper remarkably well, considering the circumstances.

_____ not a very strong believer in God.

_____ polite and obedient and always willing to try.

_____ a temperamental artist and doomed to live a lonely life.

_____ a person who will grow up with little faith in anyone and anything.

_____ a shy person who can have his feelings hurt easily.

_____ a person looking for sympathy and revenge.

_____ someone who likes to be "in" on great events but lacks the courage really to do anything worthwhile.

_____ deserves to have a crippled hand for life.

_____ _____

_____ _____

_____ _____

_____ _____ _____

VI. RELATED-TO-READING EXPERIENCES

1. Find out all you can about what skills you would have learned if, about 200 years ago, you'd have been *apprenticed* as:

a cooper	a sailmaker	a printer
a weaver	a clockmaker	a ropemaker
a butcher	a soap-boiler	an instrument maker
a shipwright	a leather dresser	a silversmith

2. Write definitions which show clearly the difference between a word in column "A" and the opposite word in column "B". Then, *without* using the word itself, write an anecdote or cite a specific example to illustrate the meanings you have discovered.

A	B
a. *conservatives*	*liberals*
b. *patriots*	*rebels*
c. *doves*	*hawks*
d. *Democrats*	*Republicans*
e. *left-wingers*	*right-wingers*
f. *Whigs*	*Tories*
g. *Unionists*	*Confederates*
h. *nationalists*	*imperialists*
i. *loyalists*	*abolitionists*

3. Plan a "Salt-Water Tea Pageant." Include songs and dances of and about the Revolution. Some of the historical statements and/or speeches on liberty and freedom could be recited. (See *Prereading Activities,* Item 2.) Longfellow's "Paul Revere's Ride," Scollard's "The Eve of Bunker Hill," Holmes' "A Ballad of the Boston Tea Party," and Emerson's "Concord Hymn"—to name a few—might be read or recited. Various members of the class could choose to come dressed as Forbes' book characters and/or other historical personages of that time and general locale.

4. Find out all you can about *Child Labor Laws* in the United States.

5. Some American cities and/or states have, or are embroiled in, a controversy over *Blue Laws.* Find out all you can about this issue. Write a statement or "Position Paper" in which you take a stand either for or against them.

If several students are interested, they may find it satisfying to prepare small guides or brochures explaining the terms and working conditions in the various apprenticeships.

6. In recent times not only harbors but whole countries have been *shut off by sea* from the rest of the world. These blockades or embargoes did not lead to such serious situations as the Boston Tea Party did. Why not? Could they have been as serious? Why? Find out all you can about one or two recent embargoes placed upon another country by the United States. Why was this done? What results did it have? What could have happened?

7. Find out all you can about the whereabouts and the activities of George Washington at the time of the Boston Revolt.

8. Find out what happened to (the fate of) Sam Adams, John Adams, John Hancock, James Otis, Doctor Warren, Paul Revere, Governor Hutchinson.

9. Make an antique trunk (See Section VII,) using the following pattern:

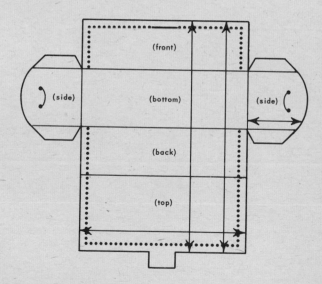

10. *Recipe for making "parchment"* (See Section VII)

    a. With a small amount of water, dilute slightly a clear-drying glue (such as Elmer's Glue-All) and brush it liberally onto both sides of that which you wish to make into "parchment."

    b. Place this on a Kleenex and then on a piece of waxed paper. Put another Kleenex on top and on top of that place another piece of waxed paper. Press firmly and allow to dry.

    c. Press with a warm iron, trim, and attach to dowel rods to simulate "scrolls."

VII. VOCABULARY THAT MAY NEED DEVELOPING

Attic Antiques: Eighteenth-Century Collector's Items

The meanings of words grow and change through use. Some words even disappear from current usage and are labeled *obsolete* or *archaic*. Most readers will read *Johnny Tremain* with greater satisfaction and deeper appreciation if they become sensitive to some of the eighteenth-century words and expressions listed below. An interesting project for some readers would involve cutting a cardboard carton in such a way as to replicate an old eighteenth-century trunk that may have been "just discovered" in someone's attic. (See pattern for making an antique trunk in Section VI, item #9.) Those who are interested may then collect these "word antiques" and their meanings and put them on "parchment" scrolls and store them in the trunk for reference and discussion. (See recipe for making parchment in Section VI, item 10.)

fagot (p. 89)	*whist* (p. 24)
knave (p. 88)	*crucible* (p. 7)
baize (p. 116)	*knapped* (p. 251)
rakish (p. 52)	*quintal* (p. 135)
surfeited (p. 248)	*sweetmeats* (p. 99)
annealing (p. 4)	*yokel* (p. 105)

cheeky (p. 11)　　　　　　*indenture* (p. 82)
tankard (p. 179)　　　　　*equitation* (p. 90)
laudanum (p. 35)　　　　　*Sabbath-breaking* (p. 41)
surtout (p. 95)　　　　　　*erstwhile* (p. 42)
seditious (p. 170)　　　　　*atrophying* (p. 96)
clericals (p. 108)　　　　　to feel *piqued* (p. 172)
brackish (p. 4)　　　　　　*paroxysm*
repoussé (p. 14)

VIII.   OTHER SELECTIONS ON A SIMILAR THEME: A SELECTED BIBLIOGRAPHY

Biography

Alderman, Clifford Lindsey. *Samuel Adams, Son of Liberty.* N.Y.: Holt, 1961.

Campion, Nardi Reeder. *Patrick Henry: Firebrand of the Revolution.* Boston: Little, Brown, 1961.

Forbes, Esther. *America's Paul Revere.* Boston: Houghton Mifflin, 1946.

Galt, Tom. *Peter Zenger: Fighter for Freedom.* N.Y.: Crowell, 1951.

Judson, Clara Ingram. *George Washington, Leader of the People.* Chicago: Follett, 1951.

Rogers, Frances, and Alice Beard. *Paul Revere, Patriot on Horseback.* Philadelphia: Lippincott, 1943.

Historical Fiction

Brink, Carol Ryrie. *Caddie Woodlawn.* N.Y.: Macmillan, 1931.

Caudill, Rebecca. *Tree of Freedom.* N.Y.: Viking, 1949.

Edmonds, Walter D. *The Matchlock Gun.* N.Y.: Dodd, Mead, 1941.

Field, Rachel. *Calico Bush.* N.Y.: Macmillan, 1931.

Keith, Harold. *Rifles for Watie.* N.Y.: Crowell, 1957.

Speare, Elizabeth George. *The Witch of Blackbird Pond.* Boston: Houghton Mifflin, 1958.

Wibberly, Leonard. *John Treegate's Musket.* N.Y.: Farrar, 1959.

Poetry

"The Concord Hymn" by Ralph Waldo Emerson, available in many editions.

"I Hear America Singing" by Walt Whitman, available in many editions.

"Paul Revere's Ride" by Henry Wadsworth Longfellow, available in many editions.

"Try, Try Again," author unknown, from *Poetry Festival,* edited by John Bettenbender, N.Y.: Dell, 1966.

"Yankee Doodle," author unknown, available in many editions.

JOHNNY TEXAS

by CAROL HOFF

Illustrated by Bob Meyers

I. THE STORY

When Johann comes from Germany to make his home in Texas, he is awed at first by the vastness of the country; but from the moment the big, friendly stagecoach driver tousles his hair and calls him "Johnny Texas," the boy's love for this wide and wonderful land begins to grow and grow. Then war upsets the family when his father is called to fight, and life becomes a lonely, daily struggle without him. When bitterness takes hold of his mother, Johnny must find a way to show her that they cannot give up.

II. PREREADING DISCUSSION QUESTIONS

The questions which follow are illustrative of the kinds which teachers can prepare for the purpose of releasing children to reveal how *they feel* about some of the same larger ideas and bigger meanings contained in the book *before* it is read.

About Growing Up
1. What are some of the things that young children find it hard to wait "until you're older" to do?
   What are some of the things that teenagers find it hard to wait "until you're older" to do?
   What kinds of things do parents never seem to believe their children are old enough to do?

About Losing Things
2. What things do people lose that make them feel the saddest? The angriest? The happiest?

3. What kinds of things does a person do in order to go about finding something he has lost?
4. What do you think a person might mean when he says, "I feel lost!"?

About Making Mistakes
5. What would you define as a "goof?" A *faux pas*?
6. What kinds of mistakes do you feel are the most embarrassing?
7. Why do people try to keep from making mistakes?
8. What kinds of mistakes are you most afraid of making?
9. What kinds of mistakes would a "greenhorn" make?
10. What kinds of mistakes would be valuable? Describe one.
11. What do you think the following means:

"To err is human; to forgive, divine."

About Being Truthful
12. How would you describe the difference between a "fib" and a "l...... ......n a "fib" and a "white lie?" Between a "white lie" and a "lie?"
13. When would keeping silent and not telling anything be considered a lie? What would be an example of a person's telling a lie by stating *only part of the truth*?

III. PREREADING ACTIVITIES

1. Write a "position statement" that tells clearly how you feel about the buying and selling of . . .

a. athletes
b. slaves
c. children (for adoption)
d. husbands or wives

2. In stories about the "Old West" (in books, movies, television), what things are fact and what things are fiction?
3. Make a list and describe (or, by drawing pictures, show) the differences in living you think an eleven-year-old boy or girl would find out West between now and about 150 years ago.

102

a. in housing	f. in clothing	k. in religion
b. in food	g. in dangers	(churchgoing)
c. in work	h. in sicknesses	l. in traveling
d. in play	i. in wishes/wants	m. in learning to
e. in school	j. in mailing letters	do things well

4. Construct models to show the kinds of dangers early settlers of the West faced and the safety precautions they took against these dangers, e.g., fires, Indians, wild animals, weather.

5. Make a time line of the wars in which the United States has been involved. (See Time Line on p. 211.)

6. Conduct a research survey and publish a list of the kinds of things that mothers worry about most.

7. By examining and reading the pictures in *Johnny Texas* before reading, *(a)* write a brief paragraph or two which anticipates and/or predicts where the story takes place, when, who the main characters are, and what the plot is; *(b)* seal in an envelope until after book is read. Compare the predictions!

8. Conduct a survey in order to discover the "Imported Habits and Customs" of people coming to the United States from other countries.

IV. POSTREADING DISCUSSION QUESTIONS

1. Johnny Texas' "Texas Paradise" seems to be summed up in his feelings which the author describes on page 29:

> ". . . It was like waking each morning to a brand new world. Sometimes in the early morning coolness as Johnny stood breathing deep of the fresh, sweet air and listening to the joyous songs of the hundreds of birds, he would look up into the blue, blue sky and imagine that it was a high, wide cup which God had tipped over on them, drenching them with happiness."

In other places, Texas is referred to as the "Land of Promise." Tell why you think Johnny's mother might have said:

"Texas? Hrumph! Johnny, you and your father here are just living in a dream world. Both of you are convinced that *the grass is always greener on the other side of the fence*! Now that we're here in Texas, look around you. Look what we've found! Just both of you open up your eyes a little and tell me how much *greener the grass is*!"

2. In what ways were the *unconquerable ants* like Johnny Texas?
3. Some children may have fun in writing "Greenhorn Situation" paragraphs.

V. HELPING CHILDREN TO REVEAL THEIR COMPREHENSION

1. Make a map of the Friedricks' voyage from Leipzig, Germany, to Harrisburg, Texas.
2. Johnny's mother worried about many things (dangers, school, church, etc.). Make a list of these "Wild West Worries" and compare them with the kinds of worries which today's mothers have. (See "Survey Report," Item 6, *Prereading Activities.*)
3. Cite examples of Johnny Texas' *(a)* being lost, *(b)* feeling lost, and *(c)* having lost.
4. Tell why you think Johnny Texas should receive "The Most Unconquerable Person of the Year" award.
5. How can you explain why there are so few human lives lost in battles such as that of San Jacinto?
6. How would you defend or punish Johnny Texas for the lies he told his mother? Such as: he didn't tell her about the snake he saw in the water; he didn't tell her about the pain and about how much he was worried about the ant bites; he didn't tell her about learning to shoot until she found out; and so forth.
7. Make a "feelings log" or diary for *(a)* Johnny Texas, *(b)* Johnny's father, Robert Friedrick, and *(c)* Johnny's mother, Clara Friedrick.
8. The author, Carol Hoff, has Johnny's mother make her decision to stay in Texas *before* her husband returns to her. Why do you think this was an important thing for her to do?

9. Suppose there were two more chapters in this book: one called "Ten Years Later" and another called "Twenty Years Later." What would be in those chapters? Who would be President? What would Johnny be doing? What would "Little Clara" be doing? What would be happening in the United States? In the world? In Texas?

VI. RELATED-TO-READING EXPERIENCES

1. Collect information, prepare and duplicate a brochure or booklet entitled "Ten Tall Texans"—nominating whom you consider to be the ten greatest Texans of all time.
2. Collect information, prepare and duplicate a brochure or booklet entitled " 'Leven Lone Star Landmarks"—nominating places or events that you consider to be the eleven greatest moments in Texas history.
3. Prepare a map of southern United States (about 1830-40). On it, locate New Orleans, Harrisburg, El Paso, Victoria, Alamo, San Jacinto, San Antonio, etc. Indicate the various trips Johnny Texas and/or his mother and father took throughout the story.
4. Do some research and find out all you can about *duels* in the United States as well as in Europe. What famous Americans were involved in duels? Why was dueling outlawed in the United States?
5. Prepare a word game (such as a crossword puzzle) using some of the unusual words and their meanings found in *Johnny Texas*. You might want to use a few of these as starters:

wharf (p. 1)	dignity (p. 26)	jubilant (p. 125)
forelock (p. 14)	dignified (p. 26)	specie (p. 126)
alien (p. 18)	greenhorn (p. 58)	mortally (p. 126)
chore (p. 22)	throng (p. 125)	peon (p. 126)

6. How does the "Slavery Issue" appear in the story although the author, Carol Hoff, touches upon it only briefly with the Negro character Tobias? How does the "Indian Issue" appear

in the story? From the research that you do, whom do you think was right about President Jackson's Indian Policy—Sam Houston or Davy Crockett? What can you find out about Sam Houston's views on slavery? If the Democrats had nominated him to run for President of the United States against Lincoln, do you think he could have won? If he had defeated Lincoln, do you think his views would have prevented the Civil War? What facts can you uncover about Abraham Lincoln's real views on slavery *before* he became President?

VII. VOCABULARY THAT MAY NEED DEVELOPING

1. *Word Balloons:* Like blowing up a balloon, a word may expand in *meaning.* For example, *run* (meaning "to move the ˈ ˌy") might be a word balloon, "blown up" with such nˌ ˌnings as "to operate a vehicle"; "to stand as a candidate for election"; or "the damage done to one's stocking." Using some of the words in *Johnny Texas* (or from other sources), some will profit by making their own word balloons.
2. *Wˌ ˌ Hunt:* Have children engage in a "word hunt" for foreign words or phrases either that are encountered but not generally used (e.g., "lift" for elevator, "tubes" for subway) or that have been adopted by Americans (e.g., "voodoo," "menu," "queue," "amok").

VIII. OTHER SELECTIONS ON A SIMILAR THEME: A SELECTED BIBLIOGRAPHY

Edmonds, Walter D. *The Matchlock Gun.* N.Y.: Dodd, Mead, 1941.
Hoff, Carol. *Johnny Texas on the San Antonio Road.* Chicago: Follett, 1953.
Jackson, Jesse. *Call Me Charley.* N.Y.: Harper, 1945. (Available as a Dell Yearling book.)
Lenski, Lois. *Judy's Journey.* Philadelphia: Lippincott, 1947. (Available as a Dell Yearling book.)

Moody, Ralph. *Riders of the Pony Express.* Boston: Houghton Mifflin, 1958.

Travers, P.L. *I Go by Land, I Go by Sea.* N.Y.: Norton, 1964. (Available as a Dell Yearling book.)

Poetry

"I Hear America Singing" by Walt Whitman, available in many editions.

"Open Range" by Kathryn and Byron Jackson, from *Cowboys and Indians,* N.Y.: Simon & Schuster, 1948.

"The Pioneer" by Arthur Guiterman, from *I Sing the Pioneer,* N.Y.: Dutton, 1926.

"Prairie-Dog Town" by Mary Austin, from *The Children Sing in the Far West,* Boston: Houghton Mifflin.

"Texas Trains and Trails" by Mary Austin, from *The Children Sing in the Far West,* Boston: Houghton Mifflin.

CALL ME CHARLEY
by JESSE JACKSON

Illustrated by Doris Spiegel

I. THE STORY

When the Mosses move to the pleasant suburb of Arlington Heights, Ohio, twelve-year-old Charley Moss decides to take a paper route—and that's where he meets Tom Hamilton for the first time. A friendship grows between the boys, who have an enterprising way of thinking up new adventures, but the relationship becomes a series of ups and downs when Charley is treated as a Negro, instead of just another boy.

[For those readers who enjoy *Call Me Charley* and elect to follow Charley Moss's further adventures through high-school graduation, there are *Anchor Man* and *Charley Starts from Scratch,* also available in Dell Yearling editions, in which Jesse Jackson continues the story of his young Negro hero. Teachers will find many of the following suggestions helpful and/or readily adaptable for use with students who choose to read either of the sequels.]

II. PREREADING DISCUSSION QUESTIONS

The questions which follow are illustrative of the kinds which teachers can prepare for the purpose of releasing children to reveal how *they feel* about some of the same larger ideas and bigger meanings contained in the book *before* it is read.

About Parental Approval and Disapproval

1. Sometimes parents don't approve of the friends you have at school or in your neighborhood. Sometimes they explain *only*

by saying: "We don't want him (or her) in our house (or apartment)!" Or "We don't approve of him and don't want you to have anything to do with him!"

Such statements are not explanations or reasons. They really are rules or orders which parents expect children to obey. Perhaps this has happened to you or to some of your friends. What do you think some of the real reasons might be? Why do you feel they could be good reasons, even though you don't like them? Why do you feel they are poor reasons?

2. Today many people your age become very angry with their parents when they won't permit them to do or have some of the things they want very much—even though *their parents did or had these same things when they were that age.* When their children discuss this with them, frequently they argue: "Gee whiz, Dad, can't you and Mom remember when you were kids?" And their parents argue back: "Yes! But times have changed. The answer is still *no*!" What reasons can you think of for parents being so "stubborn" and "unreasonable" in situations like this?

About Conformity

3. You've been invited to a Hallowe'en party and you masquerade in the best costume you've ever had. But, when you get to the party, you find out that you had misunderstood: *No one else is wearing a costume*! Tell how you think you'd feel and what you would do.

If this were *your party* and this happened to one of your guests (instead of you), how would you feel about the situation? What would you do?

4. In most families, there are customs, traditions, and habits which parents have had their minds made up about for years, such as dancing, dating, wearing lipstick, driving a car, going to bed at certain hours, celebrating religious events, associating with certain kinds of people, and so on. Even though some of these things may seem old-fashioned and silly today, children usually have no choice except to go along with their parents' ways until they are "of age." Suppose your parents didn't believe in movies, radio, television, and telephones, and made

you wear clothes which were in style about fifty years ago. How would this change your life? Knowing your parents as you do—when they have their minds made up—how do you think you might go about getting them to see things your way?

About Clubs and Organizations

5. Some people do not approve of any organizations that exclude some people. How could there be any kind of club without some rules about membership, about who can and who cannot join? How is it possible to be "fair" and "democratic" in clubs and still have rules which guarantee a membership of only the "right" kind of people?

6. Many clubs, organizations, schools, etc., have *initiations*. What can you find out about the reasons for such ceremonies? What are initiations supposed to do? What don't they do? What dangers can there be? Why do so many people—already in such clubs—favor such initiations? If a person has all the qualifications for joining an organization but refuses to be "initiated," he probably won't be admitted. In addition, his friends may think unkindly of him. What are some initiations you know from your own experience or have heard about from others? What are your opinions about initiations?

About Name-Calling

7. Why can it be difficult to tell whether name-calling is a *compliment* or an *insult*? What makes the difference? Sometimes a person's nickname is all right when used by certain people—friends and relatives—but causes a fight when used by others. Boys have such nicknames for each other as *Hambone, Cream Puff, Horsey, Dodo Ears, Fatso, Baby, Babe, Lefty, Dummy*, etc. Girls call each other *D-D, Tricksie, Finky, Bubbles, Dopey, Peaches, Brainy-Janey, Dipsy*, etc. Why does name-calling cause trouble, hard feelings, anger, fights?

8. A simple, innocent statement such as "you are a brain!" could mean many things, depending upon the *way* it is said. Try saying it in different ways in front of the class and then ask them how it "sounded" to them, that is, what *meanings* were added by the tone of your voice.

110

a. You are a *brain*. (Voice drops, lower pitch, on last word; said with defeat, disgust.)

b. *You* are a *brain*? (Impossible; unbelievable!)

c. You *are* a brain. (Thankful, grateful, pleased, congratulatory.)

d. *You're . . . a . . . b-r-a-i-n.* (Lovingly, tenderly, idolizingly.)

Have various people try their hands using other statements or phrases such as:

a. Thank you, sir
b. No.
c. It's horrible.
d. She's beautiful
e. You're a wheezle-meazle.
f. He's a big man.
g. She's a big wheel.
h. It tastes terrific.
i. I'm mad about it.
j. You're so big and tough.
k. I promise I'll remember.

About Reputations

9. Reputations can be good or bad, valuable or harmful to people. Sometimes a person has to "live up to" someone else's reputation: an older brother's or sister's school record; father's leadership abilities; mother's neat, orderly organization; grandfather's interest in medicine; Uncle Alphonso's industriousness, etc. Sometimes, even, it's difficult to live up to *one's own* past achievements or reputation; or to live up to the "proud name" you've inherited, such as William Elmont Swellworthy III; or to live up to the Joneses or others in your neighborhood. How do you feel about *living up to reputations*? What does it mean to have a "good reputation?"

10. Suppose you had straight "A's" all through school until now but this year, everything seems absolutely new, really tough to learn. Or suppose you uncle is being investigated as a Communist. Or suppose you have an older brother in prison, or a sister who always lies and cheats, or a father who earns $40,000 a year, or a mother who works scrubbing floors because your father is "sick" all the time. Or suppose you have had three other older brothers and sisters in this same school, and all of them were lazy and failed or dropped out. How do you feel about "living down" such reputations?

11. What kinds of *reputations* are desirable and helpful to you now and in the future? Does making a mistake or "goofing" give you a "bad reputation?" How? Why? Why not?
12. How are a person's *character* and his *reputation* related?
13. If your parents had come from a foreign country twenty years ago but were too busy or never went to the trouble to learn to speak or read or write English, what problems do you think this would create for you, even though your English is perfect?

III. PREREADING ACTIVITIES

1. When there are competitive contests, there can be *only one winner*—one person or one team—even though there may be hundreds or thousands of people involved. Many people believe that contests and competitions are wonderful, stimulating, rewarding, and "the American Way." Other people believe that there's much more harm in such competitive contests than there is good. Those against contests usually offer arguments like these:

   a. It's not fair. There can be only one winner, and a lot of the participants may deserve to win.
   b. In an art or music contest, a person may do things to please the judges and thus sacrifice his own creativity and style.
   c. In timed contests, a person may find shortcuts in order to be first and thus may develop bad habits for quick or careless work that he may never be able to get rid of.
   d. In almost every kind of contest, many people find it too hard to resist cheating because winning is so important.
   e. Contests teach people to work only for rewards and praise by other people and, later on, cause them to say: "Why should I spend my time doing this or that? What's in it for me?"
   f. Contests that are supposed to teach people to become more skillful or knowledgeable usually fail because most people are more interested in the game or contest than they are in learning anything else.

Find some adults in your community who have opposing beliefs about the value of contests and have them come to talk to your class. Have those in your class who are interested divide into two groups, those for and those against contests, and then let them debate the issue.

2. Suddenly your father's job requires him to move to another town in another state. This means you will have to move from your home, neighborhood, friends, and school to a strange, new place and try to make new friends. The suburb you live in is called "Snob Hill" and you and your family are the first outsiders or newcomers to move into this neighborhood in twenty-five years. Also, you don't talk the way these new neighbors talk—that is, your accent, dialect is different; your father's car isn't so new or so fine a model as theirs; your clothes are different; the food you like to eat is not even sold in the local stores; and you find that your religion is different from that found in the five houses of worship in this community. Write a story about how you think you would feel, what problems you think you might have, what you would try to do, how you would expect the people in Snob Hill to think, feel, act, etc.

3. From a small European country called "Epytoerets," a family comes and moves into a house (or apartment) next to yours. They seem to look and act the same as everyone else except for these four, very noticeable, things:

a. All the men and boys always wear *skirts*.
b. All the women and girls always wear *trousers*.
c. Everyone in Epytoerets has just *three* fingers and one thumb.
d. The color of everyone's eyes in Epytoerets is the same: orange.

As you can imagine, it will probably take a long time for the people in your community to "get used to" these people; to accept them; to like them. But, it might take even longer—*perhaps never*—because they have other characteristics or traits which worry the people in your neighborhood even more than their strange looks:

113

A. *All people from Epytoerets are known to be 100%*
   a. honest.
   b. faster and better in math than any computer.
   c. harder workers and for longer hours (14 per day) than we.
   d. accurate—none has ever made a single mistake.
   e. unforgetful—these people never forget a single thing.

B. However, it is also known that *all people from Epytoerets*
   a. have absolutely no imaginations, no creative ability.
   b. need to take twice as long as we to learn anything new.
   c. can listen to, understand and speak English, but it's impossible for them ever to be able to read or write it.

As you can see, in list "A" above, these are the things that employers like to find in the people they hire; thus, Mr. and Mrs. Ekilnu, their five children and Grandpa and Grandma Ekilnu, have become very rich and always get the best jobs offered to them, the best grades in school, etc. Very soon after they move next door to you, school begins and you meet two of the children—twins, a boy and a girl—who are your age, in the same class with you. Their names are *Lots Ekilnu* and *Very Ekilnu* and they become your best friends; and you become theirs.

Since the people in your town are afraid of strangers, they are not friendly toward the Ekilnus. Some even hate them. Others make fun of them, or are jealous and everyone—except you—dislikes them. Write a story telling about your friendship with Lots and Very—your problems, your adventures, etc.

IV. POSTREADING DISCUSSION QUESTIONS

1. How would it be possible for a patriotic American to be so *anti-Communist* that he would be *un*democratic?
2. In the play *Othello* (Act III, Scene 3) William Shakespeare wrote the following:
   "Who steals my purse steals trash;
   'tis something, nothing;

114

'Twas mine, 'tis his, and has been
    slave to thousands;
But he that filches from me my good name
Robs me of that which not enriches him,
And makes me poor indeed."

Discuss the meanings these lines have for you. Tell whether you would agree or disagree and why.

3. How can you explain the way Mr. Moss, Charley's father, felt about schooling and education?

4. Why is it that you don't find many men who are nurses, kindergarten teachers, private secretaries, telephone operators, manicurists, or hire themselves out as housekeepers? Why is it you don't find many women who fly commercial airplanes, are presidents of large corporations, drive trucks and buses, or who are carpenters, bricklayers, inventors, engineers?

5. Some readers of *Call Me Charley* would insist that the story *did not* end happily—for Charley—while others would argue that it did. How do you feel about the ending? Should Jesse Jackson have written it so that Charley would win the bicycle, get his season pass back with an apology, be elected president of the Tigers Club, and get his newspaper route back? Why do you think so?

V. HELPING CHILDREN TO REVEAL THEIR COMPREHENSION

1. Charley Moss's mother and father seem to be completely opposite in the things they did, said, believed. Explain the kinds of circumstances that could have caused one to be so hopeful and optimistic and the other so suspicious and pessimistic.

2. Hannah never seems to smile; she seems to be rough and tough and gruff most of the time—and busy minding her own business the rest of the time. Yet one just can't help but have some nice, warm, cozy feelings about her. Write what you believe to be an accurate description of Hannah—the kind of person she *really* is, her true personality, feelings, beliefs, etc.

3. In what ways do Mr. and Mrs. Reed (George's parents) and Mr. and Mrs. Moss (Charley's parents) seem to be alike?

4. Listed below are some of the important characters in the book which you probably remember very clearly. Almost all of them have certain ideas or feelings about Charley at the beginning of the story that change to almost opposite ideas or feelings by the time the story ends. In the blanks under the column marked *BEGINNING*, put either a "P.C." (*pro-*Charley) or an "A.C." (*anti-*Charley) opposite the names of the people you think held these opinions or attitudes. Do the same with the blanks marked *ENDING*. Put a "U" on any blanks if you are *undecided* or unsure. When you finish, notice those whose attitudes changed. Choose one of these and try to explain how this change happened. You may want to go back to the book and find specific evidence to cite in support of your reasoning.

	BEGINNING	*ENDING*
Tom Hamilton		
George Reed		
Hannah		
Mrs. Hamilton		
Mr. Hamilton		
Mrs. Reed		
Mr. Reed		
Mr. Moss		
Mrs. Moss		
Mr. Winter (the principal)		
Miss Barnes (homeroom teacher)		
Miss King (English teacher)		
Mr. Perkin		
Swimming Pool Manager		
Doc Cunningham		

5. Tom Hamilton became angry with his best friend, Charley, because he thought he was *yellow*, *cowardly*, *shy*, and *afraid*. The author gives many examples of this by the way he describes Charley's behavior and the way he has Charley do

116

things. If you were going to defend Charley and prove that he really was not like this but had good reasons for acting the way he did, what would your argument and your reasons be?

6. Why do you think it was so important to Charley to have people "*call him Charley*?"

7. Some people might say that the book *Call Me Charley* is one which has several different kinds of *contests*. How many "contests" do you see in this story? How many "winners" are there? Who else, besides Charley, was a winner—perhaps even a greater winner than Charley? What reasons can you give?

VI. RELATED-TO-READING EXPERIENCES

1. Shortly after the United States declared war on Japan in December 1941, Japanese-Americans, citizens and noncitizens alike, learned quickly and sternly about the ways in which friendly, peaceful people can change as a result of fear, suspicion, anger, and stereotype. They learned how a great many people can suffer for the actions of a few; how a minority group can be hated because of ancestry; how prejudice is born. Find out all you can about the treatment of Japanese people in America during World War II. Make a comparison of what you find with the feelings and actions of the people in Arlington Heights, Ohio, which Jesse Jackson chose as a setting for his fictional story.

2. Write a convincing article which tells of some of the positive, harmless values of prejudice. Some people, for example, seem to think that there is only one kind of prejudice and that it's bad.

3. In what specific ways can one man's prejudice and stereotyping of another affect that person's reputation? Prepare a list called "Anti-Prejudice and Stereotype Laws" and present it to your class for discussion and adoption. What do you expect the hardest part of this presentation to be? Why?

4. Probably the greatest number of people in the United States ever to be affected by prejudice, bias, stereotype—deprived of their civil rights—was *women*. Not very long ago women

couldn't vote, go certain places, hold certain kinds of jobs, and so forth. Find out about *female emancipation* in this country. Also, try to find out if there are still certain jobs, places, etc., restricted to women *simply because they are women.*

VII. VOCABULARY THAT MAY NEED DEVELOPING

Some readers may find it informative as well as stimulating and revealing to engage in a *semantic investigation* of the shades of meaning in the following words and prefixes:

close-minded	*biased*	*anti*-freedom
Semite (Semitic)	*pro*-horse	*dis*advantaged
un-American	*non*-Communist	*sub*servient
stereotyped	*narrow-minded*	*bigot*
"race, creed, and color"	*prejudiced*	

VIII. OTHER SELECTIONS ON A SIMILAR THEME: A SELECTED BIBLIOGRAPHY

Bontemps, Arna. *The Story of George Washington Carver.* N.Y.: Grosset & Dunlap, 1954.

De Angeli, Marguerite. *Bright April.* Garden City, N.Y.: Doubleday, 1946.

_____. *Yonie Wondernose.* Garden City, N.Y.: Doubleday, 1944.

Gates, Doris. *Blue Willow.* N.Y.: Viking, 1940.

Seredy, Kate. *A Tree for Peter.* N.Y.: Viking, 1941.

Wier, Ester. *The Loner.* N.Y.: McKay, 1963.

Yates, Elizabeth. *Amos Fortune, Free Man.* N.Y.: Dutton, 1950.

Poetry

"Abraham Lincoln 1809-1865" by Rosemary Carr and Stephen Vincent Benét, from *A Book of Americans,* N.Y.: Holt, 1933.

"Atlantic Charter, A.D. 1620-1942" by Francis Brett Young, from *Time for Poetry,* edited by May Hill Arbuthnot, Chicago: Scott, Foresman, 1961.

"The Day Will Bring Some Lovely Thing" by Grace Noll Crowell, from *Silver in the Sun* N.Y.: Harper.

COYOTE FOR KEEPS
by BURDETTA JOHNSON

Illustrated by James Ralph Johnson

I. THE STORY

A coyote pup is not the usual sort of animal children adopt as a pet, but Bob and Marie do and decide to spend their summer at their grandfather's ranch taming it. When a bounty hunter comes through the area looking for coyotes to kill, the children become involved in the dangerous task of keeping Kip safely hidden, but then another problem comes up. What will they do with their new pet when they have to go back East at the end of the summer? This is an unusual adventure story for all animal lovers.

II. PREPREADING DISCUSSION QUESTIONS

The questions which follow are illustrative of the kinds which teachers can prepare for the purpose of releasing children to reveal how *they feel* about some of the same larger ideas and bigger meanings contained in the book *before* it is read.

About Unusual Pets

1. Today it is not at all unusual to hear about someone who has just tamed a strange wild animal to keep as a pet. People have been known to walk down a main street of a town with a leash in their hands and—to the surprise of some passerby—attached to the other end an alligator, chimpanzee, panther, penguin, porcupine, and so forth. Probably there are not too many wild animals left which you haven't heard of being tamed for pets. Suppose your class wanted to be the first group of humans to

tame—for a class pet—a heretofore untamed wild animal. What unusual animals would you choose? What *one* do you think you could get your class to choose?

2. You have probably seen on television or read or heard stories about the problems that occur when someone makes a pet out of a wild animal. What are some of these problems?

About Worrying

3. Some people seem to worry all the time and are called "worry-warts"; others never seem to worry at all—about anything—and are called "carefree" or "happy-go-lucky." The *worriers* always seem to be expecting the worst to happen; they seem forever to be expecting something to happen to interfere with their plans; they often go to extremes by dreaming up all sorts of fantastic ways of how things *possibly* could go wrong. They say: "But what if . . ." or "Suppose that . . ." no matter how carefully plans have been made. Tell about such a time when you planned carefully to go somewhere or to do something— something that you wanted to do very much, something that, to you, seemed almost like a miracle that you were permitted to do or have. Tell about some of the worries you had: "It's too good to be true. . . . . I just know something's going to happen to spoil it!" When have *you* felt that way? What happened?

4. Some worriers become angry when you tell them they are silly for worrying and that they should just "enjoy themselves and face and solve problems when and *if* they occur!" The worriers argue that a person should always be thinking ahead, preparing for the unexpected so that it will be possible to *make a good decision quickly.* They say: "That's the *only* way a person can relax and enjoy himself!" What opinions do you have? Who's got the right idea, the worrier or the nonworrier? Why do you think so?

About Summer Vacations

5. Suppose you could have grandparents living in *any one* of the fifty United States, and that you had the chance this coming summer to visit them until time for school next fall. What

121

state would *you* choose? Why? Do you know whether your reasons are based on fact or could it be that you just think this is true about a particular state because you saw some parts of it on a television program. How can you learn whether or not you'd find what you want on your visit?
want on your visit?

About Wealth

6. There are many kinds of *wealth* and many different ways to be rich. How many *different kinds* of wealthy people can you describe?

7. Probably the most desirable way to be "wealthy" is to have a *combination* of different kinds of "riches." However, if you could be wealthy or rich in only *one* thing (or way), which would you prefer? Why?

III. PREREADING ACTIVITIES

1. Suppose you were employed by a travel agency and your job was to "plot out" an *itinerary* for people going *by car* to the following places, traveling about 300 miles per day. Write down *(a)* the routes, *(b)* the scenic places they can visit if they choose, and *(c)* historical landmarks (such as museums, bridges, monuments, etc.) they might want to see. Then, on a road map of the United States, mark the trip, using your town or city as the starting place.

Phoenix, Arizona   Mount Vernon, Ohio
Butte, Montana   Boulder, Colorado
Lake Itasca, Minnesota   Ogden, Utah
Carson City, Nevada   Boise, Idaho
Key West, Florida   Fairbanks, Alaska

2. The United States can boast of many famous *explorers* or pioneers, of the past as well as the present. Be an explorer yourself and try to find the "lost" and "missing" famous western explorers of the following states:

Nevada	Wyoming	Idaho	Washington
California	Montana	Arizona	Alaska
Utah	Colorado	New Mexico	Oregon

What famous explorers are "claimed by" or associated with explorations in these states? What did they discover through their explorations?

3. Tell what you can discover about *natural phenomena* that can be found in the following states; winter and summer climate; plant and animal wildlife, specifically unique to each:

Nevada	Wyoming	Idaho	Washington
California	Montana	Arizona	New Mexico
Alaska	Utah	Oregon	Colorado

4. People can *explore* in many different ways—some "explore" with test tubes while others "explore" outer space. Ordinary people, like you and me, "explore"—in some way or other— almost every day. We investigate and test new places foods, trails, people, and so forth. Make as long a list as you can of the various different kinds of explorers you can "uncover."

IV. POSTREADING DISCUSSION QUESTIONS

1. Bob and Marie decided to keep quiet about the coyote pup they found. They said they must keep it a *secret*. Why do you think they felt this way? Knowing Mr. and Mrs. Holmes (Grandpa and Grandma) as you do, do you really think they might not have permitted them to raise Kip as a pet? Why? Why not?

2. Bob and Marie thought that *not telling* their grandparents that they had found and were raising a coyote *was a secret*. Some people might say that *this kind* of secret is just another name for *a lie!*. What do you think? What is your opinion?

3. On page 35, the author, Burdetta Johnson, gives a clear picture of Bob's feeling about the West and how the coyote—*for him*—is like a magic time machine that lets him step in and out

123

of centuries at will. What do you think Bob means in this passage? How do you feel about his comparison? Think about the community in which you live. What "timeless" things, animals, places are there which someone like Bob could use to "replay the record of the past?"

> "Coyotes seemed to be able to reach into the past, pull out the excitement and adventure of frontier days, and play the background sounds all over again. They were just like wilderness record players playing the natural music of this wide-open country over and over again. To have a coyote pup for a pet would be almost like holding a little of the past, a past still living in the present. Roads and bridges had changed the looks of the land . . . but the coyotes had not changed since the days of Coronado, Kit Carson, or Billy the Kid."

4. Some people feel that capturing and taming wild animals and keeping them in captivity is cruel—worse, even, than killing them. They, like people, were meant to be free, it is argued. What are your feelings about this? Which side of the argument do you think you'd be on? Why? What are some of your reasons?

V. HELPING CHILDREN TO REVEAL THEIR COMPREHENSION

1. Write titles for the eighteen chapters.
2. On a road map of the United States, choose a city on the East Coast and mark Bob's and Marie's trip from there to the Holmes' ranch.
3. Mr. Holmes taught his grandchildren many "tricks" or "secrets" as he called them. If you think about them, they seem like lessons, or information one gets from experience, or simply learning about new things. Prepare a little booklet called "Grandpa Holmes' Wild-West Trick Book." Give each of his "tricks" a name and describe it in your own way.

For example:
    "Animal Infections" (p. 135)
    "Sagebrush Smarties" (p. 122)
    "Waterproofed Plants" (p. 121)
    "Porcupine Tips" (p. 112)
    "Flower Fuzz" (p. 121-22)
    "Alfalfa Sprinkling Cans" (p. 54)

VI. RELATED-TO-READING EXPERIENCES

1. Listen to Grofe's *Grand Canyon Suite*. The moods evoked in "Sunrise," "Sunset," "On the Trail," "The Painted Desert," and "Cloudburst" seem to fit many scenes and situations in *Coyote for Keeps*. Select some of the appropriate passages to practice for oral reading with Grofe's background accompaniment.

2. Assume the role of Bob or Marie—back in school after their summer in Arizona. Some of your classmates would enjoy hearing you tell of your trip. Prepare an illustrated "lecture" by using slides, photographs, picture postcards, and pictures cut and mounted from magazines or other kinds of publications. You might call your talk: "Arizona for Armchair Travelers."

3. Go on an "Animal-Trait Safari." Track down animals which are thought of as possessing certain *human* characteristics or traits, such as animals that are thieves or robbers, architects or builders, traders, magicians, organized into "societies," deceivers or tricksters, and so forth.

VII. VOCABULARY THAT MAY NEED DEVELOPING

1. *Lassoing Western Words 'n' Ways*

[*NOTE TO TEACHER: While enjoyment and comprehension of Coyote for Keeps is possible without digging out the specific meanings of words describing Western ways and locale, some readers will want to "lasso" these words in order to live as closely to the West as do the Johnsons. However, the reader who wants to spend a simple, vicarious summer with Bob, Marie, and Kip—with no real interest in snowy egrets, mullein plants, or rimrocks—needs to be allowed this choice.—C.F.R.*]

One interesting way to examine the exciting, colorful vocabulary in this story is to "corral" them in one of these three categories: *(a)* Animal; *(b)* Vegetable; *(c)* Mineral.

Some words readers have found interesting include:

predator (p. 24)	*pack rats* (p. 21)	*snowy egret* (p. 49)
ruminate (p. 52)	*agave* (p. 149)	*writhing* (p. 113)
mesa (p. 56)	*rimrock* (p. 33)	*bounty* (p. 51)
yodeling (p. 41)	*passel* (p. 41)	*debris* (p. 109)
vandal (p. 111)	*veered* (p. 109)	*mullein plant* (p. 48)
chagrin (p. 108)	*magpie* (p. 65)	*yucca plant* (p. 61)

VIII. OTHER SELECTIONS ON A SIMILAR THEME: A SELECTED BIBLIOGRAPHY

Coggins, Herbert. *Busby & Co.* N.Y.: McGraw-Hill, 1952.

Daugherty, James. *Of Courage Undaunted: Across the Continent with Lewis and Clark.* N.Y.: Viking, 1951.

Henry, Marguerite. *Brighty of the Grand Canyon.* Chicago: Rand McNally, 1953.

James, Will. *Smoky, the Cowhorse.* N.Y.: Scribner's, 1926.

Lamorisse, Albert. *White Mane.* Garden City, N.Y.: Doubleday.

Martin, Fran. *Nine Tales of Coyote.* N.Y.: Harper, 1950.

Poetry

"The Cowboy's Life" by James Barton Adams, from *Time for Poetry,* edited by May Hill Arbuthnot, Chicago: Scott, Foresman, 1961.

"Lone Dog" by Irene Rutherford McLeod, from *Songs to Save a Soul,* London: Chatto & Windus, 1915.

"Open Range" by Kathryn and Byron Jackson, from *Cowboys and Indians*, N.Y.: Simon & Schuster, 1948.

"The Wolf" by Georgia R. Durston, from *Time for Poetry*, edited by May Hill Arbuthnot, Chicago: Scott, Foresman, 1961.

PRAIRIE SCHOOL

by LOIS LENSKI

Illustrated by the Author

I. THE STORY

Miss Martin's little school on the prairie becomes the center of an adventure for the children when a great blizzard sweeps down and traps them inside. Waiting for rescue to come, their days are filled with suspense and excitement just figuring out ways to eat, sleep, and keep warm together in the little schoolhouse.

II. PREREADING DISCUSSION QUESTIONS

The questions which follow are illustrative of the kinds which teachers can prepare for the purpose of releasing children to reveal how *they feel* about some of the same larger ideas and bigger meanings contained in the book *before* it is read.

About Schools and Schooling
1. When someone your age returns to school after a summer vacation, what things does he expect to find *unchanged*? What things might one expect to be different?
2. Why do some people seem to think that school is so important?
3. Why are children made to go to school? Why isn't the choice of going or not going left up to them?
4. What are some of the things that people your age seem to dislike most about going to school? What are some of the things that they seem to like best?

5. What kinds of things do you think *teachers* dislike most about school? What things do you think they would like best?

6. Everyone seems to like school holidays and vacations, including teachers. Why is this so? Why couldn't going to school be the same as a vacation?

7. What kinds of people should not be allowed to come to school? Who should be excused from going to school?

8. Why are children's parents important to school success? In what ways are parents needed to help schools do a better job? How do parents help? How do they interfere?

About Blizzards and Other Natural Phenomena

9. What are some of the reasons you hear given when the President of the United States declares that a certain place is a *"disaster area?"* What does this mean?

10. Tell about a serious disaster that occurred nearby—or one that you, yourself, lived through, such things, for example, as fires, floods, hurricanes, earthquakes, tornadoes, typhoons, blizzards, etc. Did you have any warning in advance? What kinds of dangers were involved? What was the worst worry? What other kinds of worries? In what ways was living through such an emergency similar to being marooned on a deserted island? How is it possible for such emergencies to make heroes out of people?

11. When nature causes certain disasters (like those mentioned above) modern man seems to be almost helpless to prevent them. And, with all our modern means of transportation and communication, we still find that there is little to do but to "make the best of the situation." Suppose your town were suddenly cut off from the outside world and that there were no telephones, electricity, or transportation of any kind—except by foot, which was dangerous. What kinds of things would you want to buy to help you through this week-long period of isolation? What kinds of problems do you think the fire chief, mayor, and police chief would be concerned about? Which other people would be worried? Why?

12. Why do some people feel that *everyone* should know the basic things to do when someone has been hurt or injured?
13. What are some of the do's and don'ts of *first aid*?
14. What kinds of first-aid treatment do you believe to be the most important for everyone your age to know? (For example, for burns, broken bones, bleeding, suffocation, drowning, poisoning, exposure, etc.)

III. PREREADING ACTIVITIES

1. Interview some of the teachers in your school and ask them to tell you some of the things they think teachers worry about most.
2. Look around your schoolroom. Suppose there were nothing but desks and chairs, a blackboard, and a few textbooks. If you were the teacher and were given only $100 to buy the other things you needed—*for a whole year*—on what would you spend the $100?
3. Make a list of what you feel to be the twelve most important qualities a good teacher should have. If there is a college or university nearby, ask an education professor to make a similar list. Ask the superintendent or principal of your school to do the same. What kinds of things do you notice are alike? What things are different?
4. Find out all you can about the *rights* of American Indians. Can they own land? Vote? Do they have to go to school? Can they still hunt animals any time they want? Are they exempt from any of the laws that affect us? Are they fairly treated today? Mistreated?
5. Below is a "floor plan" of an *emergency room* which has been built underground, large enough for 6-8 people. The size of the room is 12' X 12' and both airtight and watertight. It is strong enough to withstand any amount of wind or heat or explosion. Use supermarket advertisements from your local paper and a mail-order catalogue and go on a "shopping spree" to supply and equip this *emergency room* for your family for one

month. On the floor plan, show how you would arrange the furniture, store supplies, etc. On the "Emergency Room Order Form" order the supplies and equipment you would need and total the cost. Be sure you can explain why the things you order are *absolute necessities* and not just "nice" things to have.

a. Emergency Room Floor Plan

12'

12'

Entrance

b. Emergency Room Order Form

Name _____

Date _____

Amount	Item	Reasons/Uses	Cost

IV. POSTREADING DISCUSSION QUESTIONS

1. What are your opinions about the different beliefs Mama and Papa Wagner had about raising children?
2. Why did such "small things" seem so wonderful to these prairie children? (The kinds of Christmas presents they wanted and received; the fair; watching a Diesel-engine train; going to town; etc.)
3. There's an old saying: "Don't put off until tomorrow that which you can do today." Tell why such a saying is almost a "life or death" rule for people who live the kinds of lives these prairie children did.
4. Tell why you feel *forgetfulness* could be a matter of life or death for children attending the Prairie School.
5. On page 152, Miss Martin was thinking to herself: "But all this was *borrowing trouble*." What did she mean? Tell about times when you have "borrowed trouble."
6. In many cities, when people grow old, they want to move away from the hustle and bustle, out in the country, maybe, or to a little cottage or home, and live peacefully. Darrell's and

131

Delores' grandparents, instead—as did most of the old folks in Corson County—*moved to the city.* Do you think their reasons for doing so are good ones? Why?

7. What did you think of when you read about the different kinds of foods the various people in the story ate? In what ways are they the same as the food you eat? How are they different? Why?

8. People who live in regions like the one in this story—as well as those near the sea—seem to become "natural weather forecasters," even young children. What examples of this can you find in the story? How accurate are such forecasts? What forecasts have you been taught to make? Is there any scientific evidence to back these "hunches" up?

V. HELPING CHILDREN TO REVEAL THEIR COMPREHENSION

1. Explain why it was necessary for Mr. Wagner to have business agreements with the Indian, Charlie Spotted Bear.

2. Make a model of the Prairie School and the teacherage.

3. Papa and Mama Wagner (Darrell's and Delores' parents) seemed to have different opinions about the importance of the animals they owned, although in the story they never discussed those differences with each other. Suppose such a conversation had taken place at the hospital. Write this discussion in play-script form and plan to dramatize it.

4. If you were Ruby Englehart's teacher, what would you decide Ruby needs most to learn? How would you go about teaching her? Write a report to Mr. and Mrs. Englehart explaining your reasons.

5. Compare Miss Martin's teaching job with that of your teacher. What things are the same? What things are different?

6. If Darrell and Delores Wagner spent next winter with you, what do you think would impress them the most? How would their lives in and out of school be different? Have them write a letter (or keep a diary) to their parents back home in Corson County, South Dakota, telling about these differences.

7. In this story, *coal, rope,* and *water* seem to be the most important things a teacher like Miss Martin could have—more important, even, than books, paste, chalk, etc. How do you explain this?

8. *A "Report Card" for Miss Martin:* On the blanks below, put an "X" opposite all those things *you* believe a good teacher should be. After you finish, draw a circle around the "X's" which you think apply especially to Miss Martin. If you find you haven't placed an "X" on one of the blanks, but yet it applies to Miss Martin, draw a circle around the blank but don't put an "X" in it.

A good teacher should . . .
— have no favorites or "teacher's pets."
— never get angry.
— always be fair to everyone.
— pass everybody.
— dress properly.
— know all about first aid.
— always use the best language.
— always be cheerful in front of students.
— never lose his temper.
— not punish students.
— give everyone good marks.
— know how to be a good cook.
— permit students to choose to learn what they want to learn.
— not be friendly with students outside school.
  think of his students before himself.
— not have dates.
— always be clean and orderly.
— be young and strong and healthy.
— not permit students to argue or be sassy.
— always have better suggestions and solutions than his students.
— not allow children to waste time by looking out the windows.
— not allow children to whisper or talk in school.
— know about cars, animals, and machinery.

VI. RELATED-TO-READING EXPERIENCES

1. Obtain a copy of *The Farmer's Almanac.* Make a list of the things you find in it that you think would be especially helpful to you if you were Darrell or Delores.

2. Suppose a new teacher "from the East"—unaccustomed to prairie life—were coming to substitute for Miss Martin for a year. Prepare a "survival" booklet that you think would be helpful. In it should be a few "recipes" for improvisation such as (1) an emergency communication system, (2) how to make soap, (3) how to conserve water, (4) how to make water safe for drinking, (5) how to make "food" out of simple things like grain, flour, salt, herbs, etc., (6) how to take care of frostbite, (7) how to keep warm or cool under extreme conditions, (8) how to keep from getting lost in the dark or blinding storms, (9) how to take care of animals, (10) emergency first aid, (11) how to forecast the weather, etc.

3. Find someone in your community who has attended or taught in a "one-room school." Have your teacher help you prepare questions you might want to ask in an interview with such a person. One question might be, for example: How would it be possible for a teacher to teach each child everything as an individual person since the students will be all ages and in all grades?

4. Plan to have a program based upon the story you have just read, *Prairie School,* taking place in the little school where you and your teacher and Charlie and Pearl Spotted Bear and their children have been marooned by the "worst blizzard ever." Open the program with the song of the prairie children, "Born of the Wind," which you will find at the beginning of the book. Some students may wish to write other verses for it once they begin to live and learn about the roughness and toughness of prairie life via their dramatization. During dress rehearsal have someone take colored slides of certain scenes and actions. These may be used subsequently for retelling the story to others. A tape recording may be made afterwards by the children and synchronized to go with the telling of the slides.

5. Suppose Miss Martin had been stranded in Aberdeen and had not been able to return to the Prairie School for a month after the Christmas vacation. What if you were the substitute teacher for that time. What kinds of plans would you have made for teaching these children? What problems would you have been prepared to handle?

VII. VOCABULARY THAT MAY NEED DEVELOPING

Although most of the words suggested below do not actually appear in Lois Lenski's story *Prairie School*, they are very much related to the actions, thoughts, and feelings of the characters and situations in the story. Many deal with concepts or with things taken for granted and are not easily defined. Searching for definitions, instances, and implications for words such as these can challenge children's thinking and provide greater appreciation of the literature they read about tough and high-spirited children who face different kinds of problems in growing up.

inventive	*catastrophe*	*show* (*movie*, p. 100)
innovative	*disaster*	*impulsive*
improvisation	*luxury*	*impatient*
ingenuity	*necessity*	*exaggeration*
imagination	*register* (p. 93-94)	*monotony*
emergency		

VIII. OTHER SELECTIONS ON A SIMILAR THEME: A SELECTED BIBLIOGRAPHY

Buck, Pearl. *The Big Wave.* N.Y.: John Day, 1948.

Day, Véronique. *Landslide!* N.Y.: Coward-McCann, 1963. (Available as a Dell Yearling book.)

DeAngeli, Marguerite. *Skippack School.* Garden City, N.Y.: Doubleday, 1939.

Dejong, Meinderet. *The Wheel on the School.* N.Y.: Harper, 1954.

Sperry, Armstrong. *Call It Courage.* N.Y.: Macmillan, 1940.

Wilder, Laura Ingalls. *Little House in the Big Woods.* N.Y.: Harper, 1953.

_____. *Little House on the Prairie.* N.Y.: Harper, 1953.

_____. *Little Town on the Prairie.* N.Y.: Harper, 1953.

_____. *The Long Winter.* N.Y.: Harper, 1953.

Poetry

"Adventure" by Harry Behn, from *The Little Hill*, N.Y.: Harcourt, 1949.

"Indian Children" by Annette Wynne, from *For Days and Days*, Philadelphia: Lippincott, 1919.

"Open Range" by Kathryn and Byron Jackson, from *Cowboys and Indians*, N.Y.: Simon & Schuster, 1948.

"Snow in the City" by Rachel Field, from *Piping Down the Valleys Wild*, selected by Nancy Larrick, N.Y.: Delacorte, 1968.

BLUE RIDGE BILLY
by LOIS LENSKI

Illustrated by the Author

I. THE STORY

Billy Honeycutt is a lively mountain boy who rides a mule to the mill, fights with the Buckwheat Hollow boys, goes on a panther hunt and discovers the mystery of the hideout at No Man's Cove—but more important than anything else, he wants to make his own music. He dreams of the day he'll own the banjo hanging in Jeb Dotson's general store, and sets out to find the means to buy it.

II. PREREADING DISCUSSION QUESTIONS

The questions which follow are illustrative of the kinds which teachers can prepare for the purpose of releasing children to reveal how *they feel* about some of the same larger ideas and bigger meanings contained in the book *before* it is read.

About Keeping Faith
1. Tell about a time when you were blamed for something you *didn't do,* just because all of the evidence *pointed your way,* was "stacked" against you. How did you feel? How did your friends act toward you? How did your parents act? What did they do and say?
2. Suppose your *very best friend*—someone you've known and trusted for several years—did the following things:

    a. during an important test in school, looked at someone else's paper;

    b. found someone's purse on the playground, which had a one-dollar bill in it for lunch money, opened the purse, looked around to see if anyone was watching, closed the purse, suspiciously walked over to a tree, and hid the purse behind it;

    c. after you had told him (or her) a very personal, private secret, he talked and laughed with someone who dislikes you and is trying to get even with you. The next day, your "secret" is known all over the school;

    d. told you that he (or she) couldn't go to the movies with you because his dad had a lot of work for him to do; so, you go to the movie anyway. Then you see him come in with someone else.

You just can't believe these things; you know there *must* be some explanation. It can't be true, you've trusted him for so long and he's never before cheated, stolen, broken a promise, or lied to you. But now, all the evidence points against him. Perhaps you were wrong about him. What would you do? How would you feel? How difficult do you think it would be to keep on trusting him as a best friend under these circumstances? Suppose he were innocent and you asked him for an explanation. How do you think that would affect your friendship?

3. No matter how old we get, our parents get older and wiser and we have learned to respect, trust, and have faith in their decisions. We have been told, for many years, that "our parents know best!" But sometimes parents make decisions for us or about us that seem unfair, cruel, unwise, or old-fashioned. Tell about such a time. Try to remember your feelings. Were you hurt, angry, disappointed? What did you do? Tell how you tried to believe that *your parents were right,* even though you didn't like the decision. Why is this so hard to do? Can you remember how it turned out? Were they right?

About Parental Discipline
4. How do you feel about the kind of father who doesn't want his son to be a "sissy" and makes him do hard work to

138

toughen him up, won't let him play games with friends or go places "for fun" because he's supposed to *act like a man*?

5. How do you feel about the kind of mother who wants to make sure her daughter is a polite, well-mannered "little lady" and won't let her take part in any sports, wear slacks or shorts, or belong to the Girl Scouts?

6. Some parents strongly disapprove of their children's spending time painting or drawing, singing in a choir or playing an instrument, or taking part in a play. "It's foolishness, nonsense, and a waste of time!" many of them say. "People ought to spend their time on *worthwhile* things, things that will keep you fed, put clothes on your back, and get you a decent place to live in." Why do people feel this way? Tell why you would agree or disagree.

7. Suppose you had worked hard one summer—as a baby sitter, mowing lawns, picking fruit, for example—and saved the money you earned to buy something you've always wanted: a pair of skis (water or snow). When your mother finds out, she burns them because she says they are too dangerous; so you have nothing left but a memory and a wish. How would this make you feel? What would you try to do about your feelings? What would be the hardest thing for you to do?

III. PREREADING ACTIVITIES

1. Prepare a "language map" of the United States. On it, place words, phrases and idioms, regional pronunciations etc., peculiarly unique to certain areas. For "supporting evidence," children may use books of fiction and nonfiction, people in the community who *have lived* in those regions, live radio/television broadcasts, local newspapers, etc.

2. From time to time, local, state, and national laws are made in the "best interests" of all of the people. However, sometimes these laws interrupt and interfere with the habits, customs, and ways of small groups of people. For example, now it is illegal for private citizens to make and sell medicine, cigarettes, beer or whiskey; it is also unlawful for people to "practice

medicine"—or "doctor" other people—without a license; and it is against the law for children *not* to go to school and for children to be working as adults. These laws are good laws, but they are broken every day by people who feel they are *bad* or that they *don't apply to them.* Suppose someone in your community has been arrested and brought to court for breaking three or four of the above laws, and you are the judge listening to the arguments for and against the defendant. Before you reach your decision, make a list of these arguments; then write a statement telling why you believe the defendant to be guilty or not guilty.

3. Choose one of the following statements. Write a brief, clear statement about why you support or do not support these ideas or philosophies. Prepare to read your "position paper" to a group of your friends.

The following statements are quotes taken from Lois Lenski's "Foreword" in *Blue Ridge Billy:*

a. "An artist looks at the outward surface of things. He is primarily interested in what meets the eye. He looks for beauty, character, action, design and pattern, but he rarely goes more than skin-deep. A writer, on the other hand, has to understand reasons and motives. With all the inquisitiveness of a four-year-old, he keeps asking, 'Why? Why? Why?' He must find out the hidden meanings of all he sees and hears."

b. "Terms like 'minority groups' and 'underprivileged peoples' imply superiority and condescension on the part of the person who uses them."

c. "Often people who are very poor in worldly goods have great richness of spirit."

d. "There is a fundamental lesson to be learned from life: 'that whatever you give comes back to you a hundred times over.' "

e. "Tolerance makes all men brothers."

f. "When people's speech is different from the correct, grammatical school-reader English, it should not be changed, for this would be a travesty on all the beauty and character in the lives of these people."

IV. POSTREADING DISCUSSION QUESTIONS

1. Rudolphus Honeycutt, Billy's father, had firm beliefs about the importance of good hard work and no foolishness, and he expected the members of his family to have the same feelings. At one point, Mr. Honeycutt said: "Music won't grow corn and beans" (p. 130). At other times Mr. Honeycutt said: "Think money grows on bushes, don't you? Work never stunted a young un yet" (p. 129). And, "I never seen a good fiddler or banjo picker that was worth his salt for anything else. Fiddlers are not worth shootin' " (p. 128). And, "What have I got me a wife and young uns and a son almost growed for, if not to tend the crops? I'm a hunter and a horse-swapper and a logger—not a farmer" (p. 142). What kind of a man is this? Why do you think he believes as strongly as he does about the value of work? Do you think this is a good way or a necessary way to be successful? Why do you think Mr. Honeycutt seems to believe that good hard work and success *don't mix with music*?

2. After failing to evict Granny Trivett and Sarey Sue, Pappy seems to change—both in his attitude about music and in the way he treated his son. Tell whether you think he really changed and in what ways. Why?

3. In many families, usually it is the father who "rules the roost" although the wives tend to say, "Sure they do—but I just let my husband *think* he's the boss. I'm the one that makes all the decisions around here!" What kind of a wife and mother was Mrs. Honeycutt? Certainly she wasn't afraid to speak up and, throughout the story, it seems as if she never wins an argument or gets her way—except in the Granny Trivett "caper." Even if

Granny hadn't found the paper in her chimney, Mr. Honeycutt knew he had been beat. How can you explain why Billy's mother just sat by during the dulcimer-burning incident?

4. Read the quotations below. Tell why you think they are or are not related to the story. Which might be a good description of one or more of the characters in the story? Why?

   a. "The best things in life are free."
   b. "All work and no play makes Jack a dull boy."
   c. "It's hard work—not pleasure—that buys the bread."
   d. "Keep the faith, baby."
   e. "Lazy fokes's stummucks don't git tired."
   f. "Music hath charms to soothe the savage breast, to soften rocks, or bend a knotted oak."

V. HELPING CHILDREN TO REVEAL THEIR COMPREHENSION

1. In the Foreword, the author, Lois Lenski, tells us that this story takes place *before* the coming of the automobile to the region. Since the automobile had been invented and was in use in other places in the United States, why do you think it took so long to come to Ashe County? Think back through the story—quickly scan the chapters once again: suppose there had been a few automobiles or trucks owned by people in Solitude. How might the author have had some of the people "use an automobile" in this story? Who would they have been? What would the circumstances have been? Write down your opinions in a paper you might want to call "The First Automobile in the Blue Ridge Mountains." By the way, what *kind* would it have been?

2. Just as one might expect of any normal boy or girl, Billy Honeycutt disobeyed his parents several times in this story. Make a list of those instances (refer to the book, if you want) and then—for each—write a brief paragraph telling whether or not you think his disobedience was "right" or "wrong" and why. If you were Billy, would you have done the same thing?

3. One of the worst things that happened to Billy Honeycutt in this story was the punishment he received from his father for (1) not hoeing the beans as he was told to do; (2) not keeping his mother's water bucket filled; and (3) going to Jeb Dotson's store without permission. As a result, his father

   a. burned the dulcimer he had made.
   b. took his money from Jeb Dotson.
   c. bought a dog with the money Billy worked hard for in order to buy a secondhand banjo.
   d. named the dog "Banjo" and brought it home.
   e. made Billy carry bucket after bucket of water which he dumped on the ground.
   f. kicked him and sent him to bed.

   Billy's father believed that this punishment would teach his son *who the boss was in their house.* Suppose you had been there and were able to "step in" and suggest some other kind of punishment for Billy—one that "suited his *crime.*" What would you have suggested that you think Mr. Honeycutt would have agreed with? Or suppose you were President of the Association for the Prevention of Cruelty to Children (APCC) and happened to witness this scene. Write a report of this incident to the sheriff, demanding Mr. Honeycutt's arrest and punishment. Describe what you think would be a *just* punishment for him.

4. You have just won a contest and your prize is a free summer vacation in Ashe County, Virginia, in the Blue Ridge Mountains and you have your choice of living with one of the following:

   a. Granny Trivett   *b.* Uncle Pozy   *c.* Jeb Dotson
   d. Uncle Jamie   *e.* Mr. and Mrs. Rudy Honeycutt

   Write a letter to the one you choose, thanking him, introducing yourself to him, telling him when you're going to arrive. Obtain a road map which has all of the states that are in the Blue Ridge Mountain area as well as your own state. On the map, show the route you will travel in order to get to Solitude, Virginia.

Now, since you know a lot about these people, their way of living, their personalities, and so forth, write a composition—using your imagination to the fullest—telling all about your summer vacation. What did you do? What problems did you have? What was the hardest thing for you to get used to? What friends did you make? What adventures? Work? Fun? What did you miss most from "back home?" You might want to call your story "My Blue Ridge Mountain Summer."

5. Make a display or exhibit and call it "The Blue Ridge Mountain Museum." Make and put in it models of the "curiosities" you found in the book. A few suggestions to get you started are a dulcimer, a banjo, Jeb Dotson's store, the clothes the people wore, an inside view of the Honeycutts' home, a basket like those made by Uncle Pozy, the Cowcumber tree, the "Half-Way-Up" House, different kinds of roots and herbs and their uses, and so forth.

6. Make a Blue Ridge Billy "Photograph" Album containing your sketches *and* brief word-picture descriptions of the characters in the story and a few of some of the most unusual happenings or sights.

7. Suppose Walt Moseley were your father and that you had been with Billy, Glen, Jack, and Rick on the panther hunt the night when they caught the men moving the still. Describe how you might have felt after learning this about your father. What would you have done about it? Why?

VI. RELATED-TO-READING EXPERIENCES

1. Conduct a mock trial. Mr. Izzie Evah Badd is on trial for using poor, nonstandard, ungrammatical English over the radio. His defense lawyer is Mr. Heezah O. Kaye. The prosecuting attorney's name is I. M. Knutz. The judge's name is Yorah Fyne Enfair. Select a jury that is impartial and, using witnesses, present Mr. Badd's case before the court.

2. Collect and prepare a "recipe" booklet containing "ole timey" herb potions, lotions, and remedies. Why not call it *Granny's Yarb Miracles*?

3. Rewrite Chapter XI, changing all of the "mountain" words and phrases to the kind of English you speak in school. Read this aloud to a group of your classmates; then read the chapter again, the way Lois Lenski wrote it. Have them discuss the differences.

4. On page 147, Lois Lenski writes, "She had nothing—only dreams to believe in. When you had nothing at all, you could have everything in dreams . . . even if they never came true." Suppose you have been selected to give the "kick-off speech" for a fund-raising campaign to help poor and needy orphans in your town. Using the author's quote above, and the ideas and feelings it has for you, write your speech and deliver it to your class by broadcasting it over the public-address system.

VII. VOCABULARY THAT MAY NEED DEVELOPING

1. Write *travel brochures, advertisements,* and/or *encyclopedia entries* in "mountain" words and phrases (pp. 202-03) and regional dialect. Send for several travel brochures about places in America. Then, *rewrite* all of the *written* information so that it would appeal to the folks living in Ashe County, Virginia. Attach your "Mountain Translations" to the brochure. Find an advertisement (for a musical instrument, beverage, bicycle, for example) and rewrite all the *written* information it contains so that it will tempt the people living in Ashe County and make them want to buy. Attach your "Mountain Translations" to the original advertisement. Using an encyclopedia, look up such words as *laurol, possum, ghost, herbs, relatives, square dance.* Rewrite the descriptions and definitions as they might have appeared if they had been written by and for the people living in the Blue Ridge Mountains.

2. Some readers will enjoy testing Lois Lenski's statement (p. 202) about the pure Old English or Anglo-Saxon words used by Chaucer and Shakespeare being preserved in the mountains—handed down by word of mouth from Elizabethan

145

days and earlier. A good way for some to begin their research to test this hypothesis would be to start with *Bartlett's Familiar Quotations.*

VIII. OTHER SELECTIONS ON A SIMILAR THEME: A SELECTED BIBLIOGRAPHY

Credle, Ellis. *Down, Down the Mountain.* N.Y.: Thomas Nelson, 1934.

George, Jean. *My Side of the Mountain.* N.Y.: Dutton, 1959.

Henry, Marguerite. *Benjamin West and His Cat Grimalkin.* N.Y.: Bobbs-Merrill, 1947.

Krumgold, Joseph. *And Now Miguel.* N.Y.: Crowell, 1953.

Lenski, Lois. *Cotton in My Sack.* Philadelphia: Lippincott, 1949. (Available as a Dell Yearling book.)

Stuart, Jesse. *The Beatinest Boy.* N.Y.: McGraw-Hill, 1953.

Poetry

Boni, Margaret Bradford, editor. *Fireside Book of Folk Songs.* N.Y.: Simon & Schuster, 1947.

Botkin, B.A., editor. *The Pocket Treasury of American Folklore.* N.Y.: Pocket Books.

Chase, Richard, compiler. *Hullabaloo, and Other Singing Folk Games.* Boston: Houghton Mifflin, 1949.

Ives, Burl, editor. *The Burl Ives Song Book.* N.Y.: Ballantine.

Ritchie, Jean. *Singing Family of the Cumberlands.* N.Y.: Henry Z. Walck, 1955.

_____. *The Swapping Song Book.* N.Y.: Henry Z. Walck, 1952.

Sharp, Cecil J, compiler. *English Folk-Songs from the Appalachian Mountains.* N.Y.: Oxford, 1953.

STRAWBERRY GIRL

by LOIS LENSKI

Illustrated by the Author

I. THE STORY

Set in the little-known backwoods region of Florida, *Strawberry Girl* is Birdie Boyer's story; of how she and her fierce Cracker pride battled nature, animals, and feuding neighbors to become the best "strawberry girl" the backwoods ever knew.

II. PREREADING DISCUSSION QUESTIONS

The questions which follow are illustrative of the kinds which teachers can prepare for the purpose of releasing children to reveal how *they feel* about some of the same larger ideas and bigger meanings contained in the book *before* it is read.

About Industriousness
1. Many people like the work they do and, consequently, they work hard to "get ahead"—to have a better life, better clothes, home, car, food, vacations, etc. Why is it then that some people dislike them for their *industriousness*? What causes people to say: "Look at them! Who do they think they are? Hrumph! They ought to be ashamed, puttin' on airs like that. What makes them think they're so much better than the rest of us?"?
2. People who study hard and get good marks in school are not always well liked—especially by those who do as little studying as possible, get poor marks, and hate school. How can you explain this?

3. Why is it that lazy people—who do as little work as possible and have very little money and other things they want (things they could have if they tried harder)—often become envious and bitter toward those who do have the things they want?

4. If you were in charge of a small group of people who were assigned a job to be completed by a certain time (making the scenery for a play, for example) and there were two or three who did very little—or "goofed off" as much as possible—what would you do since they want to "get some of the praise and credit" without really doing very much?

5. What would you think of a person who told you he was looking for a job—*any* kind of job—that paid the *highest* salary for the *least* amount of work?

About Hospitality

6. Why is it so difficult sometimes to make a stranger feel welcome

   a. in your neighborhood?
   b. in your club?
   c. in your school?
   d. in your classroom?

7. Tell about a time when you were a stranger or a newcomer and why you felt uncomfortable, strange, or uneasy. In what ways did you feel out of place? Different? What caused this? Did it turn out to be your imagination or were people really suspicious?

8. What are your opinions about a person who says: "Why should I help you out? What's in it for me?"?

About Apple-Polishing

9. In your opinion, can there be such a thing as a "good" *apple-polisher*—that is, a kind of *apple-polisher* that you could approve of?

10. Wherever there is competition, you can be almost positive that there will be an *apple-polisher* or two around somewhere. Why don't people seem to like *apple-polishers*? How many different ways can you describe about how people *apple-polish*?

11. Sometimes people say that *apple-polishing* is necessary—that "it's the *only* way!" What reasons could they have? What opinions do you have about this?

About Feuds

Sometimes neighbors just don't seem to get along with one another—the adults and their children argue, fight, avoid each other; they call one another names and often go out of their way to annoy or make trouble for each other. The *reasons* for these "feuds" usually seem silly and ridiculous to other people. What kinds of "neighborhood feuds" can you describe? What other feuds do you know about (in business, families, school, sports, etc.)?

III. PREREADING ACTIVITIES

1. Some television programs are presented in acts and scenes and have a *prologue* before Act I and an *epilogue* following the last act. After watching four or five of these programs, tell what you believe to be the purpose or function of *prologues* and *epilogues*. What do they add or contribute? Why aren't they included in the regular acts and scenes instead of being separated from them?

2. In many communities throughout the United States, a group of people get together and decide to welcome all newcomers into their community by calling on them, giving them free gifts, and advice, and answering their questions. The *Welcome Wagon* is one of the most well-known of these groups. Find out if there is such a welcoming committee in your community. If so, learn all you can about it: Who sponsors it? Why? Who pays for the free gifts? What kinds of gifts are they? What kind of a person is it who calls on strangers who move into a community?

If there is no committee like this in your community, what do neighbors do in order to try to make strangers feel welcome?

3. Make a list of the fifty states. Do some research and find out (1) what the state's nickname is and (2) what people who

come from that state are called. For example: Ohio: The Buckeye State; Ohioans or Buckeyes. New York: The Empire State; New Yorkers.

4. Some families are "poor" and seem to have very little even though the income—or money earned by them—is exactly the same amount as that in your family. One reason could be that the money is spent foolishly—"thrown away on unnecessary things." Another reason might be extreme "penny-pinching." In such situations, one feels sorry for the adults but even worse about the children in the family. Write a sad story about a make-believe or imaginary friend of yours who lives in such a family. Tell how his life is, what he has to do without, and why. Try also to describe the way you think he might feel about the situation: Would he (or she) want things to be any different? Would your help be wanted? Would *pride* get in your way?

IV. POSTREADING DISCUSSION QUESTIONS

1. Tell why, to whom, and in what ways you think the following quotations are related to the story *Strawberry Girl*:

   a. "It's the early bird that gets the worm."
   b. "They are always trying to keep up with the Joneses."
   c. "Love thy neighbor as thyself."
   d. "Am I my brother's keeper?"
   e. "Some people are always putting on 'airs.' "

2. What do you think that life might be like for the Slaters (and the Boyers, too!) when Sam Slater decided to give up raising cattle?

3. In what ways do you think *pride* hindered the coming of better relationships between the Boyers and the Slaters? What evidence can you find in the book to support your opinions?

4. Lois Lenski's first illustration in the book appears opposite the title page. If you compare this with the picture she drew for the cover, you can see that one makes you feel happy while

the other makes you feel a bit sad and uneasy. Why do you think she chose to put this picture here? Who are the people in the picture? Where are they? What is about to happen? What do you think is behind the expressions on their faces?

And, before you leave this page, look across to the title page and the decorative illustration Lois Lenski put beneath the title. Is there any significance to this drawing?

5. It seems that, for as long as man has inhabited this planet, *fences* have been the cause of problems, disputes, hard feelings, wars, etc. Should fences, walls, boundaries, barriers, etc., rules and laws give people the right to own property and prevent trespassing by others? Suppose all over the world it were possible to remove *all* barriers of all kinds. What is your opinion about how this would or would not help men to live peaceably with one another?

V. HELPING CHILDREN TO REVEAL THEIR COMPREHENSION

1. Suppose the feud between the Boyers and the Slaters wound up in court and you were the judge listening to both sides of the argument. Make a list of the arguments of both families. Then, as judge, tell what your decision would be for each of the problems.

2. Now that you've finished the story and know the Boyers and the Slaters pretty well, what things can you think of that might have prevented the trouble from developing between the two families? Why did the Slaters resent the Boyers' moving in next door? How did the Boyers "get off on the wrong foot" with their new neighbors?

3. What kind of a boy do you think Shoestring Slater *really* was? How do you think he felt about Birdie? He seems to have a real "mean streak" in him, but some people might think he has an equal amount of good in him, too. Write *two* descriptions or characterizations of Shoestring Slater, using as many facts from Lois Lenski's story as you can remember or find. Instead of simply saying, for example, that *Shoestring's lazy*, try to write your characterization by including several of the following:

a. Describe Shoestring's good and mean character by telling *what he is not*.
b. Repeat what others say about Shoestring.
c. Describe the way Shoestring does things.
d. Tell about an episode to prove a point about Shoestring's good and mean character.
e. Compare Shoestring with other people or things that are good and mean.

4. In her Foreword, the author, Lois Lenski, tells us that "the 'Crackers' lived a primitive life, an endless battle went on—a conflict with nature, with wild life, and with their fellow men." Without their problems with the Slaters, life for Strawberry Girl Birdie and her family still would not have been "easy." Tell about some of the other "battles" the Boyers had to "fight." Write this as a *human-interest article* to be published in your local newspaper to show people how they can succeed if they just don't give up.

5. Suppose you are the one and only local newspaper reporter in the area. Write the stories, complete with headlines, for the following news events:

a. The Slaters' fight with Mr. Pearce, the teacher.
b. The big fire that burned the school.
c. An editorial about *fences* and *open-range rights.*
d. The new refrigerator cars for strawberry growers.

6. Make large advertising posters (about thirty-six inches by twenty-four inches) announcing the following:

a. Brother Jackson's Camp Meeting in Tallahassee
b. Barney Barnum's Saturday Bargains
c. Bihu Boyer's Cane-Grinding Frolic
d. Miss Liddy Evans' Millinery Specials

7. Mrs. Boyer, Birdie's mother, seems to be nowhere in the story, *yet she seems to be everywhere*! At various places, we find that she's clever and wise enough to stop what could have been

a serious fight; she's gentle, friendly and generous—but proud and firm; and she seems to have a lot of different kinds of talent. If you were going to nominate Mrs. Boyer for the "Woman-of-the-Year Award," what convincing things would you say about her? Write your nomination.

8. Birdie Boyer's brothers and sisters don't seem to play a very important part in the story. Suppose one of them (Robert, called Bunny; Bihu, called Buzz; Daniel Alexander, called Dan; Dixie Lee Francine, called Dixie; Dovey Eudora, called Dove) summarizing the story, from his point of view, from the time they all moved into the old Roddenberry house. What do you think he would consider to be the most important events, problems, and fun? Why do you think so? (Since the author doesn't tell us much about any of these children, a lot of your ideas will probably have to come from your imagination and from the way you understand the thoughts and feelings of other children in the story.)

VI. RELATED-TO-READING EXPERIENCE

1. Write a *ballad* which you might call "The Ballad of Birdie Boyer" based on what you feel to be some of the most significant events in the story. You may want to keep the tune of one of your favorite ballads in mind as you write the verses or, better yet, why not try your hand at writing an original tune?

2. Find out all you can about the early colonization of Florida—the Spanish influence, the Indians, pirates, etc. What can you learn of some of the old laws that still exist in Florida, the Homestead Act, for example?

3. Examine the *forewords, prologues,* and *epilogues* of a few books. What reasons can you think of for including these as separate from the "chapters?" Do all authors seem to use these devices in the same way, for the same purposes?

4. Almost every religion and every religious sect or denomination can reveal "miracles" which have occurred to one or more of the members of the congregation. Some of these may be in the category of cures for the sick or injured; others might be in the

area of help given to those who cannot resist the temptations of alcohol, gambling, etc.; and still others could include the changing of "Scrooge-like" beliefs and attitudes to those which are more neighborly and loving. Talk with some of the leading religious leaders in your community and ask them to tell you about one or two of the most outstanding "miracles" from their experiences in ministering to human beings. In what ways would you compare Sam Slater's miraculous change as a result of Brother Jackson's powerful preaching with any of these miracles?

5. Secure a few strawberry plants (as well as blackberry and raspberry, if possible). Find out all you can about how to raise them. Can you get them to bear fruit in your classroom?

6. Select one of the simple recipes for making taffy from a cookbook and make plans to have a taffy pull at your next school party.

VII. VOCABULARY THAT MAY NEED DEVELOPING

1. *Communications Capers with "Cracker Codes"*: Some readers will enjoy making and keeping "Cracker Dictionaries" as they read *Strawberry Girl* and then "translating" Birdie's letter:

"Dear Friend,
    "My name's Birdie Boyer and I'm a Cracker. I shore dunno iffen you-uns kin fetch us ary help or not since hits sich a fur piece between our schools, but my teacher, Miss Annie Laurie Dunnaway, said thar purely ain't no harm in askin'.
    "Thar war a fire and hit burned our school. Now we have a new school but I'm afeard thar's nary thing for us to larn from. We'd be beholden to you-all iffen thar war somethin' you'd like to git from Floridy that we kin swap for some books—ary thing at all. We kin have a "Give Boot—Take Boot" 'tween our schools iffen hit pleasures you.
    "We kin send you-all purty little live cooters and other critters, too, like bitty 'gators. Also, thar be strawberries,

154

purty bed-kivers, lard for your Ma's cookin', and flowers and taffy I made myself. (I daresn't tell you-all how good the taffy be 'cause hit'll sound biggety!)

"Jest write me soon iffen thar's ary thing you-all want to take boot for so's we kin git school books.

Love,
Birdie Boyer"

2. *Television Linguistics Research:* Certain television programs are set in regions where language—idioms, pronounciation, etc.—may be different from the colloquial speech of the local community (*Gomer Pyle, Daniel Boone, Green Acres, The Beverly Hillbillies,* and *Andy Griffith,* for example). Some children will enjoy compiling collections of regional language ways and patterns as a way to understanding and appreciating cultural differences as well as preserving hum dignity. A simple "Notebook Page" like the one below mi it encourage some to begin their collections:

Date	Program	Who Said It	The Way They Say It:	The Way We Say It:	Region

VIII. OTHER SELECTIONS ON A SIMILAR THEME: A SELECTED BIBLIOGRAPHY

Estes, Eleanor. *The Hundred Dresses.* N.Y.: Harcourt, 1944.
Jackson, Jesse. *Call Me Charley.* N.Y.: Harper, 1945. (Available as a Dell Yearling book.)
Lawrence, Mildred. *Sand in Her Shoes.* N.Y.: Harcourt, 1949.

Lenski, Lois. *Judy's Journey.* Philadelphia: Lippincott, 1947. (Available as a Dell Yearling book.)

Seredy, Kate. *The Good Master.* N.Y.: Viking, 1935.

Stuart, Jesse. *Red Mule.* N.Y.: McGraw-Hill, 1955.

Poetry

"The Ballad of the Harp-Weaver" by Edna St. Vincent Millay, from *The Harp-Weaver and Other Poems*, N.Y.: Harper, 1950.

"Berries" by Walter de la Mare, from *Collected Poems, 1901-1918,* N.Y.: Holt, 1920.

"Neighborly" by Violet Alleyn Storey, from *Child Life,* December 1926.

"Portrait of a Neighbor" by Edna St. Vincent Millay, from *Piping Down the Valleys Wild* selected by Nancy Larrick, N.Y.: Delacorte, 1968.

ELEPHI, THE CAT WITH THE HIGH I Q

by JEAN STAFFORD

Illustrated by Erik Blegvad

I. THE STORY

Elephi Pelephi Well Known Cat Formerly Kitten lives in a city apartment with a nice but slightly boring couple. Desperate for a playmate and some intelligent conversation, he manages to smuggle in a small foreign car which had been stuck in a snowdrift. When Elephi's new companion is discovered in the storeroom, there is lots of confusion and some rollicking fun!

II. PREREADING DISCUSSION QUESTIONS

The questions which follow arc illustrative of the kinds which teachers can prepare for the purpose of releasing children to reveal how *they feel* about some of the same larger ideas and bigger meanings contained in the book *before* it is read.

About Boredom

1. Tell about a situation in which you were *extremely* bored: *(a)* Where was it? *(b)* Who was there (if anyone)? *(c)* How could such a situation have developed? That is, how did *you* get involved in it? (Presumably, if you had a choice in planning things, you'd have made certain that the situation would have been more fun for you.)

About Disobedience

2. Certain rules are made with the expectation that people will follow or obey them. Parents and relatives make such rules as well as teachers, friends, coaches, firemen, policemen, neighbors, Scout leaders, etc. When people *disobey,* usually they

believe that they are "right" in doing so—that is, they feel they have a "very good reason" for their disobedience. Tell about a situation you know of in which you feel disobedience was (or was not) justified.

3. Sometimes people do not know that they are breaking any rules or laws. Very often they say: "But I didn't know I was doing anything wrong!" Or "It was just my dumb luck. I couldn't help it!" Or "I didn't understand what the rule meant!" Or "I didn't know that what you said applied to *me*!" How do you feel about such a person's being punished for his disobedience?

4. There are some people who are disobedient and seem to enjoy the "thrill" of not getting caught or putting the blame on someone else. Describe how you feel about such people.

About Unusual Companions

5. One of the most cherished rights of all people in a free country is the right one has to choose his companions, his friends, his playmates, his possessions, whether they are animal, human, vegetable, or mineral. However (unless one lives all alone on a deserted island, for example), there are always some restrictions which either allow or prohibit the choices a person has. It could be one's age, where he lives, with whom he lives, his health, etc., that limit his choices. For example, if a person's brother is allergic to cats, then no cats are allowed so long as he lives with his brother. Some parents will not allow their children to have certain plants, chemicals, or toys in the house. And there are certain clubs, organizations, teams, and games in which one's best friend (good-luck charm or toy) isn't allowed. Generally speaking, the more unusual—the more "offbeat"— the person or thing is, the less welcome. What could you describe as one of your most unusual companions (or possessions) which you were forced to give up?

III. PREREADING ACTIVITIES

One way the author manages to bring humor—sometimes obvious, frequently subtle—to the pages of *Elephi* is through her skillful use of stereotype and personification. Children may be helped to become more sensitive to this style of writing and thus gain deeper appreciation from their reading if their thinking can be directed toward some of the common stereotypes and cliches with which they are already familiar.

1. There are people who have certain traits (looks, habits, personalities, mannerisms, abilities, etc.) or characteristics which can be likened to those of animals or things. What responses come quickly to mind when one says:

sly as _____	hungry as _____	cute as _____
big as _____	cunning as_____	pretty as_____
fat as _____	quiet as _____	dumb as _____
slippery as _____	clever as_____	quick as_____
evil as _____	slow as _____	fast as _____
smart as_____	bright as_____	good as _____
innocent as _____	bad as_____	wicked as _____
noisy as _____	crazy as _____	wise as _____
shiny as _____	cool as_____	sharp as_____

2. There are people with pets who frequently notice *human* traits or qualities about them and tell stories about the very-difficult-to-believe things their pets do. Although there are different opinions as well as facts about the abilities and intelligence of animals, some people attribute certain "human" qualities and activities to animals. Of the pets you've known or heard about, which ones would you put in the blanks below?

A pet who is able to . . .
a. *talk,* such as _____
b. *count,* such as _____
c. *remember,* such as _____
d. *think,* such as _____
e. *dance,* such as _____
f. *be polite,* such as _____
g. *paint* or *draw,* such as _____
h. *rob* or *steal,* such as _____

i. *marry,* such as _____

j. *play human games,* such as _____

k. *make successful plans,* such as _____

l. *read peoples' minds,* such as _____

m. *understand human speech,* such as _____

n. *keep house,* such as _____

o. *work for money,* such as _____

p. *build a house,* such as _____

q. *hold a grudge,* such as _____

r. *take revenge,* such as _____

s. *become an actor,* such as _____

t. *fight in a war,* such as _____

u. *roller-skate,* such as _____

v. *take a bath,* such as _____

3. If you were writing a story that had characters in it like those described below, what names (first and last and a middle name, too, if you can think of a good one) do you think would be *most appropriate* for your imaginary characters?

a. A woman who talks constantly and never lets a person get a word in edgewise: Mrs. _____

b. A man who always speaks with a loud, booming, mean, and stubborn voice: Mr. _____

c. A married couple who are *extremely* odd—slightly crazy—"as nutty as a fruit-cake":   Mr. & Mrs. _____

d. A doctor or dentist of whom you're terribly afraid because you are *positive* he will hurt you: Dr. _____

e. A person (boy or girl) of your own age who is a "nut"—a fanatic—about a sport (or, a certain food, game, or hobby):   _____

f. A man whose first and last
names give a *very good clue*
about the type of job he has or
the type of work he does: Mr._____

4. What kinds of things do you know of that have been smuggled
or sneaked into a house or apartment without parents' knowledge? Why would such things have to be smuggled in?

5. People find many ways to "escape" from boredom. If you
were giving advice to your best friend about how to escape
from boredom, how many ideas could you come up with?
First, be sure to describe briefly what your friend's boring
situation is! (Solutions might include getting oneself excused,
creating a disturbance, daydreaming, etc.)

A.

SIX SIMPLE WAYS TO GET ONESELF
EXCUSED FROM A BORING SITUATION

The situation is _____
_____
_____

1.
2.
3.
4.
5.
6.

B.

SIX SIMPLE PLANS FOR ESCAPING
FROM A BORING SITUATION

The situation is _____
_____
_____

    1.
    2.
    3.
    4.
    5.
    6.

C.

SIX IDEAS FOR CREATING A DISTURBANCE
IN A BORING SITUATION WITHOUT BEING
CAUGHT

The situation is _____
_____
_____

    1.
    2.
    3.
    4.
    5.
    6.

SIX SURE-FIRE AIDS TO ESCAPE A
BORING SITUATION BY DAYDREAMING

The situation is_____
_____
_____

1.
2.
3.
4.
5.
6.

IV. POSTREADING DISCUSSION QUESTIONS

1. Depending upon the *situation* and the *kinds of feelings* people
have toward one another, *name-calling* could be considered
proper in one instance and improper in another. Calling a
person (animal or thing) a name, for example, could be very
(a) rude, insulting, derogatory; *(b)* affectionate, kind, personal;
(c) harmful, painful—if repeated out of context; *(d)* flattering,
complimentary; *(e)* harmless as well as helpful to an individual
for "blowing off steam"—if he does it in private.

It is easy to laugh with author Jean Stafford as she makes use
of name-calling in one way or another on nearly every page in
the book. How do you feel about this kind of humor? Here
might be a few examples to start with:

Elephi (about his owners, the Moneypennys): "And, also,
they were cuckoo" (p. 6).

Elephi (about the laundryman): "He was a dope" (p. 21).

Elephi (about Mr. Blaster): "He was a big, fat drip with
whiskers" (p. 26).

Elephi (about Cadillac): "a stuffed shirt" (p. 54).

Whitey (about Cadillac): "old Smarty Pants" (p. 47).

Whitey (about Dandy Lion): "hasn't the brains of a potato" (p. 44).

Cadillac (about Whitey): "a shrimp, peanut, microbe" (p. 47).

Mr. Blaster (about Whitey): "a flop, and a dope, and a drip, and a jellyfish, and a watch fob" (p. 50).

2. On pages 5, 6, 11, 18, 21, 28, 30, 32, and 47, the author uses parentheses for expressing certain ideas. Reread—orally or silently—then discuss: Why does the author enclose these words in parantheses? What additional meanings could she expect you to gain as a result? In what way(s) are the meanings of the parentheses different in different places in the story?

3. What kinds of mischief could a pet (such as a dog, cat, white rat, etc.) get into if his owners left the house or apartment for a whole day and forgot to pen him up?

V. HELPING CHILDREN TO REVEAL THEIR COMPREHENSION

1. Describe (by picture and/or words) Elephi's "office" (p. 28).

2. In addition to his many other abilities, suppose Elephi could write and that he kept a diary for the first year of his life. What would be written in such a diary on some typical days?

3. Suppose Elephi had kept handy a list called "15 Ways to Mess up a House" which he added to from time to time. What could such a "helpful" list contain?

4. Suppose Whitey were not the only friend Elephi had smuggled into the Moneypennys' apartment. Knowing Elephi as you do, and the habits of the people around him, write another episode in which Elephi smuggles another unusual friend into the apartment to keep him company.

5. Elephi Pelephi Well-Known Cat Formerly Kitten was well-known to the various humans in the story. Yet each probably viewed him in a different way and had his own words to describe him and his behavior. What words (adverbs,

adjectives), phrases and/or sentences do you think would reveal the ways the following people felt about Elephi?

Mr. Cuckoo	Mrs. Cuckoo	Madella (the maid)	Sam (the handyman)	Walter (the building supt.)

6. Elephi is able to do many *un-catlike* things. However, the author, Jean Stafford, is very careful to keep Elephi *true to his species.* How many feline attributes can you list that the author wisely has allowed Elephi to retain? In a way, these catlike qualities are *limitations* because they pose problems for Elephi to surmount (e.g., his inability to open the door in order to escape).

VI. RELATED-TO-READING EXPERIENCES

1. Most people seem to be able to make the best of the boring situations in which they frequently find themselves. In each of the situations below, list as many things as you can think of which you might try in order to escape if you found the circumstances boring. How do you think Elephi would have behaved in each of these situations? How do you think your pet would try to escape from such boredom if his IQ were as high as Elephi's?

Some boring situations:
a. a long trip
b. standing in line
c. being sent to one's room for punishment
d. being sent to bed early
e. being forced to hear a story for the umpteenth time

165

f. being forced to sit and listen to a school lesson which you already know

g. having to sit and listen to a speech or sermon which you don't understand

h. having to sit politely with adults while they talk about things which don't interest you.

2. What do you think the following statements mean and how do you feel about them?

a. "Ignorance of the law is no excuse."
b. "Finders keepers."

3. Compare the personality and the behavior of Elephi with that of another cat hero about which you've read.

4. If you could "place your order" and have a *friend* made to suit all y⸗ur wishes and specifications, what would you request?

VII. VOCABULARY THAT MAY NEED DEVELOPING

The charm, humor, and believability the reader finds in *Elephi* are due to the masterful way Jean Stafford uses *figures of speech*: simile, metaphor, personification, hyperbole, and metonymy. One doesn't mind, even, the frequent use of clichés since they appear to come from Elephi and, therefore, are uniquely fresh rather than trite. Miss Stafford is always in control and her readers go along with her, believing and laughing at the incredible cat situation played to the tune of a universal human theme: escape from boredom. Succinctness and vividness of style, then, are reflected in the author's ability to use words in an unusual or nonliteral sense.

1. Although it is not suggested here that children be taught lessons to help them identify various types of figures of speech, it may prove valuable for some to examine the ways *familiar* words take on *different meanings* when used in new ways:

"the buses grumbled and groaned" (p. 12)

"It looked like somebody with a dozen legs who had fallen headlong into the basket and couldn't get out" (pp. 12-13). "It was as if a hippopotamus had got into the Cuckoos' bathtub" (pp. 13-15).

"It would be scary for it to be forsaken in the storm. The car would be buried alive" (pp. 16-17).

"thrown up his paws in dismay" (p. 28).

"catnapped by a treacherous furrier who took a fancy to his elegant suit" (p. 21).

"I have never in all my live-long days known anyone more vexatious" (p. 18).

"villainous witch's companion" (p. 18).

"If it weren't for herself and the dinner herself is making for me" (p. 22).

"cuckoo, cuckooness" (p. 7).

"a clumsy lot" (p. 10).

"a peerless poultice" (p. 37).

2. After reading the story, some students may wish to engage in a closer investigation of *figures of speech* and try to discover differences between them and categorize those which they find in their reading (or hear or make up). This method of inquiring into the way language works makes learning more meaningful and dependable than providing children with ready-made definitions.

VIII. OTHER SELECTIONS ON A SIMILAR THEME: A SELECTED BIBLIOGRAPHY

Guillot, Rene. *The King of the Cats.* N.Y.: Lothrop, Lee & Shepard, 1963.

Lawson, Robert. *Rabbit Hill.* N.Y.: Viking, 1944.

Neville, Emily. *It's Like This, Cat!* N.Y.: Harper, 1963.

Newberry, Claire Turlay. *April's Kittens.* N.Y.: Harper, 1940.

Selden, George. *The Cricket in Times Square.* N.Y.: Farrar, Straus, 1960.

Poetry

"The Duel" by Eugene Field, from *Poems of Childhood*, N.Y.: Scribner's, 1904.

"Motor Cars" by Rowena Bastin Bennett, from *Around a Toadstool Table,* Chicago: Follett, 1930.

"The Owl and the Pussycat" by Edward Lear, available in many editions.

"The Rum Tum Tugger" and "Macavity: The Mystery Cat" by T.S. Eliot, from *Old Possum's Book of Practical Cats,* N.Y.: Harcourt.

MR. WIDDLE AND THE SEA BREEZE

by JO ANN STOVER

Illustrated by the Author

I. THE STORY

Mr. Widdle, in pursuit of perfect happiness, builds himself a village, plants in it three unusual inhabitants, and settles down to live strictly according to schedule. When a particularly strong sea breeze and a strange little man named Bump Jump visit the village, Mr. Widdle's entire schedule goes awry, and he is forced to discover a surprising new life in which happiness does not depend on schedules.

II. PREREADING DISCUSSION QUESTIONS

The questions which follow are meant to be illustrative of the kinds which teachers can prepare for the purpose of releasing children to reveal how *they feel* about some of the same larger ideas and bigger meanings contained in a particular book *before* it is read.

About Schedules

1. What kinds of schedules can you think of and how would you list them in order of importance—from the most necessary and helpful to the most useless and bothersome?
2. In what ways are schedules necessary? In what ways do schedules interfere with the work people do?

About Happiness

3. People say they are happy—or could be happy—for many different reasons. Why would a person make statements like these:

"If I could only be that lucky, I'd be the happiest person alive!"

"*That* was the happiest time of my whole life!"

"I've never been so happy as I was when I was *there*."

4. What kinds of things do people want which they think will make them happy?
5. There are things which people are sure will bring them happiness, but, after they have them, they are still unhappy. What could some of these things be and why do you think that they really don't make people happy?

About Ownership

6. Almost everyone likes to have things which are his, things which he owns—possessions which belong to no one else. Sometimes these things are given to a person, sometimes they are bought, and sometimes they are made or constructed by the person himself. These things become a person's "treasures"—his property. Sometimes they are expensive and worth a lot of money. Sometimes they cost very little and are valuable only to the person who owns them.
   What kinds of possessions can you think of that most people have?
7. What kinds of unusual possessions can you think of that are valuable only to the person who owns them?
8. What kinds of possessions do children have?
9. In our country, what kinds of things are people *not* allowed to own?
10. What do you think could be just about the most *impossible* thing a person could own?

About Perfection

11. Although many people seem to believe that it's impossible to be perfect, almost everyone believes that it is a good thing to *try to be as perfect as you can*—to keep trying always to be perfect. When a person decides *for himself* that he wants to do better—to take pride in the perfection of his work—it probably

170

is a good thing. But how do you feel when somebody decides *for another person* that he should be perfect in the things he does? What are some examples of these kinds of things?

12. Sometimes when a person decides for himself to be as nearly perfect as he can—*in everything*—it makes the lives of other people who have to live or work with him very unhappy. Describe such a person and tell about how his perfection affects the lives of others.

III. PREREADING ACTIVITIES

1. Describe or draw a picture of your idea of an ideal town or city—a dream world, a place you might call "Dreamsville, U.S.A."

2. Suppose you had the following things as pets—a mosquito, a panther, an eagle, a dandelion. What names would you call them by?

3. Here is a description of a very unusual person. He is unusual not only because of his looks, but because of his profession. The only work he does is putting cracks in things like dishes, sidewalks, walls of buildings, and so forth. He is 3 feet 9-3/4 inches tall; 348 months, 2 weeks, 4 days, and 18-1/3 hours old; he has short red hair, blue eyes, and skin that is golden yellow. He wears a pointed pink cap, a blue shirt with no sleeves or buttons, and a pair of golden-yellow trousers which come just below his knees and are held around his waist with a piece of rope instead of a belt. His shoes are red with two tiny hammers fastened at the very tips of the pointed toes. Whenever he walks, he takes exactly ten steps and then stamps his feet—first the left and then the right—ten times before taking the next ten steps. As he puts it: "You see, this is how I put cracks in things!"

   What do you think would be a good first and last name for this unusual little man?

IV. POSTREADING DISCUSSION QUESTIONS

1. Although the author, Jo Ann Stover, seems to be no place in the book, one who reads it gets the strange feeling that she is every place. For example, she keeps reminding us over and over again about how important it is to "watch something growing everyday." What do you think the author might be trying to tell us or get us to believe?

2. All of the unusual and interesting characters (including the animals) in *Mr. Widdle and the Sea Breeze* have names except the *storekeeper*. It is unlikely that the writer forgot to name him or that she couldn't think of a name for him. Therefore, she must have had some reason for calling him simply "Storekeeper" throughout the whole story. What do you think some of these reasons might be? If you were to name him, what do you think would be a name that best suited his personality and his behavior?

3. The Sea Breeze and Bump Jump seem to have the same effect on the people of Widdleville. Since Bump Jump was really the one that "rescued" everyone, the Sea Breeze seems very unimportant. Why, do you think, shouldn't the story have been called *Mr. Widdle and Bump Jump* instead of *Mr. Widdle and the Sea Breeze?*

4. What kinds of people do you know about who might be thought of as people with professions like Bump Jump's?

5. In what ways would you agree with Mr. Widdle's "recipe" for happiness? In what ways would you disagree? When he said that he'd learned how to be happy, do you think that his method would work for anyone who wanted to try it today?

V. HELPING CHILDREN TO REVEAL THEIR COMPREHENSION

1. Making a model of Widdle Hill.
2. Making two maps, one of Widdleville and the other of Ellivelddiw.

3. Writing character sketches for a "Who's Who" of Mr. Widdle, Miss Drew, Bump Jump, Mr. Bobby, The Storekeeper, Pretty Bit.

4. Writing autobiographies for Gillie, Rhubarb, and/or the hornet: "My Life as a Sea Gull in Widdleville" or "My Life as a Cat (or Hornet) in Widdleville."

5. Having children reread or reflect on their Prereading Discussion Responses and asking them to share their ideas about *perfection, schedules, ownership,* and/or *happiness* as a result of their experience with *Mr. Widdle and the Sea Breeze.*

6. Having children reexamine the unusual names they gave to the mosquito, the eagle, the panther, and the dandelion. Can they now think of names which they feel the author, Jo Ann Stover, might have given them if they had been characters in the book?

VI. RELATED-TO-READING EXPERIENCES

1. "An ill wind blows no good."
   "She's just full of hot air, that's all."
   "He's just flapping his lips and making wind—nothing else."
   "The boss just breezed in."
   What kinds of meanings are in statements such as these?

2. How would the following people react to a sea breeze?

   a. a captain of a large ocean liner
   b. a person out sailing in a small sailboat
   c. a lighthouse keeper
   d. a cotton farmer living along the Atlantic coast
   e. a housewife in Kansas hanging her wash outside to dry
   f. a weather forecaster
   g. a person who used to live close to the sea but who has lived away from it for twenty years.
   h. a person who hates the sea.

3. What feelings or ideas do you have about people who make the following statements:

173

a. "When my ship comes in, I'm going to buy you the finest things money can buy."

b. "I'm still searching for that pot of gold at the end of the rainbow and, when I find it, I'll be sitting pretty on easy street."

4. King Midas was granted his wish and everything that he touched turned to gold. As you know, he regretted that wish. What kinds of similar wishes are made by people today—wishes which you think they'd be sorry about if they were to come true?

VII. VOCABULARY THAT MAY NEED DEVELOPING

The inhabitants of Widdleville are examples of extreme personality stereotypes. However, the Sea Breeze and Bump Jump cause them to behave in ways completely opposite to their usual behavior. Since a good portion of this book effectively contrasts one extreme with another some children will benefit in knowing how writers make use of synonym and antonym—of contrasts and comparisons—to make their point.

1. After the students have read the story, they may want to find those words which best describe certain characters in the book.

2. One activity that may prove interesting and valuable for some students would be to have them find as many words as they can that mean just the *opposite* of a person who is—slovenly; bold; boisterous; tardy; courageous; humble. Some children may want to add some of the author's words to their original lists of antonyms after they have read the story.

VIII. OTHER SELECTIONS ON A SIMILAR THEME: A SELECTIVE BIBLIOGRAPHY

Andersen, Hans Christian. "The Emperor's New Clothes," from *The Complete Collected Stories,* translated by Jean Hersholt. N.Y.: Heritage, 1952.

Atwater, Richard and Florence. *Mr. Popper's Penguins.* Boston: Little, Brown, 1938.

Becker, Edna. *900 Buckets of Paint.* Nashville, Tenn.: Abingdon.

Coatsworth, Elizabeth. *The Cat Who Went to Heaven.* N.Y.: Macmillan, 1959.

Grimm Jacob and Wilhelm. "The Fisherman and His Wife," from *Grimm's Fairy Tales,* Garden City, N.Y.: Doubleday, 1956.

Seuss, Dr. *The 500 Hats of Bartholomew Cubbins.* N.Y.: Vanguard, 1938.

Thurber, James. *Many Moons.* N.Y.: Harcourt, 1943.

Poetry

"Jonathan Bing" by Beatrice Curtis Brown, from *Piping Down the Valleys Wild,* selected by Nancy Larrick, N.Y.: Delacorte, 1968.

"A Nautical Ballad" by Charles Edward Carryl, from *Davy and the Goblin,* Boston: Houghton Mifflin, 1962.

"Someone" by Walter de la Mare, from *Piping Down the Valleys Wild,* selected by Nancy Larrick, N.Y.: Delacorte, 1968.

"The Tale of Custard the Dragon" by Ogden Nash, from *Favorite Poems Old and New,* edited by Helen Ferris, Garden City, N.Y.: Doubleday, 1957.

"Who Has Seen the Wind?" by Christina G. Rossetti, from *Piping Down the Valleys Wild,* selected by Nancy Larrick, N.Y.: Delacorte, 1968.

ALL-OF-A-KIND FAMILY

by SYDNEY TAYLOR

Illustrated by Helen John

I. THE STORY

Five high-spirited little girls have simple but happy times together growing up on New York City's Lower East Side at the turn of the century. An understanding mother and father, rich in kindness though poor in money, add to the warmth and humor of their day-to-day adventures.

[For those readers who enjoy *All-of-a-Kind Family* and elect to follow the further adventures of this wonderful, traditional Old-World Jewish family as they all grow a little older and wiser, move into a new neighborhood, and manage to cope with the continuous parade of challenges of living in the United States in the early 1900's, Sydney Taylor continues the chronicle in *More All-of-a-Kind Family* and *All-of-a-Kind Family Uptown,* also available in Dell Yearling editions. Teachers will find many of the following suggestions helpful and/or readily adaptable for use with students who choose to read either of the sequels.]

II. PREREADING DISCUSSION QUESTIONS

The questions which follow are illustrative of the kinds which teachers can prepare for the purpose of releasing children to reveal how *they feel* about some of the same larger ideas and bigger meanings contained in the book *before* it is read.

About Household Chores and Responsibilities
1. What kinds of work "to help out around the house" are you expected to do? Why do so many parents make their children

176

take on certain responsibilities or work duties around the home?

2. What kinds of "chores" or duties do you especially dislike? How—in what ways—have you tried to "tolerate" these responsibilities which have been assigned to you? Give an example of a boring, unpleasant household duty you have to do and tell of the ways you've tried to make the time go fast while doing it. Tell of other ways that you've tried to make such chores "games."

3. If, at your house, one of your job responsibilities is to wash and dry the dishes, iron, carry out the garbage, or go to the store daily to pick up groceries for your mother, what reasons would be allowed for your skipping these duties for a day?

About Family Life and Religion

4. Who decides about the kind of religion a person accepts, believes in, and follows? Who makes this kind of a decision for very young children? Tell why you believe this is a good practice. Tell about the problems or disadvantages, if any, in deciding on a religious faith in this way.

5. Why does it seem true that, in many families, if one's grandparents happen to have been members of a certain political party (Republican or Democrat, for example), then the whole family tends to follow, generation after generation?

6. In the United States we have many ways of worshiping God. Tell why you think it would be a good idea to have or not to have *one* religion, a "national religion," for everyone in the United States. Do you know of any countries of the world that have a national religion? Which ones? Do you know of any problems this has caused? Any advantages?

About Sibling Comparisons

7. Younger brothers and sisters very frequently are compared with older brothers and sisters. If you have an older brother or sister, tell some of the times and ways you've been compared and why you felt it unfair and/or embarrassing. Tell about a time when you expected one of your friends to be exactly like his older brother. Tell how you were right or wrong in your expectation.

8. In our society whenever twins, triplets, quadruplets, or quintuplets are born to a married couple, these parents seem to follow the traditional custom of dressing their children alike, giving them names that look and sound almost the same, etc. Sometimes, even, this happens in large families when the children are born about a year apart. How do you think you would feel dressing like your brother or sister, going to the same places, doing the same things with him (or her) day after day? Do you think this is a good or a bad custom? Why is it that most schools do not want to have brothers and sisters in the same class and try, if at all possible, to separate them?

About Children in America

9. It is not unusual to hear parents and grandparents today make such remarks as: "I don't know what's wrong with children today. They never can be satisfied; they just want, want, want all the time. Why, when I was a child, we found things to do and had fun *without* movies and radio and television. We invented games and made our toys out of scraps and junk and, if we had a penny, we thought we were rich! It's too bad that this generation has been so spoiled." When you hear such comments, how do you feel? When would your parents be most likely to say things like that to you? Why? Do you think you could be any different even if you wanted to be? Why? Why not?

III. PREREADING ACTIVITIES

1. Prepare a questionnaire and conduct a survey in order to learn about some of the similarities and differences in children of families of four or more.

   a. What is each child's special, most favorite game, sport, TV program, hobby, pastime, etc.?
   b. What is each child's special talent—something he (or she) likes and can do better than any of his (or her) brothers or sisters?
   c. What is each child's weakness or something he seems to need most to improve?

d. What habits do they have that seem to annoy their other brothers and sisters the most?

e. And so forth.

2. Different families have different dates or times during the year when they celebrate special occasions or events. Write a description of what you believe is the most important time of the year for your family. Why is this such a special time? What happens? What do you do?

3. Different families have different ways of punishing their children for "not behaving" or not doing what they should do. With the help of a few of your friends who are interested, write a booklet called "A Parent's Guide to FAIR Punishment of Children." On one side, you might put "Violation" and on the other, "Justice." For example:

Violation	Justice (1st offense, 2nd, etc.)
Not eating vegetables	
Not eating salad	
Not eating meat	
Growling about going to bed	
Talking after going to bed	
Getting lost	
Forgetting to do something	
Losing a school book	
Not turning off the water	
Not turning off the lights	
Not squeezing the toothpaste properly	
Losing your overshoe or boot	
Tracking in mud	
Borrowing something without asking	

4. Make a list of as many religious sects or faiths as you can. Try to find out some of the ways they are different. What customs and important dates differ from religion to religion? What customs and dates are the same?

5. Almost everybody, at one time or another, has a hero or "idol" whom he looks up to, likes, and tries to imitate. Sometimes this person is a relative, famous athlete or actor, or a friend or classmate. Tell about a person you felt you wanted to be like—someone you admired and imitated. What reasons did you have? What kinds of "qualities" or abilities did this person have that made you feel the way you did? Write a paper nominating this person for the "Hero-of-the-Year Award."

IV. POSTREADING DISCUSSION QUESTIONS

1. Tell why you think the sayings listed below do or do not apply to the story you have just read. To what person(s)? To what situation(s)?

   a. "Birds of a feather flock together."
   b. "They're as thick as thieves."
   c. "A family that prays together, stays together."
   d. "It's better to give than to receive."

2. The author (on p. 41) describes Charlie, and then, (on p. 42) tells about Papa's feelings of loneliness. Tell why you think this could be considered an omen.

3. Since 1912, many things have changed. Some things, however, never seem to change. There are several kinds of love stories in this book. One of them is Charlie's love and search for his "lost" Kathy. How would you compare it with romances you know about today? How different are they? What are some of the other love themes? Do they appear to you to be about the same? Why?

V. HELPING CHILDREN TO REVEAL THEIR COMPREHENSION

1. There are many things which we have today—called "modern conveniences"—which people in 1912 did not have. The author, Sydney Taylor, describes what things were available and what people living then used. What are some of the differences? What inventions came along after this story ends? Find places in the story where people would have done or seen different things if the All-of-a-Kind Family were living next door to you today. (For example, Mama didn't telephone Dr. Fuchs herself [p. 113]; horses pulled the fire engine [p. 139]; streetcars; shooting fireworks; central heating.)

2. Even though the five girls were alike in so many ways, they were different also. Write "word photographs" which describe Ella, Henny, Sarah, Charlotte, and Gertie. In what ways are they different, especially in their likes and dislikes. Which one would you most enjoy as a friend? Why?

3. Write an epilogue to the story which briefly looks ahead about ten years after the birth of Little Charlie. Tell how the family might be just a little different; a few things that they might do differently.

4. The author, Sydney Taylor, makes it very clear at the beginning why this family is called "all-of-a-kind." However, at the end of the book, Mama gives Papa his wish: a little boy is born, and it seems as if the family is no longer all-of-a-kind. Perhaps it should be called "Not-So-All-of-a-Kind Family!" When Ella suggested this, Mama disagreed by saying that an "All-of-a-Kind Family" means *more* than having five daughters. Suppose you were Mama writing to her parents in Europe. Try to explain to them about your "new" all-of-a-kind family.

5. Suppose, instead of girls, the story had been about five boys: "Papa's boys!" Many things would have been the same—the religion, the love in the family, etc. But, obviously, some things would have been different. For example, what would five *boys* have purchased with their after-lunch pennies when

shopping with Mama? What would have pleased five *boys* on a rainy-day visit to Papa's place of business? What would Mama and Papa have called their five sons?

6. Suppose Papa wanted to hire someone to help him in his business. What kind of a person would he want? Write a "job description," telling what kind of business it is, the kind of work involved, what the pay would be (in 1912, remember!), the number of hours the person would have to work, etc. Also, write a "help-wanted" advertisement to put in the local paper.

VI. RELATED-TO-READING EXPERIENCES

1. Find out all you can about *public health* and *quarantines.* What kinds of quarantines are common today? What are the "childhood diseases" doctors always seem to want to know about? What kinds are almost nonexistent today—not nearly so important as they were fifty years ago? What is an *epidemic*? Why do schools require *injections* and *vaccinations*? When one plans to visit certain countries outside the United States, usually he is required to get a series of shots. What are some of the reasons for this? Why are certain kinds of plants, animals, foods not permitted to enter the United States? Why do some of the states *in* the United States (Florida, Hawaii, for example) have strict rules about certain kinds of plants coming in and out of the state?

2. At one time, in the United States, a penny could buy quite a lot of things. There used to be, for instance, a penny ice-cream cone. Make a list of the things you like to buy today with the money you earn or save. Then, do some research through old newspapers and magazines and try to find out how much these things would have cost you fifty or sixty years ago.

3. Only in recent times have most states in our country enacted fireworks laws. Try to find out about these laws in your state. Also, ask your parents and grandparents about them and about how they used to celebrate the Fourth of July. Ask them about their opinions of the reasons for fireworks laws. Suppose you wanted to change the law so that you could

celebrate the Fourth as people fifty or sixty years ago used to do. What would your arguments be? Or tell why you'd be in favor of the way fireworks are sold and displayed today? Fireworks also are used for other celebrations. What are they and why?

VII. VOCABULARY THAT MAY NEED DEVELOPING

In *All-of-a-Kind Family* Sydney Taylor uses many interesting words to describe Jewish festivals, foods, holidays, holydays, etc. In every instance the author uses synonymous or parenthetical phrases to provide meanings for those words which for some readers may be unfamiliar. Many children will find it profitable as well as interesting to investigate the ways in which writers define unfamiliar words in the *context* of their sentences and paragraphs. For example, on page 55 the author writes:

> "Wait a minute, children," Mr. Basch called. He walked over to the back of the store where he kept *slabs of smoked salmon* (he called it *lox)* and cut off two pieces of *moist, salty skin.* This was a rare treat.

Listed below are a few of the other words children might use to develop this context skill.

Haggadahs (p. 124)	*Rosh Hashana* (p. 166)
Torah (p. 94)	*Succos* (p. 166)
gefüllte (p. 73)	*Teiglech* (p. 93)
Haman Taschen (p. 92)	*Yom Kippur* (p. 37)
afikomen (p. 128)	*Passover* (p. 114)
Purim (p. 91)	*kittel* (p. 125)
matzoth (p. 124)	*Tanta* (p. 177)

VIII. OTHER SELECTIONS ON A SIMILAR THEME: A SELECTED BIBLIOGRAPHY

Clark, Ann Nolan. *In My Mother's House.* N.Y.: Viking, 1941.

DeAngeli, Marguerite. *Bright April.* Garden City, N.Y.: Doubleday, 1946.

_____. *Henner's Lydia.* Garden City, N.Y.: Doubleday, 1936.

Fitch, Florence Mary. *One God: The Ways We Worship Him.* N.Y.: Lothrop, Lee & Shepard, 1944.

McCloskey, Robert. *Homer Price.* N.Y.: Viking, 1943.

Sheehy, Emma Dickson. *Molly and the Golden Wedding.* N.Y.: Holt, 1956.

Sorenson, Virginia. *Plain Girl.* N.Y.: Harcourt, 1955.

Poetry

"Father" by Frances Frost, from *The Little Whistler,* N.Y.: McGraw-Hill, 1949.

"Neighborly" by Violet Alleyn Storey, from *Child Life,* December 1926.

"Shop Windows" by Rose Fyleman, from *Gay Go Up,* Garden City, N.Y.: Doubleday, 1930.

"Song for My Mother" by Anna Hempstead Branch, from *The Shoes That Danced and Other Poems,* Boston: Houghton Mifflin, 1905.

I GO BY LAND,
I GO BY SEA
by P. L. TRAVERS

I. THE STORY

When German bombs began to fall in 1940, Sabrina Lind, with her young brother James, left home and parents in England to spend the war years with close friends in America. Sabrina kept a very personal diary, recording the swift departure and the dangling feeling of separation and strangeness afterward, the long journey across the ocean, and their adjustment to a new life, where a warm welcome, exciting new adventures, and new friends helped to alleviate homesickness and constant worry for their parents' safety. With warm touches, both tragic and humorous, Sabrina learned to accept changes in a life turned topsy-turvy.

II. PREREADING DISCUSSION QUESTIONS

The questions which follow are illustrative of the kinds which teachers can prepare for the purpose of releasing children to reveal how *they feel* about some of the same larger ideas and bigger meanings contained in the book *before* it is read.

About Parental Decisions
1. What reasons can you give for parents' sending their children away to live with someone else for a long period of time?
2. Suddenly your parents decide to send you about six thousand miles away to live *indefinitely* with some relatives you've never seen. The only reason they give you is a statement such as the following:

"Now don't you worry your head about it. We've taken care of everything and we know what's best for you, dear. Besides, you'll really have such a good time that the time will pass very quickly and before you know it you'll be on your way back home again."

How do you think you might feel? What might you say? What thoughts would you think, *but not say*?

About Trips and Traveling

3. Tell about the longest trip that you've taken. From where to where? About how far? Who was with you? How did you travel?

4. When you've been on a trip that was particularly boring and uninteresting to you, what kinds of things have you done to pass the time?

5. What things do you like most about the trips you've taken (for example, the packing, unpacking, the departing, the arriving, the trip itself, others)? What things have you enjoyed least?

About Prayers and Praying

6. Sometimes young people your age say prayers not only at the usual places and customary times (such as before meals, at bedtime, in church or synagogue, etc.,) but, also, at times and places and for other than the ordinary, expected reasons. What might some of these be?

7. When people pray, sometimes they make up their prayers; sometimes they recite prayers which they've learned or memorized. When and for what reasons would a person make up his own prayer?

About Personal and Private Writing

8. What kinds of *diaries* do people keep? On what occasions? What reasons can you give for people's keeping diaries? What kinds of diaries are written with the expectation of having them read by other people? (Strangers? Close friends only?) What kinds are written in absolute secrecy and privacy—for the writer's eyes only?

9. When people write things down only for themselves, what kinds of care and attention do they give to spelling, grammar, etc? Why? How is this different from the way one writes a report for a teacher? A letter?

III. PREREADING ACTIVITIES

1. Try to remember a trip you've taken recently. Think of the most unforgettable person you met or saw. Describe him (or her): What did he look like? What was he wearing? What was he doing that made such an impression? What did he say (to you or to others)? Would you describe him as likable? Disagreeable?
2. Describe what you would call the *most dangerous* incident (or narrow escape) in which you've ever been involved on a trip you've taken. It may be something that happened after you arrived at your destination.
3. Prepare a "Boredom Survival Kit"—about the size of a shoebox—and a directions booklet to go with it. How many games, activities, "things to do," etc. can you include in it to help keep someone your age entertained while on a long journey? Be sure to include many activities that can be done alone. What differences would their be in Boredom Survival Kits when one is traveling by *(a)* ship, *(b)* automobile, *(c)* train, *(d)* bus, *(e)* plane? (A good reference: E.O. Harbin's *Fun Encyclopedia,* Nashville, Tenn.: Abingdon Press.)
4. People have many reasons for praying. When a person prays, naturally *he feels* his reason for doing so is a *good* one. Here are a few things some people say are *good reasons* for praying. What are your opinions? On the blanks below, put an "A" for Agree, "D" for Disagree, "SA" for Sometimes Agree, and "SD" for Sometimes Disagree.

_____ money
_____ bicycle
_____ good health
_____ faith

187

_____ to be first on moon

_____ to rid the world of Communism

_____ bad luck to one's enemies

_____ a friend's recovery from an illness

_____ to win a fight

_____ to win a football game

_____ a bigger allowance

_____ to live to be 105 years of age

_____ revenge on a cruel, evil, mean person

_____ a certain person to be elected president

_____ free college education for everyone

_____ good grades

_____ the end of war

_____ food

_____ happiness

_____ a vacation

_____ a good job

_____ courage

_____ safety

_____ to pass a test

_____ new clothes

_____ forgiveness

_____ strength

_____ intelligence

_____ protection

_____ to win a contest

_____ to find some money

_____ to win a medal

_____ to be famous

_____ to win a bet

_____ to believe in God

5. With the help of one or two of your friends, prepare a small, pocket-size booklet (to be dittoed or mimeographed) called: "How _Not_ to Make Friends and Influence People." It would contain advice about how _not_ to treat strangers or visitors—things that will _not_ make them feel comfortable, welcome, or "at home."

6. When people come from other countries to visit the United States for the first time, they bring with them many strange (to us) ideas about the people here and the ways we do things. One good reason for this is that they think all of us are like the people they see in American movies or on American television. Also, for the same reason (due to television, movies, or the books we've read), we have ideas about people, places, and "funny" ways of foreign countries which seem strange to *them*. Think of a foreign country you would like to visit that you know something about, such as England, Russia, France, Italy, Greece, China, etc. Make a list of all the "odd" or "funny" or "strange" things or customs you think you would expect to find there (language, words, dress, food, etc.). After you finish your list, try to find someone you know who's lived in that country for a while and have him mark your statements "true" or "false" and explain his reasons to you.

7. On a map of the world, find the various places (on land) which are six thousand miles from where you now are living—in any and all directions—and list them. From your point of view, which place would be the most desirable for you to live for the next *four years*? Why? Which, in your opinion, would be the least desirable? Why? Make a travel brochure advertising the place of your choice, its advantages, beauty, etc.

IV. POSTREADING DISCUSSION QUESTIONS

1. In what ways did Sabrina and James behave as you would have behaved if you were in their place? In what ways would you have said or done or felt things differently?

2. Sabrina lets us in on her ideas and opinions by giving us different kinds of definitions—some are "funny"; some are quite surprising. For example, she says that *California* is America's *vegetable garden* (p. 99). Investigate some of her others; find those which a group of you would like to discuss; read them aloud. Here are a few to get you started:

189

Sabrina's definitions of . . .

a. a drugstore (p. 83)
b. refugees (p. 84)
c. American social studies (in school) (p. 143)
d. the necessary requirements to pass a medical exam to be allowed to come to the United States (p. 17)
e. school (pp. 142-45)

V. HELPING CHILDREN TO REVEAL THEIR COMPREHENSION

1. Readers will notice that each "chapter" or "diary entry" starts with ". . ." instead of the date, and then is followed by the month. Travers explains the reason for this omission on page 6. Now that the dates no longer need to be kept secret, some readers may enjoy replacing them.

2. Write a Part Three: *I Go By Air,* telling of Sabrina and James Linds' *flight home.* When was it? From where did they leave? What did they do during their trip? What interesting traveling companions did they meet? How did they feel?

3. On page 57, Sabrina says: "I do not want a new world. I want the old world with everything in its own place and no changes." Do you feel she really meant this? Why? Why not? When have you ever felt this way? What if you made such a wish, and it came true? What if Sabrina's wish had come true and remained that way for 25 years? How would your life today be different?

4. On pages 29 and 30, Sabrina tells us that she made a wish upon the first star she saw that night, but that she couldn't tell the wish (even to her diary) because it would be bad luck. What do you think the wish might have been? Why? Do you think it could have come true? Why? Why not?

5. Write a dialogue—a discussion that *could have taken place* if you were in Sabrina's shoes and your parents told you that they were sending you away for a while (see p. 13-15). What reasons, arguments, pleading would *you* have used?

6. Describe a day aboard the ship which brought Sabrina and James to the United States. What schedules did they have? What did they do?

VI. RELATED-TO-READING EXPERIENCES

1. A lot of people feel they can predict the future. A lot more people go to them with all sorts of questions to learn about the future. How large a list of different kinds of people and things that predict the future can you make? How reliable, do you think, is Georgina's method for finding out who the person is whom you're going to marry? How is this like or different from the "she loves me, she loves me not" daisy game? (See pp. 101-02)
2. On page 12, Sabrina says that there are lots of signs and portents of things that are about to change. Things seem queer, funny, *unusual*—like a "calm before a storm." Tell of a time when you've had these feelings, when you've noticed such things—and then found that they were a warning of something bad or an indication of something wonderful that happened to you afterwards.

VII. VOCABULARY THAT MAY NEED DEVELOPING

[NOTE TO TEACHER: Although P. L. Travers tells us that this is an authentic, factual story, some teachers may find it controversial and discomforting. Truth is like that sometimes. A child's growing up, separated from his parent during a time of great crisis such as World War II, is awesome, but nonetheless real. British spellings of English, idiomatic speech, and use of such words as wireless for radio and chemists for drugstore are as vital to the book's realism and authenticity as Sabrina's personal, diary spelling. I have never met a child who became a poor speller or reader because he was exposed to regional dialects, vocabulary, and idioms, and misspellings in books.—C.F.R.]

1. Not only people, but animals and things as well as "ideas" have been called *refugees*. Have children probe deeply into the many and varied meanings of this word as well as *refuge, alien, foreigner, displaced person, turncoat, evacuee, escapee, war orphan, immigrant, exile,* and *banished*. What kinds of things are people *refugees* from?
2. *British English: A Foreign Language.* Begin a collection of "translations" or *British to American English Dictionary.*

wireless (p. 36)

napkins (p. 34)

half-tablet (p. 36)

pig's trotters (p. 49)

a cast in her eye (p. 44)

to crack the crackers (p. 155)

the paravanes (p. 41)

winding their putties (p. 64)

her stays creaked (p. 16)

the yellow-hammer (p. 12)

to tickle trout (p. 20)

perambulator (p. 32)

the chemists (p. 83)

tommy cooker (p. 26)

rescuer (p. 26)

pram (p. 42)

the pictures (p. 42)

the cinema (p. 70)

curraghs (p. 30)

bully beef (p. 35)

hard tack (p. 35)

cheque (p. 23)

lift (p. 15)

queue (p. 18)

eider down (p. 19)

tam-o'-shanter (p. 32)

a pillar box (p. 16)

VIII. OTHER SELECTIONS ON A SIMILAR THEME: A SELECTED BIBLIOGRAPHY

Angelo, Valenti. *The Bells of Bleecker Street.* N.Y.: Viking, 1949.

_____. *Big Little Island.* N.Y.: Viking, 1955.

Boston, Lucy M. *A Stranger at Green Knowe.* N.Y.: Harcourt, 1961.

Carlson, Natalie Savage. *The Family Under the Bridge.* N.Y.: Harper, 1958.

_____. *The Happy Orpheline.* N.Y.: Harper, 1957

Hoff, Carol. *Johnny Texas.* Chicago: Follett, 1950. (Available as a Dell Yearling book.)

Poetry

"Adventure" by Harry Behn, from *The Little Hill*, N.Y.: Harcourt, 1949.

"Dreams" by Langston Hughes, from *The Dream Keeper*, N.Y.: Alfred Knopf, 1932.

"Mother to Son" by Langston Hughes, from *The Dream Keeper*, N.Y.: Alfred Knopf, 1932.

"Valentine for Earth" by Frances Frost, from *The Little Naturalist*, N.Y.: McGraw-Hill/Whittlesey House, 1959.

CHARLOTTE'S WEB

by E. B. WHITE

Illustrated by Garth Williams

I. THE STORY

This is the story of a little girl named Fern who loved a little pig named Wilbur—and of Wilbur's dear friend, Charlotte A. Cavatica, a beautiful, large gray spider who lived with Wilbur in the barn. With the help of Templeton, the rat, who never did anything for anybody unless there was something in it for him, and by a wonderfully clever plan of her own, Charlotte saved the life of Wilbur, who, by this time, had grown up to be quite a pig.

II. PREREADING DISCUSSION QUESTIONS

The questions which follow are illustrative of the kinds which teachers can prepare for the purpose of releasing children to reveal how *they feel* about some of the same larger ideas and bigger meanings contained in the book *before* it is read.

About Persuasion
1. Why do people tend to buy more things that are advertised than those which are not advertised? In what ways do people advertise? Which kinds of advertising do you think are most convincing, that is, most successful? What things are necessary in advertising to make people want to do something (or buy or have something)? What kinds of things can you think of that are *not* advertised? Can you give an example of some advertising that "backfired?"
2. When a person doesn't have very good feelings or ideas about himself, we say that he has a poor *self-concept.* Suppose

194

someone you loved very much—a brother or sister, perhaps, or a friend—were sad, lonely, and extremely unhappy because he felt *(a)* ugly; or that *(b)* he had no friends; or that *(c)* he was not popular; or that *(d)* he lacked the ability to do something as well as others—in sports, music, art, school subjects, and/or contests of all kinds. What would you do to help him feel different about himself? What would you say?

About Human Relationships

3. Almost everyone has a *reputation* for something although a person's reputation at home, at school, in the neighborhood, in clubs and on teams, or with friends may be quite different. What kinds of *reputations* do different people have? From where does a *reputation* come (that is, how does one get a *reputation*)?

4. Some people talk about having a "bad reputation," which is hard *to live down.* What examples can you give about how a person tries to "live with" or to "live down" a bad reputation?

5. Sometimes a person gets a reputation for something, such as being *clever,* or *brave,* or *smart,* or *honest,* quite by accident— or by "being lucky." Then, usually, he finds he has to try hard *to live up to it.* What would make such a person feel he has "to live up to his reputation?" What might such a person do to try to live up to it?

6. If, for example, a person has a reputation for dressing well, being neat, buying only "the best," etc., how does it affect the way he does things (or the things he allows to be seen) when people other than his family or close friends are present?

7. When a person has a reputation to live up to, it probably means that it affects the way he acts, talks, or behaves when he is with *other people, doing things that are different from that for which he's noted.* What examples could you give? If a person has a reputation for being a good artist or football player, for example, what might other people expect as a result? What might the person do in these other situations to live up to his reputation?

8. Explain why you feel it is or, *isn't* possible to have a "poor personality" *and* a "good reputation."

About Love

9. Sometimes it is easier to let another person know that you *love* him (or her) by *showing* him that you do. How many specific and different ways can you think of in which people *show* their love? What kinds of things do people do for others in order to prove their love?

10. What are some of the *risks* people take or *dangers* they sometimes face when doing something for someone they love? Frequently a person will suffer many *hardships* for someone he loves. Name some examples of this.

11. Great poets, great writers, and great lovers have used many words to express the complex feelings all wrapped up in the simple, four-letter word "L O V E." *Adore, worship, idolize, cherish* are four examples. Since people always seem to be searching for other words to use instead of "I love you," it's as if they don't like the word "love" or are dissatisfied with it. What explanations can you give? How do *you* feel about it?

III. PREREADING ACTIVITIES

1. Using the Personality Checklist below (or, better yet, make one yourself by asking people to tell you some of the things they look for in a person with a "good personality"), give yourself a rating or score of 0 to 10 on *each* of the items. Total them, fold the paper and put it into an envelope and seal it. Put your name on the outside and put it in a safe place (or give it to your teacher) until later. (See V. Helping Children to Reveal Their Comprehension, Item #1.)

Personality Checklist		TOTAL: ☐
Friendly ....☐	Polite ....☐	
Happy ....☐	Understanding ....☐	
Helpful ....☐	Dependable ....☐	
Patient ....☐	Thoughtful ....☐	
Kind ....☐	Generous ....☐	

196

2. Make a list of some of the specific things (such as toys, habits, and/or interests) which people *outgrow*. Give as many reasons as you can explaining why such things—which at one time were *very important*—become unimportant or even useless.

3. When compared with humans, most animals have a short life-span. It's even shorter for most insects. It is believed that some animals and insects know when they are going to die because they seem "to prepare" for it. If such animals could think or have feelings as we have, what kind of a mood do you think they would be in during their last few days or hours? (Some children may want to find an insect that lives only for a year or less and write, in prose or poetry, "The Story of My Life and Death.")

4. What advantages and disadvantages can you think of for making promises which you're not sure you'll be able to keep?

5. Fortunately, most of the human beings in the world hate killing. However, we do kill animals for food. We hunt and fish. We kill "useless" animals as well as those which would harm us or destroy our property. We usually don't feel very bad when we swat a fly to his death or poison mice or burn out hornets' nests. How can we explain these feelings which seem to oppose each other?

6. Sometimes a person is able to do something very difficult— something he didn't dream possible for him to do—simply because someone else had *faith* in him, believed in him, encouraged him on. Describe an experience like that which you have had.

7. Sometimes the power of suggestion is mightier and more influential than one's strongest opponent. (For example, certain colors can make people feel hot or cold; some sounds make people shiver, and so forth.) The word *propaganda* is used to mean "a planned and systematic attempt to get a lot of people to think or feel the same way about an idea, course of action, and/or an object or thing." Make a collection of various propaganda techniques. Even if the idea is a good one, why do or don't you feel there should be limits as far as propaganda is concerned? What, in your opinion, would be the difference between "good" and "bad" propaganda?

8. What do you feel about the possible effects of this statement:

"If you keep telling him he's stupid loud enough, often enough, and long enough, he will begin to believe it and act accordingly!"

9. Probably the major reason that competitions and contests are so exciting is the fact that *there can be only one winner*—all others must lose. This means we've got a lot of "losers" in the world. What is it that causes a person to keep on trying even though he never seems to win? What keeps losers from giving up hope?

IV. POSTREADING DISCUSSION QUESTIONS

1. When people vote fo leaders, rules, ideas, etc., how much of their vote, do you f el, is influenced by the personality and reputation of the candidate who is running for election or sponsoring the motion? How much of their vote is influenced by the candidate's ability or the quality of his idea?

2. On page 41, Wilbur says: "Well, I've got a new friend, all right. But what a gamble friendship is! Charlotte is fierce, brutal, scheming, bloodthirsty—everything I don't like. How can I learn to like her, even though she is pretty and, of course, clever?"

   What would you say to Wilbur to convince him he's not exactly right and that he should try to change his opinions?

3. Suppose you know that you are average or better than average in *all* f your school subjects *except math.* However, on the first si math tests of the year, you "just happen" to make the *highest marks of anyone in the whole school*! This causes you to get a reputation in school because everyone—the teachers, students and even your parents—now believe you are the *top* mathematician in the whole school! What would you do about this reputation? How do you think it would affect what you did and how you did it?

4. At the beginning of the story, Fern seems to be with Wilbur all of the time. Then, gradually, she finds other things to do,

other interests (including a boy, Henry Fussy). Although she keeps in touch with things going on in the barn, it appears as if she's all too glad to let Charlotte have the responsibility for saving Wilbur. What are your opinions? Does this mean she doesn't care so much for Wilbur as she used to?

5. In what ways and for what reasons could *Charlotte's Web* be called a *love* story?

6. "Keep the faith, baby!" might have been a slogan used by anyone in the story to help Wilbur gain confidence in himself. In what ways did *faith* play an important part in helping Wilbur to change his poor self-concept?

7. Charlotte's "advertising campaign" used the *power of suggestion* very effectively. Suppose Fern, instead of Charlotte, had printed signs: *"Terrific!" "Some Pig!" "Radiant!"* Would this have been as effective? Why?

V. HELPING CHILDREN TO REVEAL THEIR COMPREHENSION

1. Using the Personality Checklist (see III. Prereading Activities, Item #1), rate the following characters in *Charlotte's Web* and total their scores. (Do each one separately.) Then open the envelope which contains the rating you gave yourself and compare it with those of the characters in the book. How do you explain the similarities and the differences you find? (Suggested characters would include Charlotte, Fern, Templeton, Wilbur, Avery, the sheep, the goose.)

2. Suppose each of the following has been asked to design a medal for Charlotte—a medal with a simple design that was exactly *right* for her, one that summed up her many qualities, traits, and/or abilities: Fern, Wilbur, a fly that had escaped from Charlotte's web, Templeton, and Mrs. Arable (Fern's mother). From the medals you see below, choose the one you think each designed and explain the reasons for your choice.

3. Make a finger puppet[1] of Charlotte and let her give a speech to a group of people who hate and fear spiders, attempting to convince them of how friendly, lovely, lovable, and useful she is.

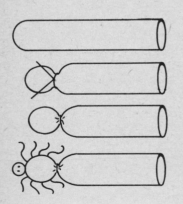

[1]A simple finger puppet may be made by cutting the finger from an old glove.(The index or forefinger of a woman's cloth glove works best.) Stuff about a half inch of the closed end with cloth or paper and tie it off with heavy black thread. Next, attach a bead, round button, small cork, eraser, etc., to the other end to serve as Charlotte's head. Then fasten the legs—eight small pieces of rubber band, wire, pipe cleaner, or construction paper— to the body in the appropriate places (see drawings on pp. 38, 66, 92).

4. Suppose Charlotte's plan had failed! If you were in Fern's shoes, what plans would you have made to save Wilbur? What would you do first? What results would you expect? What would you do second? What results would you expect? And so on.

5. If, instead of Charlotte, Templeton (or the sheep or the goose) had become Wilbur's best friend, describe the kind of plan you think he would have devised to save Wilbur.

VI. RELATED-TO-READING EXPERIENCES

1. Prepare an advertising campaign to make a person (or a group of people) change his mind about *not* wanting something.

2. Suppose you wanted to buy or to do something of which you feel sure your parents would disapprove. What are some of the things you would try to "sell them" on the idea *before* you ask?

3. It is often easier and more convincing to describe a person or thing indirectly than coming right out and saying, for example: "Charlotte is a wonderful spider. She is very kind, helpful and intelligent. She spins webs, as all spiders do, but she has the talent to put messages in her webs. She loved her home in the barn, and she loved Wilbur, too."

Write a paragraph or two describing *Wilbur's* characteristics by:

a. telling how he does things, including how he thinks and what he thinks about.

b. telling an episode to prove a point about Wilbur's character and personality.

c. comparing Wilbur with other animals or humans who have the same kinds of traits.

d. telling what Wilbur is *not*.

e. telling Wilbur's own characterization of himself.

f. telling what others say of Wilbur.

g. telling of the exceptions Wilbur has when compared with others of his species.

201

4. Some students may profit from a compa...
of spiders and other insects—noting simila...
in habits, habitat, food, life-span, etc.

5. Using E. B. White's description of Char...
description of herself, some children ma...
become amateur entymologists and dr...
Charlotte. Once they complete their ...
check an encyclopedia to see true dra...
compare the differences.

6. Compose music for the two songs: "Sleep ...
Only" (p. 104) and "Summer Is Over and ...

7. Write a new episode, "The Next Year in ...
one of Charlotte's children becomes the ...
perhaps all three: Joy, Arenea, and Nellie...

8. Write an episode from your past experie...
statement on page 69 to be true: "Ch...
hang onto things tighter than their parent...

VII. VOCABULARY THAT MAY NEED ...

1. Some children may enjoy and benefit fr...
the prefix "be" in such words as ...
*be*witched, *be*moan, etc. From *their* lists ...
them try to generalize about the prefix "...
it has on the *meanings* of words.

2. In what ways are these sentences alike? ...
different?

I *love* blue. I *adore* blue. I *like* blue. I'm ...

In the same way, some children may pr...
the similarities and differences among ...
being mad about such things as steak, th...
Lincoln convertibles, Uncle Jonas, soc...
money, God, being lazy, my count...
traveling.

4. Suppose Charlotte's plan had failed! If you were in Fern's shoes, what plans would you have made to save Wilbur? What would you do first? What results would you expect? What would you do second? What results would you expect? And so on.
5. If, instead of Charlotte, Templeton (or the sheep or the goose) had become Wilbur's best friend, describe the kind of plan you think he would have devised to save Wilbur.

VI. RELATED-TO-READING EXPERIENCES

1. Prepare an advertising campaign to make a person (or a group of people) change his mind about *not* wanting something.
2. Suppose you wanted to buy or to do something of which you feel sure your parents would disapprove. What are some of the things you would try to "sell them" on the idea *before* you ask?
3. It is often easier and more convincing to describe a person or thing indirectly than coming right out and saying, for example: "Charlotte is a wonderful spider. She is very kind, helpful and intelligent. She spins webs, as all spiders do, but she has the talent to put messages in her webs. She loved her home in the barn, and she loved Wilbur, too."

   Write a paragraph or two describing *Wilbur's* characteristics by:

   a. telling how he does things, including how he thinks and what he thinks about.
   b. telling an episode to prove a point about Wilbur's character and personality.
   c. comparing Wilbur with other animals or humans who have the same kinds of traits.
   d. telling what Wilbur is *not*.
   e. telling Wilbur's own characterization of himself.
   f. telling what others say of Wilbur.
   g. telling of the exceptions Wilbur has when compared with others of his species.

4. Some students may profit from a comparative research study of spiders and other insects—noting similarities and differences in habits, habitat, food, life-span, etc.
5. Using E. B. White's description of Charlotte and Charlotte's description of herself, some children may find it exciting to become amateur entymologists and draw their version of Charlotte. Once they complete their drawings, have them check an encyclopedia to see true drawings of spiders and compare the differences.
6. Compose music for the two songs: "Sleep, Sleep, My Love, My Only" (p. 104) and "Summer Is Over and Gone" (p. 113).
7. Write a new episode, "The Next Year in the Barn," in which one of Charlotte's children becomes the central character. (Or perhaps all three: Joy, Arenea, and Nellie)
8. Write an episode from your past experiences which proves the statement on page 69 to be true: "Children almost always hang onto things tighter than their parents think they will."

VII. VOCABULARY THAT MAY NEED DEVELOPING

1. Some children may enjoy and benefit from an examination of the prefix "be" in such words as *be*friend, *be*grudge, *be*witched, *be*moan, etc. From *their* lists of such words, have them try to generalize about the prefix "be" and the influence it has on the *meanings* of words.
2. In what ways are these sentences alike? In what ways are they different?

I *love* blue. I *adore* blue. I *like* blue. I'm *mad* about blue.

In the same way, some children may profit by trying to note the similarities and differences among *love, adore, like,* and *being mad about* such things as steak, that dress, my parents, Lincoln convertibles, Uncle Jonas, social studies, my dog, money, God, being lazy, my country, my best friend, traveling.

3. What similarities and differences are there in the *meanings* of the following words? *notorious, infamous, well-known, notoriety, popular, popularity, reputation, renown.*

VIII. OTHER SELECTIONS ON A SIMILAR THEME: A SELECTIVE BIBLIOGRAPHY

Grahame, Kenneth. *The Wind in the Willows.* N.Y.: Scribner's, 1933.
Lawson, Robert. *Rabbit Hill.* N.Y.: Viking, 1944.
Seredy, Kate. *The Tenement Tree.* N.Y.: Viking, 1959.
Ward, Lynd. *The Biggest Bear.* Boston: Houghton Mifflin, 1952.
White, E. B. *Stuart Little.* N.Y.: Harper, 1945. (Available as a Dell Yearling book.)

Poetry

"The Ant Village" by Marion Edey and Dorothy G⋅ ꜀er, from *Open the Door,* N.Y.: Scribner's.
"Firefly" by Elizabeth Madox Roberts, *Piping Dowr the Valleys Wild,* selected by Nancy I⋅⋅ ꜀, N.Y.: Delacorte, 1968.
"Mice" by Rose Fyleman, from *Piping Down the Valleys Wild,* selected by Nancy Larrick, N.Y.: Delacorte, 1968.

STUART LITTLE

by E. B. WHITE

Illustrated by Garth Williams

I. THE STORY

"When Mrs. Frederick C. Little's second son arrived, everybody noticed that he was not much bigger than a mouse. The truth of the matter was, the baby looked very much like a mouse in every way." The rather extraordinary arrival of Stuart in the Little house in New York City begins a funny and tender story of an heroic figure. In spite of his small size—just over two inches—Stuart gets around a good bit in the world. But he does have some trouble now and then, such as the time he was rolled up in a window shade and when he got dumped into a garbage scow. His great adventure comes when, at the age of seven, he sets out to seek his dearest friend, Margalo, a beautiful little bird who stayed for a few days in the Little's Boston fern.

II. PREREADING DISCUSSION QUESTIONS

The questions which follow are illustrative of the kinds which teachers can prepare for the purpose of releasing children to reveal how *they feel* about some of the same larger ideas and bigger meanings contained in the book *before* it is read.

About Big and Little

1. To a person your age, adults seem forever to be saying: "You're not big enough!" or "You're too little!" or "Wait until you grow up!" or "You're not old enough!" By this time, it must be easy for you to remember many such statements or excuses made by your parents, teachers, and

others. What are some of these things you weren't permitted to do because you were too little or too young? What are some of the things which, even today, you aren't permitted to do, to go to, or to have because you're "not old enough" or "not big enough?"

2. Probably it hasn't been very long since someone scolded you or reminded you: "You are *too big* to be doing such and such a thing!" or "You've outgrown such foolishness!" or "Act your age!" or "You're too old still to be wanting such things!" Tell about a time when such a statement was made to you. Who made it? Why? Do you think you were too big or too old?

3. Not all *midgets* are in carnivals or circuses. Many, in fact, live in homes and neighborhoods just like yours. They go to school just as you and like to do the same kinds of things you do. Suppose, in your classroom in school, sitting in the seat next to you, there was a midget. He (or she) is 2-1/2 feet tall, which is not quite so tall as a yardstick. Now suppose this person was your best friend for a week, going with you everywhere, doing the things you do. Due to his size, what kinds of problems do you think he might have? How would you help him solve them?

About Love

4. You probably have heard people say that there are many kinds of *love*. Perhaps you, yourself, have had different kinds of feelings of *love*. Suppose a stranger visiting our country (who understands English) would hear you say the following things:

a. "Man! What a game. I *loved* every second of it."
b. "Gee Barbara, I simply *love* your dress."
c. "Well, maybe my dog isn't a thoroughbred, but I *love* him more than anything in the whole world."
d. "Daddy, you're the greatest person ever! I *love* you!"
e. "What the world needs now is *love*, sweet *love*."
f. "Gosh I hope I win the contest. I'd *love* to have that bike."
g. "I *love* chocolate ice cream."

205

h. "When I fall in *love* and get married, I'd like to live in an apartment in a big city like New York."

i. "Oh, that? That's just puppy *love*."

j. "I *love* my country. It's the greatest place on earth."

What would you say to this foreigner if he asked you to explain what Americans mean when they say *love*?

5. In movies and on television, one often hears someone say: "This is something I've just got to do. I can't help the way I feel. I've got to keep trying and searching—forever, if necessary. Nothing else matters." A lot of people in real life feel this way, too. They are dedicated to a single thing, person, or idea. How many reasons can you think of that would cause a person to make a statement such as this?

6. All over the world—from ancient times to the present—people have gone on long pilgrimages or voyages. As a result, many suffered great discomfort, hardships, and even death. For what kinds of searches would people today take long voyages? How might you describe their reasons as *love*? What are they hoping to find? Why do they think it's so important?

About World Leadership

7. Tell what your opinion might be if someone suggested that the solution to all of the problems of the world is to have a *King of the World* or a *Chairman of the World* or a *World President*.

About Important Things

8. If your teacher told you and your classmates that the *only* thing you would study for a *whole year* would be whatever all of you decided was *the most important thing*, what would you suggest or vote for as being the most important thing?

III. PREREADING ACTIVITIES

1. Suppose your mother and father "adopted" a chimpanzee and raised him as a member of the family—exactly the way they raised you. He would, of course, be your brother and he would

sit at the table with you, sleep in a bed, play with you, dress and wash, and go on trips, parties, etc., with you and your parents. In fact, you and your parents would have been treating him as a human for so long that you would not think of him as a chimpanzee. Make a list of some of the things that you think he would not be able to do. Make a list of some of the embarrassing things he probably would do. Describe a situation which tells how you think other people in your neighborhood may feel toward your "brother." How do you think they would feel about you and your family?

2. Suppose you had a magic ring that would make you *two inches* tall *for one hour* if you rubbed it once, or *ten feet* tall *for one hour* if you rubbed it twice. (When the hour is up, you would be the size you are now—until you rubbed the ring again.) Write a story telling what happened to you while you were two inches tall. What were some of the advantages? What dangers? What did you do? Or, if you prefer, write about your adventures while you were ten feet tall.

IV. POSTREADING DISCUSSION QUESTIONS

1. Using Stuart's definitions of *law* and *advice,* how many other rules can you think of which you feel Stuart would have accepted? (p. 93)

2. What do you think: Did Mr. and Mrs. Frederick C. Little and their son, George, really believe that Stuart was a mouse or simply a human "mini-midget?"

3. How do you explain the fact that no one seemed to think it very strange that a mouse could talk, sail boats, drive a car, buy things, build a canoe, etc.? We, the readers, know that this is a story of fantasy, make-believe, a talking-animal story, but why don't the humans in the story think that this is very odd?

4. Stuart's brother, George, asked him where he had been after his adventure in Central Park. Stuart replied that he had just been "knocking around town." Why didn't Stuart want to tell George about his adventure? How did these two brothers feel about one another?

207

V. HELPING CHILDREN TO REVEAL THEIR COMPREHENSION

1. Stuart begins his journey on page 75. Make a road map of his journey showing his various stopping-off places.

2. Suppose Stuart Little's next idea is to go to a newspaper office and place an ad in the paper, telling Margalo how he feels, where he is, and that he is on his way to find her. Write such a personal advertisement.

3. Suppose a letter arrives for Stuart Little from Margalo the day after Stuart leaves home. What do you think such a letter would say? Pretend you are Margalo and write such a letter.

4. Due to Stuart's size, the Littles had to make him special things: clothes, a bed, a chair, etc. Using a shoe box, make a diorama showing Stuart Little in his "room" at home.

5. Stuart Little is very fussy about being "proper," doing the right thing with the proper manners. This is especially true when he learns about Harriet Ames, asks her for a date, and spends an evening with her (Chapters 13 and 14). Prepare a booklet called *Stuart Little's Do and Don't Date Book.*

6. One of Stuart's adventures is as a substitute teacher. Suppose your regular teacher were absent from school today and, instead, Stuart were hired to take over! Write a letter to the superintendent of schools in your district, telling him how good (or bad) you thought this substitute teacher (Stuart) was. What, for example, were Stuart Little's ideas about education and learning? What was his system of teaching? How did you feel be..._ -- in ..is class? And so forth.

VI. RELATED-TO-READING EXPERIENCES

1. From an old sock, make a hand puppet[1] and name him Stuart Little. Choose what you feel to be one of the most exciting and/or interesting of Stuart's adventures. Then plan to have Stuart (your hand puppet) tell this adventure to some kindergarten, first- or second-graders in your school.

[1]*How to make a hand puppet:*

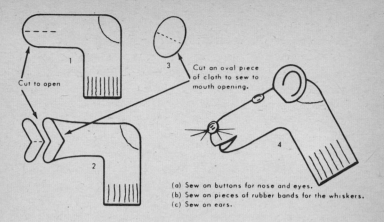

Cut to open

1

3

Cut an oval piece
of cloth to sew to
mouth opening.

2

4

(a) Sew on buttons for nose and eyes.
(b) Sew on pieces of rubber bands for the whiskers.
(c) Sew on ears.

2. Obtain a white mouse from a pet store in your town. Prepare
   an escape-proof home for him. Observe him carefully and prepare interesting toys and games for him to use. Write a biography about your mouse friend after you've had time to study
   and observe him for several weeks.

3. Find out all you can about other mouse and rat heroes. Collect
   information and pictures about them and compare them to
   Stuart Little. (Mickey Mouse, Amos [in Lawson's *Ben and
   Me*], Anatole, Templeton [*Charlotte's Web*] etc.) Suppose
   each of these mice were running for president of your class.
   Have a "political campaign" (posters, radio broadcasts,
   speeches, etc.) for a week, then prepare a ballot and have your
   class vote for the candidate of their choice.

4. Go on a "Musical Love Search." From the thousands of new
   and old songs about *love,* collect as many as you can. Try to
   get a small group of people together and decide on the "Top
   Twenty Tunes." Probably you will want to consider the titles,
   the tunes, and the lyrics as criteria to help you in your decision.

VII. VOCABULARY THAT MAY NEED DEVELOPING

1. On page 33, Dr. Paul Carey and Stuart Little play a word game. Choose a partner and decide on any topic you want—boats, cars, food, sports, etc. See how long you can keep this game going.
2. *Pun Fun: balsam* (p. 95) for "bawl some"; *rhinestone* (p. 85) for "gallstone."
3. *shinnying* (p. 2), *wrapper* (p. 13), *belittle* (p. 10), *pariah* (p. 72).

VIII. OTHER SELECTIONS ON A SIMILAR THEME: A SELECTED BIBLIOGRAPHY

Lawson, Robert. *Ben and Me.* Boston: Little, Brown, 1939.
———. *Mr. Revere and I.* Boston: Little, Brown, 1953.
Selden, George. *The Cricket in Times Square.* N.Y.: Farrar, Straus, 1960.
Stafford, Jean. *Elephi, The Cat with the High IQ.* N.Y.: Farrar, Straus, 1962. (Available as a Dell Yearling book.)

Poetry
"Mice" by Rose Fyleman, from *Piping Down the Valleys Wild,* selected by Nancy Larrick, N.Y.: Delacorte, 1968.
"The Mouse" by Elizabeth Coatsworth, from *Compass Rose,* N.Y.: Coward-McCann, 1929.

THE PURPOSE OF USING BIOGRAPHIES
IN THE CLASSROOM

Through biographies, children encounter great people whose destinies have shaped the future. Not only are these encounters meaningful in expanding the readers' understanding of a rich cultural heritage, but, in addition to learning about the facts of time, place, people, and circumstance of historical and contemporary happenings, they also become intimately and sensitively *involved* in them. They come to feel, sense, understand, and identify with the pressures and the problems, the accomplishments and the defeats, the ideas and the causes, the events and the activities which have set the stage and provided the scenery for man's continuous attempt to make life good. Because of this involvement, children establish a "toehold" on a piece of the past, and as they pause momentarily to touch and to be touched by greatness, these encounters -these very personal experiences—become vibrant moments of immediate reality.

Joan of Arc dies	Pocahontas dies	The first English dictionary	George Washington born	Betsy Ross born	French and Indian Wars begin	Beethoven born	Boston Tea Party	Revolutionary War begins	Baltimore 1st U. S. Capital
1431	1617	1721	1732	1752	1754	1770	1773	1775	1776

1760

| | | | | | French and Indian Wars end | | | Paul Revere's ride | Declaration of Independence |

The Time Line

The Time Line, shown and referred to on the following pages, is a visual aid to the concept of total historical sequence. It shows the place in time for major figures and events, some of which are covered in the si biographies, some of which are not. The teacher might duplicate a Time Line similar to this one, adding to it as events and people are uncovered by children in their classroom experiences, or children may wish to plot their own Time Lines, investigating dates, people, places, events, etc. As the biographies are read, other figures than the one on whom the book focuses, and other situations and events, will be discovered. While the teacher is free to call children's attention to any or all of these, the purpose here is to illustrate the type of activity which allows children to research and investigate on their own, and appraise their discoveries in historical perspective.

212

Philadelphia 2nd U. S. Capital	Revolutionary War ends	N. Y. C. becomes U. S. Capital	Davy Crockett born	Constitution ratified	Bill of Rights ratified	Cotton gin invented	Sam Houston born	Parachute invented
1777	1783	1785	1786	1788	1791	1792	1793	1797

Learning Experiences through Biographical Comparisons

After children have read two or more biographies, their insights into the lives of historical figures can be reinforced and extended through biographical comparisons. Such activities will also enable children to express their understanding of great moments of history. Of the following suggested activities, some deal with specific Yearling *Discovery* titles while others are quite general. Most activities can easily be adapted to both the biographies a child has read and the teacher's goals. Through such activities as these children can search for and find relationships that break down stereotypes, offer perspectives, and bridge generations.

1799	1807	1809	1812	1814	1815	1819	1820	1821
George Washington dies	Houston goes to live with Cherokees	Abraham Lincoln born	War of 1812 begins	"Star-spangled Banner" written	War of 1812 ends	Julia Ward Howe born	Florence Nightingale born	Clara Barton born
		Louis Braille born					Susan B. Anthony born	

1. Discuss the apparent contradiction in the following:

   a. "Sticks and stones may break my bones, but words can never hurt me."
   b. "The pen is mightier than the sword."

   Write a brief paragraph or so telling which of the two statements above might have been a philosophy held by each of the following: Washington, Lincoln, Keller, Nightingale, and Kennedy. Why do you think so?

2. Apparently, being able to read and doing a lot of reading played a most important part in the careers of Washington, Houston, Lincoln, Nightingale, Keller, and Kennedy even though their *reasons* or purposes for reading and *what* they

Beethoven dies	Louisa May Alcott born	Alfred Nobel born	Horatio Alger born	Mark Twain born	Battle of San Jacinto	Betsy Ross dies	First telegraph message sent	Texas admitted to Union
1827	1832	1833	1834	1835	1836		1844	1845
					Battle of the Alamo	Davy Crockett dies		

read were not always the same. How did each feel about the importance of reading? How did reading help them, specifically, to achieve the success they eventually found? How do you feel about the importance of reading in people's lives today? In the lives of our country's leaders? Is it still as necessary? Why? Why not?

3. From among the following, select one and nominate him (or her), in writing, for a *Peace Prize*: Washington, Lincoln, Houston, Nightingale, Kennedy.

4. Note and compare the many occupations which the following persons had in common: Kennedy, Houston, Lincoln, Washington.

5. Suppose you could write to Houston, Lincoln, and Kennedy, asking them for their views on slavery. Write three letters to

1846	1847	1848	1849	1852	1853	1856	1859
Mexican War begins	Joseph Pulitzer born	Belle Starr born	Safety pin invented	Louis Braille dies	Crimean War begins	Crimean War ends	First oil well drilled
First organized baseball game	Mexican War ends	Gold discovered in California					

yourself, from each of these men, explaining their feelings and positions.

6. In their lifetimes, Washington, Houston, Lincoln, Nightingale, Keller, and Kennedy all suffered a great deal of physical pain. Who do you think suffered the most? Who, because he (or she) was able to endure so much pain, was able to benefit the most people?

7. Do some research and tell how the families of Washington, Lincoln, Houston, Nightingale, Keller, and Kennedy encouraged and helped them to greatness. Tell, also, how their families almost prevented some of them from achieving the greatness which eventually came to them.

8. In many ways, the home and family life of Washington, Houston, Lincoln, Nightingale, Keller, and Kennedy, were the

216

1860	1861	1863	1865	1866	1866	1867	1871
Jane Addams born / Annie Oakley born	Civil War begins	Battle of Gettysburg	Abraham Lincoln assassinated	Anne Sullivan (Macy) born	Dynamite invented	Alaska purchased from Russia	The Great Chicago Fire
Pony Express formed		Sam Houston dies	Salvation Army organized / Civil War ends			Madame Marie Curie born	

same; in other ways they were different. Do some research and note and compare such things as *(a)* the size of the family when they were children, *(b)* the size of the families they had after they married, *(c)* stepparents and stepbrothers and stepsisters, *(d)* family deaths and tragedies, *(e)* family wealth, *(f)* family mobility.

9. Select one of the six people in this biography series. Then, do some research and find, note, and compare the lives of other great people who made their accomplishments during approximately the same period of time—perhaps hundreds or thousands of miles away. What, for example, famous artists, musicians, inventors, kings and/or queens were living and working at the same time? What other important events were taking place?

217

1876	1877	1879	1880	1881	1882	1882	1886	1888	1889
First telephone message	Phonograph invented	First successful electric light	Helen Keller born	President Garfield assassinated	Franklin D. Roosevelt born	Jesse James shot	Statue of Liberty unveiled	Louisa May Alcott dies	Belle Starr dies
Custer's last stand		Will Rogers born		American Red Cross founded	Anna Pavlova born				

10. From your research, explain what the state of Texas has in common with Sam Houston and Presidents Eisenhower, Kennedy, and Lyndon Johnson.

11. Do some research into the lives of all United States Presidents. Which of them had military careers before being elected President? You might entitle your research paper: "From Private to President."

12. It is interesting to notice and compare the kinds of games famous people spent their time playing when they were young and how these games seem to be related to their careers as adults. Study the childhood games of these famous people. What opinions do you have about the effect they had on their eventual greatness?

Alfred Nobel dies	First P. T. A. organized	Spanish-American War begins and ends	Horatio Alger dies	President McKinley assassinated	Wright Bros. first flight	Susan B. Anthony dies	Mark Twain dies	Florence Nightingale dies	Joseph Pulitzer dies
1896	1897	1898	1899	1901	1903	1906	1910	1910	1911
		Amelia Earhart born					Julia Ward Howe dies		Jane Froman born

13. Suppose, as Washington, Houston, Lincoln, Nightingale, Keller, or Kennedy, your one last wish is to say "Thank you!" to the world. Write such a speech and deliver it before your classmates.

14. Collect and compare the witticisms and sayings of Benjamin Franklin, Abraham Lincoln, Will Rogers, and Mark Twain.

15. Collect and compare the "Notable Quotes" of Washington, Lincoln, and Kennedy.

16. Collect and compare "Songs of War" from 1700 to the present.

17. Collect and compare "Slogans of War" from 1700 to the present.

18. Collect and compare "Slogans of Politics" from 1700 to the present.

Clara Barton dies	World War I begins	John F. Kennedy born	World War I ends	First radio broadcast	Annie Oakley dies	Anna Pavlova dies	Madame Marie Curie dies	Jane Addams dies	Anne Sullivan (Macy) dies	Amelia Earhart dies
1912	1914	1917	1918	1920	1926	1931	1934	1935	1936	1937
	Panama Canal opens							Will Rogers dies		

19. Try to find some copies of *almanacs*. Go to the library and see if you can locate a copy of *Poor Richard's Almanac*. What does an *almanac* contain? Why were they so popular in early America? Why do many people still read them?

20. Collect and display coins or stamps commemorating the lives and work of these historic people.

21. Locate the various cities which have been United States Capitals and find out why so many were needed.

22. Find out what the six or eight most common causes of death in the world were from 1600-1700; 1700-1800; 1800-1900; and 1900 to the present.

23. Make and compare models of ships, forts, weapons, dwellings, modes of transportation from 1700 to the present.

World War II begins	First commercial TV broadcast	Franklin D. Roosevelt dies	United Nations formed	Korean War begins	Korean War ends		First U. S. satellite in orbit	President John F. Kennedy assassinated
1939	1941	1945	1945	1950	1953	1957	1958	1963
		World War II ends				Sputnik I, 1st man-made satellite in orbit		Valentina V. Tereshkova: 1st woman astronaut

24. Make "Career Maps" which reveal important geographical locations of famous people and/or events of historic significance.

25. Construct a "Salt Map"[1] f the United States. On it place teepees with the names of the tribes and the dates, depicting the areas which they claimed as their territories in early America.

---

[1] Salt-map recipe: 3 parts salt, 1 part flour; add water slowly until consistency of dough.

GEORGE WASHINGTON
by STEWART GRAFF

Illustrated by Robert Doremus

I. THE STORY

Young George Washington loved his home in Virginia, where he learned to ride and hunt; he was strong and rugged, and at twenty became an officer and surveyor in the Virginia militia. When the Revolution began, Washington was made commander of the first American army. His soldiers were ragged and poorly trained, but Washington ⸱. a great leader. He worked hard to get food and guns for his men. He taught them to march and to shoot. Best of all, he gave them the spirit to fight. When the Revolution was over and the thirteen colonies became the United States, George Washington was elected the first President. Under his leadership, America grew strong. When he died, one of his old soldiers wrote about him, "First in war, first in peace, and first in the hearts of his countrymen."

II. PREREADING DISCUSSION QUESTIONS

The questions which follow are illustrative of the kinds which teachers can prepare for the purpose of releasing children to reveal how *they feel* about some of the same larger ideas and bigger meanings contained in the book *before* it is read.

About Historical Fame
1. Many great men in history were fathers of children. However, other historical figures have been considered "fathers" in other ways, such as: (1) writers of famous documents; (2) famous inventors; (3) heroes; (4) originators of ideas; (5) first great leaders of countries; and (6) the first people to pioneer in

dangerous, unknown places—"conquering" Mt. Everest, swimming the English Channel, flying nonstop around the world, etc. Who are some of these men and what did they do? How do people decide on the famous people they want to call "father" in history books?

2. How does a person become famous? Is it something he decides to do at a young age and then works for? Is it by accident? Is it due to the good things he does for a lot of people? Can it be due to evil or bad things he does against society and the world?

About Wealthy Parents

3. If a child's parents are so wealthy that he would never have to work to earn money in order to live and do the things he wants to do, how would this help a person to become a successful and well-loved leader? What are some of the disadvantages which you think would stand in such a person's way as a result of his parents' money?

4. What important things does a poor person who suddenly becomes wealthy need to learn? What important things does a wealthy person need to learn in order to live and work happily with most of the other people in society who have much, much less?

5. One of the great attractions which brought thousands of people to the United States, one of the great hopes which most people in this country have, could be called "the Great American Dream": a poor person *can* become wealthy; a person from "plain, ordinary" parents *can* be elected to the highest office in the land, the Presidency of the United States. Do you think this "rags to riches" idea applies in America today? In America of the past?

About Taxation

6. What is a tax? What kinds of taxes affect people your age and the money they have to spend? Who decides who has to pay taxes? How much taxes? What is to be taxed? Who gets the tax money? What is tax money to be used for? What is a hidden tax? What would be an example of an unfair tax? Can an

owner of a store or business tax his customers? What is the difference between *paying interest* and *being taxed*? When someone says, "You've taxed my patience long enough!" or "My poor brain is overtaxed!," what do you think they mean?

About Determination

7. When some people lose or are defeated in something they try hard to do and to succeed in, they give up and try something else. Some others will feel angry and/or ashamed and run away. Others will keep on trying and failing until they are so discouraged that they feel convinced they cannot possibly win. Still others who are defeated make new plans, try different ways, and keep on with their attempts—over and over again until they succeed or are unable to try or resist any longer. What causes people to react to defeat so differently? Why are some so stubborn while others give up so easily? Which typ. do you think is best? Why? What things influence the number of "tries" a person makes before he gives in?

III. PREREADING ACTIVITIES

1. Choose a parent or grandparent (or other relative), or a contemporary personage (such as a sports hero, movie or TV star, politician or public official, etc.) for whom detailed information is abundant and available, and/or with whom correspondence or an interview is possible, and *(a)* make a "Career Map" of their schooling and occupations from childhood to the present; or *(b)* make a "Time Line" of dates and significant events and accomplishments in their lives from childhood to the present; and/or *(c)* make a study of their various hobbies or interests and/or childhood dreams or aspirations to find out whether or not these contributed—and to what degree—to happiness and success in their present professions or occupations.
2. There are many different kinds of "teachers" in a person's life while, in turn, each person himself becomes a "teacher" to

many others. Frequently a leader has to be a teacher in order to do his job effectively. Of the many different kinds of leaders you can think of (such as a Scoutmaster, choir director, bandleader, chairman of a group, president of a club, etc.), choose one and list as many different "teaching jobs" he has to do as a result of his leadership role.

IV. POSTREADING DISCUSSION QUESTIONS

1. In what ways, do you think, did George Washington's father, his brother Lawrence, his family's wealth and social position help him to become a major, colonel, general, and finally President of the United States?

V. HELPING CHILDREN TO REVEAL THEIR COMPREHENSION

1. Make a "Career Map" of George Washington's schooling and occupations from 1732 to 1799.
2. Make a "Time Line" of the dates of significant events and accomplishments of George Washington (successes and failures) from 1732 to 1799.
3. As George Washington, write letters explaining how you feel during those historical moments in your life when you experience defeat as well as victory: at times of death; during school; after your marriage; before and after battles, conferences, peace missions; during times of pain and hardship; and as President of the United States and/or Representative from Virginia. You may choose to write to different people or to one person, such as your wife, Martha; your son, Jackie; your daughter, Patsy; or Governor Dinwiddie, Thomas Jefferson, Alexander Hamilton, John Adams, James Madison, or to Benjamin Franklin Bache, editor of *The American Daily Advertiser* in Philadelphia.

VI. RELATED-TO-READING EXPERIENCES

See "Learning Experiences with Biographical Comparisons," (pp. 213-221.)

VII. VOCABULARY THAT MAY NEED DEVELOPING

Word meanings vary, expand, and are changed by time, place, situation—that is, word meanings change and grow by the *people who use them.* A modern-day *colonist* is different from a *colonist* of two or three centuries ago. So, too, is a *colonial* empire or a nation (or industrial firm) that desires to *colonize. Colonial* furniture and architecture may have stable meanings while words like *colony* and *colonization* are used in connection with certain kinds of insects, illnesses, ghettos, conquests, organized clubs and groups, etc. Some students may profit from making studies or comparisons of words and their historical, early-American meanings and the new and different meanings and usages they have today. Other interesting words might include:

continent, continental, military, militia, mercenary, mercenaries, revolution, revolutionary, revolutionist, representation, convention, congress, Congress, congregate, treaty, and *fox hunt.*

VIII. OTHER SELECTIONS ON A SIMILAR THEME: A SELECTED BIBLIOGRAPHY

Alderman, Clifford Lindsey. *Samuel Adams, Son of Liberty.* N.Y.: Holt, Rinehart, 1961.

d'Aulaire, Ingri and Edgar. *George Washington.* Garden City, N.Y.: Doubleday, 1936.

Forbes, Esther. *America's Paul Revere.* Boston: Houghton Mifflin, 1946.

———. *Johnny Tremain.* Boston: Houghton Mifflin, 1943. (Available as a Dell Yearling book.)

Judson, Clara Ingram. *George Washington, Leader of the People.* Chicago: Follett, 1951.

Lawson, Robert. *Mr. Revere and I.* Boston, Little, Brown, 1953.

Poetry
"Paul Revere's Ride" by Henry Wadsworth Longfellow, available in many editions.

"Washington" by Nancy Byrd Turner, from *Child Life,* February 1930.

SAM HOUSTON

by JEAN LEE LATHAM

Illustrated by Earnest Kurt Barth and Hobe Hays

I. THE STORY

As a boy, Sam Houston grew up near the Cherokee Indians; he knew
and loved these people well. Houston became a soldier and fought
bravely with General Andrew Jackson in the War of 1812. He later
served as Governor of Tennessee and was President Jackson's trusted
adviser. The lure of adventure took Sam to the territory of Texas.
He became leader of the new Texas army that was fighting for
independence from Mexico. Although the Texans were vastly out-
numbered, Sam led them to victory at the Battle of . an Jacinto. He
became President of the Republic of Texas, then a United States
Senator, and Governor after Texas was admitted to the Union. Bril-
liant, courageous, and loyal, Sam worked hard for his two loves: the
Union and the Indians.

II. PREREADING DISCUSSION QUESTIONS

The questions which follow are illustrative of the kinds which teachers can prepare for the purpose of releasing children to reveal how
they feel about some of the same larger ideas and bigger meanings
contained in the book *before* it is read.

About Childhood Dreams and Aspirations

1. When people are young, they have many ideas of what they'd
   like to be "when they grow up." Sometimes these ideas change
   frequently; sometimes they stay and one hears a person say:
   "Why, it seems as though I always wanted to be a doctor."
   While they are young, many children "play" those roles they
   want to assume when they are older, such as doctor, fireman,

teacher, milkman, postman, policeman, nurse, movie star, soldier, and so forth. In what ways do you feel these games and dreams have (or don't have) an influence on what a person actually becomes once he is grown up?

2. What, in your opinion, are some of the reasons that children feel like running away from home?

About Determination

3. When a person says, "I've made up my mind! I'm *determined* I'm going to do it, regardless of the consequences!"—what things might change his mind? What things might prevent him from carrying out his plans? Do you think a *determined* person can be stopped? How can a person be stopped if he has made up his mind to rob or kill? How can a person be prevented from succeeding in school (or in sports) even though he is determined to succeed?

About Paying Debts

4. People "get into debt" in many ways and for many reasons:

   a. "I'm up to my ears with debts and you want to buy a new car!"
   b. "I'll be indebted to him forever."
   c. "He's paid his debt to society."
   d. "Now I owe you a debt which I won't be able to pay back until your car is on the blink.'
   e. "Someday I'll repay the debt of gratitude I owe my parents for their encouragement."
   f. "Could I be in debt to you for five dollars until payday?"

Debts can be for such things as money, favors, loans of all kinds, kindnesses, jail terms, love or hate, and feelings of deep appreciation. How do you feel about the statement: "A person must always pay back all of his debts!"? What debts are hard (if not impossible) to pay back and why? What is so terrible about *not* paying one's debts?

5. In what ways is the following statement related to debts?

"Now you're one up on me!"

6. What do you know about the "debtors' prisons" that used to exist in England? Why would some people be in favor of them? Why would some people be against them?

III. PREREADING ACTIVITIES

1. Starting with a *Private* (for the Army and Marine Corps) and with a *Seaman* (for the Navy), make a sequential chart of all the military ranks.
2. Find out about the number and kinds of schools, hospitals, teachers, nurses, and doctors in America from 1800 to 1850.

IV. POSTREADING DISCUSSION QUESTIONS

1. Military tradition, obedience, and respect along with a "slip of the tongue," led to the betrayal of Santa Anna and his capture. Tell of an experience you know about where a person felt like "cutting his tongue out." What are some of the "little slips" or mistakes that often cause spies to reveal themselves or, "lose their cover?"
2. Sam Houston had many *wounds* in his lifetime (the death of his father, broken bones, arrow and bullet wounds, Texas' entering the Civil War as a slave state). Some people never seem to recover from such injuries. How do you feel about the idea that, "because of his many 'wounds,' Sam Houston became strong and as tough as his old friend, 'Old Hickory Jackson'?"

V. HELPING CHILDREN TO REVEAL THEIR COMPREHENSION

1. Sam Houston earned many "promotions" in his lifetime, not only as a soldier but in nearly every "occupation" he tried, from "The Raven" brother of the Cherokees to United States Senator. What would "Sam Houston's Profile" look like when plotted on a graph between the years 1790-1890 and listing all Army ranks as well as Indian, clerk, student, lawyer, Congressman, Governor, President of Texas, and U.S. Senator?
2. Frequently the lives or paths of great men come together and thereafter are remembered as "significant moments in history." The historical path of Sam Houston crossed those of many other great people, such as: Ulysses S. Grant, Andrew Jackson, and General Santa Anna. What would a front-page newspaper story and headline be like after such historic occasions?
3. Every man has a "geography" of his own—that is, there are certain regions, places, cities, etc., which a person remembers for certain reasons (like one's "home town"). Very often places "remember" certain people for the "marks" they made while living or working there. On a map of the United States, find a way to indicate Sam Houston's "Geographical Biography." (Children will want to search for these significant places on their own. However, a few of these would include Virginia, Tennessee, Washington, D.C., the Hiwassee River, Hiwassee Island, Horseshoe Bend, the Tallapoosa River, the Arkansas River, Nacogdoches, Washington-on-the-Brazos, the Alamo, San Antonio, Houston, Goliad, Gonzales, the San Jacinto River, San Jacinto, New Orleans, and Huntsville.)

VI. RELATED-TO-READING EXPERIENCES

See "Learning Experiences through Biographical Comparisons," pp. 213-221.

VII. VOCABULARY THAT MAY NEED DEVELOPING

1. Some students may gain deeper insight into the strong motivation and unique personality of Sam Houston by investigating what the following words have in common and what nuances in meaning make them different:

determination	*dedication*	*stubbornness*
dogged	*obstinate*	*optimism*
tenacious	*persistent*	*relentless*

2. Things, people, ideas, problems, rules, and so forth often are called *tough.* Some children will profit from an investigation of synonyms for *tough.*

VIII. OTHER SELECTIONS ON A SIMILAR THEME: A SELECTED BIBLIOGRAPHY

Daugherty, James. *Daniel Boone.* N.Y.: Viking, 1939.

James, Marquis and Bessie. *Six Feet Six: The Heroic Story of Sam Houston.* N.Y.: Bobbs-Merrill, 1931.

Le Sueur, Meridel. *Chanticleer of Wilderness Road: A Story of Davy Crockett.* N.Y.: Alfred Knopf, 1951.

Rourke, Constance. *Davy Crockett.* N.Y.: Harcourt, 1934.

Vance, Marguerite. *The Jacksons of Tennessee.* N.Y.: Dutton, 1953.

Poetry

"Barbara Frietchie" by John Greenleaf Whittier, available in many editions.

"Daniel Boone" by Arthur Guiterman, from *I Sing the Pioneer,* N.Y.: Dutton, 1926.

"The Defense of the Alamo" by Joaquin Miller, available in many editions.

ABRAHAM LINCOLN
by ANNE COLVER

Illustrated by William Moyers .

A Discovery Book in the Yearling Biography Series

I. THE STORY

Young Abe worked hard, as all pioneer children did, but still he found time to go to school and learn to read faster than anyone. He found time for mischief, too, and once made footprints on his mother's ceiling! As he grew older, he worked and studied even harder, and people came to know him for his fair and honest ways and his great sense of humor. Abraham Lincoln had always believed that all men should be free. When, as President, the slavery problem threatened to divide the nation in half, Lincoln kept his position. A great war broke out, killing many Americans on both sides and causing great damage, but when it was over the nation was reunited and slavery was abolished forever.

II. PREREADING DISCUSSION QUESTIONS

The questions which follow are illustrative of the kinds which teachers can prepare for the purpose of releasing children to reveal how *they feel* about some of the same larger ideas and bigger meanings contained in the book *before* it is read.

About Mobility
1. Today it is not unusual for a person to be born in one city, state, or country and then move to live somewhere else. Many people these days have several "home towns," go to several schools, and work in places far from their parents' homes and childhood memories. What are some of the reasons for this? For a boy or girl your age, what are some of the *disadvantages*

you can think of which result from your parents' finding it necessary to move from one neighborhood to another; from one city or state to another? What are some of the *advantages*?

2. Even if money were no problem, sometimes a person who "doesn't have the right kind of *upbringing*," or who "isn't from the right kind of family," or who "doesn't have the right manners, speech, or clothes" isn't invited to certain social events, allowed to join certain clubs, or permitted to go to certain places. What does such a person do to become socially acceptable? Why do you feel that such a situation is fair or unfair, democratic or undemocratic? Why do people on different levels of society have different "rules"? Suppose you were born into a family that has been considered *high society* for many years and because of that, you had very few friends. You are still your plain, kind, sweet self and yet everyone thinks you are "stuck up," "snobby," and that "you look down your nose at them." How would you feel about their opinions of you? What would you try to do?

About Being Different

3. We all know that no two people are the same: some are very tall and some are very short; some are clumsy, awkward, and untidy, while others are dexterous, graceful, and neat; some have unusual talents in art or music while others seem to be mechanical wizards. When a person has several extreme or "odd" qualities about him, people notice him and remember him because "he is so different!" Some people who don't think they are very different, *try to be different.* Other people who think they are too different, *try to hide their differences.* What kinds of extreme differences can you think of that might get in a person's way of being happy and successful? What kinds of extreme differences can you think of that would be helpful to a person's plans for happiness and success?

About Being a Reader

4. Parents, teachers, friends, relatives, businessmen—almost everybody—says that the most important skill *everyone* needs for a successful future (regardless of what one decides to be) is *to be*

233

able to read well: fast, accurately, critically. Yet, in school as well as out of school, many people do not like to read, do not read, and will not read if they can avoid it. They would rather listen to radio or to records, watch television, go to movies or plays, play games of all kinds, and so forth.

a. What are some of the reasons for this? Can anything be done about it or is it "just natural" for people to feel this way?
b. What are some of the important things which people *have to read* in their daily lives whether they want to or not?
c. What occupations or kinds of jobs could a person get that required very little or no reading?
d. What kind of reading does a housewife have to be good at? An auto mechanic?
e. In what ways does *being able to read* make life for a person your age better, happier, more interesting?

III. PREREADING ACTIVITIES

1. Choose one of the following topics and write an article for a magazine read by people your age:

   a. "Clothes Make the Man"
   b. "Actions Speak Louder Than Words"
   c. "A Little Knowledge Is a Dangerous Thing"
   d. "Money *Can't* Buy *Everything*"
   e. "The Grass Always Seems Greener on the Other Side"

2. Suppose you were a visitor to a small village in Australia and you found that, although the people were very intelligent, no one could read. They had never heard of reading; they had never seen a book, magazine, letter, newspaper—anything in printed letters and words. Make a list of the kinds of occupations (work or jobs) which you *would not find* people doing. Make a list of the other differences which you notice as you compare them with how you live: *(a)* What kinds of games and

entertainment *don't they have*? *(b)* What would the insides of
their shops, homes, schools, buildings look like? *(c)* What
kinds of things would a person your age be doing? *(d)* What
would people your age be learning? Who would be teaching
you?

3. One thing that adults keep asking children is "What are you
going to be when you grow up?" For many people your age,
(and even older) this is a hard question to answer. Why is it so
difficult to know what you want to be or what you are going
to be when you grow up?

4. Many years ago, *stepmothers* and *stepfathers, stepbrothers* and
stepsisters usually were considered to be angry, mean, cruel,
unloving, hateful. Many stories—such as *Cinderella,* for
example—were written that made such people seem ugly and
evil. Write a story in which you make such a person kind,
helpful, understanding and loving.

IV. POSTREADING DISCUSSION QUESTIONS

*[NOTE TO THE TEACHER: Children may profit from the
discussion which ensues from these open-ended questions, if
they are helped to recall some of the opinions and feelings
they expressed during one or more of the "Prereading Activities."]*

1. As a young boy and a young man, Abraham Lincoln very
easily could be described affectionately as an "odd ball." His
size, looks, habits, etc., all set him off as "being different." In
what ways do you think these differences helped and/or
hindered his career?

2. Lincoln was about as stubborn in some of his ideas as he was
honest and kind in his deeds: Although his father said he was
"wasting his time reading," he read. Although many disagreed,
he was stubborn in his beliefs that a country couldn't be "half
free and half slave." Although he was busy, he played with his
children and allowed them to be around him—even though it
angered some of his friends who came to the White House on

235

serious business. How do you suppose Lincoln knew he was being "stubborn" about the *right* things?

VI. HELPING CHILDREN TO REVEAL THEIR COMPREHENSION

1. Some people today might call Abraham Lincoln a "Jack-of-all-trades, master of none" if they had known him as a young man. As you know, he tried out many jobs: farmer, carpenter, Indian fighter, storekeeper, lawyer, postmaster, surveyor, and politician. He also worked in a sawmill and on riverboats. Yet, eventually, he was elected President of the United States! How can you explain this? Why couldn't Lincoln make up his mind? Find out about the past work experiences of the President we have today. Do you think he was as undecided as Lincoln? Why or why not?

2. One of Lincoln's many nicknames is "Honest Abe." Tell why you think "Kind Abe" also might be an appropriate nickname. (Children may wish to refer to the "Pig Episode," or to the "Captured-Indian Affair," or to his feelings about slavery and freedom and/or to the "Josephine-and-Her-Trunk Situation.")

3. Abraham Lincoln is remembered as much for his wonderful *sense of humor and wit* as he is for most of his other remarkable accomplishments. Yet, there was much tragedy in his life: the death of his mother and of his sons, Willie and Little Eddie, saddened him nearly as much as the hundreds of men who died on the battlefields in the Civil War. Suppose you were Robert Todd Lincoln's best friend at college and he showed you the letters he received from his father which told how he felt. What would Lincoln have put in those letters to his son?

VI. RELATED-TO-READING EXPERIENCES

See "Learning Experiences through Biographical Comparisons," pp. 213-221.

VII. VOCABULARY THAT MAY NEED DEVELOPING

1. Some children may benefit from an investigation of the various meanings and forms of the following and situations in which they are used:

to swear	*to promise*	*to take an oath*
to pledge	*to affirm*	*to witness*
to notarize		*to make legal or official*

2. Words and word meanings change from generation to generation. Words such as *running board* and *glove compartment,* for example, are "historical hangovers." Whereas *running board* is obsolete, the *glove compartment* in one's car contains almost everything except gloves. Some children will enjoy researching these oddities and compiling their own lists of these Historical Hangovers—used in the context of yesteryear *and* comparing them to the vernacular of today. Some words from *Abraham Lincoln* might launch such a study:

parlor   chore   swap   beau (beaux) *fourscore   imp*

VIII. OTHER SELECTIONS ON A SIMILAR THEME: A SELECTED BIBLIOGRAPHY

Bailey, Bernadine. *Abe Lincoln's Other Mother: The Story of Sarah Bush Lincoln.* N.Y.: Julian Messner, 1941.

Daugherty, James. *Abraham Lincoln.* N.Y.: Viking, 1943.

d'Aulaire, Ingri and Edgar. *Abraham Lincoln,* Garden City, N.Y.: Doubleday, 1939.

Fisher, Aileen. *My Cousin Abe.* N.Y.: Thomas Nelson, 1962.

Yates, Elizabeth. *Amos Fortune, Free Man.* N.Y.: Dutton, 1950.

Poetry

"Abraham Lincoln" by Mildred Plew Meigs, from *Child Life,* February 1936.

"Abraham Lincoln 1809-1865" by Rosemary Carr and Stephen Vincent Benét, from *A Book of Americans,* N.Y.: Holt, Rinehart, 1933.

"Lincoln" by Nancy Byrd Turner, from *Child Life,* February 1929.

"Nancy Hanks 1784-1818" by Rosemary Carr and Stephen Vincent Benét, from *A Book of Americans,* N.Y.: Holt, Rinehart, 1933.

FLORENCE NIGHTINGALE
by ANNE COLVER

Illustrated by Gerald McCann

A Discovery Book in the Yearling Biography Series

I. THE STORY

When she was a child in England, Florence Nightingale's favorite game was playing hospital with her dolls. As a young girl she often nursed people in her own village. Her family thought nursing was not a suitable occupation for a young lady, but Florence became such a good nurse that the British government sent her to Russia during the Crimean War. The wounded soldiers never forgot Florence's courage and kindness. She not only changed methods of wartime nursing, but later started the first school for training nurses in London.

II. PREREADING DISCUSSION QUESTIONS

The questions which follow are illustrative of the kinds which teachers can prepare for the purpose of releasing children to reveal how *they feel* about some of the same larger ideas and bigger meanings contained in the book *before* it is read.

About Propriety

1. What are some of the reasons that some girls are called "tomboys?"
2. What are some of the things which most people think are improper for young girls to do? For grown women?
3. What kinds of work (occupations, jobs, professions) generally considered "for men only" do women find it difficult, if not impossible, to do? What kind of work is generally considered "for women only?"

4. What kinds of things do girls your age want to do but find their parents won't allow them because "they are not suitable" activities for young ladies to engage in?

About Innovation

5. When a person has an idea about a better, safer, or easier way to do something, what problems might he face? How might people react, especially if they are satisfied with things as they are? For example, what pro and con arguments could there be for these ideas: making certain streets one-way; having children learn from teachers in school for half a day, and from television for the other half; making everyone *use* seat belts; making everyone use a "Water Pik" instead of a toothbrush; making laws about the purchasing of guns; etc.?

6. It is said that people *naturally* resist change; that they would rather stick with the *status quo* than change their ways of living. In what ways would you agree or disagree with such a statement? What are some examples? How would you explain why most women are happy and eager to change when it comes to such things as clothing and hairstyles?

7. "But Mom! Things are not the same as they were when you were a little girl! This is a new generation and things are different." Statements like this probably occur daily in most American homes. What are some of the reasons behind such statements?

About Famous Females

8. Throughout history there have been many women who have made important contributions to the world. Some of them have been queens, explorers, inventors, scientists, and so on. Some, even, have been famous criminals or desperadoes, such as Belle Starr. Nominate any woman, living or dead, for a list entitled "The World's Ten Most Valuable Women Awards." Give reasons for your nomination.

About Girls' Games

9. What kinds of toys and games do girls your age want to play with?

10. When little girls are growing up, they often pretend to be different kinds of people. What are some of the most common "pretend games" played by girls?

III. PREREADING ACTIVITIES

1. How many television shows have women as their *main* stars or characters? Do you think this is as it should be? Why? Of all the books you've read or you know about, how many have been written by women? How many different women's voices do you hear (and how often) on your favorite radio station? How many women politicians, lawyers, doctors, dentists, shop owners can you name? What reasons can you give to explain your answers to these questions?
2. Just a few decades ago, women in the United States were not so free as they are today; there were places to which they could not go, things they were not allowed to do, and things which they *could* do but were considered "not very nice." Ask your parents, grandparents, friends, and neighbors about these things. In each of the three areas mentioned above, how many new freedoms for women can you find and list?
3. If a girl's parents wanted her to become a teacher and she wanted to become an engineer, how would she go about trying to do what she really wanted to do without hurting her parents?

IV. POSTREADING DISCUSSION QUESTIONS

1. What arguments can you give—for and/or against—about women being:

   (a) army generals, *(b)* astronauts, *(c)* prizefighters, *(d)* football players, *(e)* garage mechanics, *(f)* judges, *(g)* United States Presidents, *(h)* ditch diggers, *(i)* announcers on television, etc.?

2. Tell why you would agree or disagree with the following statement: "Today, in this country, men are more free than women."
3. What examples can you give of the type of freedom women have or don't have in other countries of the world?
4. What things can men do better than women? Why do you think so?

V. HELPING CHILDREN TO REVEAL THEIR COMPREHENSION

1. Florence Nightingale's father once said to her (p. 23): "Don't cry. Some people must always be poor. You are too little to worry about the world. It will never be any better." That was more than 100 years ago. You are now living in a world he never dreamed possible. Suppose you could get a message through to Mr. Nightingale. In your letter, which of his predictions and advice would you agree with? With what would you disagree?
2. Florence Nightingale's parents often told her (p. 31): "You will never need to work. You will have plenty of money." Now that you know her, try to put yourself into Florence's shoes. You are sitting up all night with a patient who is very ill. Suddenly you think of a way to make your parents understand why you didn't stay at home and live off their money. So, you begin your letter: "December 12, 1854. Dear Mamma and Papa, . . ."
3. For about one-third of her life, the people who loved her most kept trying to convince Florence Nightingale to give up her "silly ideas"; they were disappointed in her. But nearly everyone else thought that Florence was a wonderful, marvelous, talented person. However, when they tried to show Florence how they felt, she would always avoid them. Some people said it was because she was shy. Florence said it was because she was too tired or because she wasn't brave enough for celebrations. What do you think? Why do you think the people

closest to her thought of her ideas as *silly* while thousands of others (including the Queen of England)—who didn't know her so well—thought of her ideas as *great*?

VI. RELATED-TO-READING EXPERIENCES

1. The Nineteenth Amendment to the Constitution of the United States was called the "Women's Suffrage Amendment" because it "gave women the vote." As a result of this new right won by women, other "freedoms" seemed to open up for them (or to be taken by them) even though the *only* new right guaranteed women by this new law was the *right to vote.* How can you explain why women felt they had even more freedom in other things?
2. See "Learning Experiences through Biographical Comparisons," pp. 213-221.

VII. VOCABULARY THAT MAY NEED DEVELOPING

1. Some students may profit from an investigation of word origins and derivations as well as meaning changes in such words as:

   hospital: hospice, hostel, hospitium, hotel, inn, shelter, refuge, infirmary, sick bay
   hospitable: hospitality, hospitably
   hospitalize: hospitalization
   ambulate: ambulant, ambulator, ambulatory, perambulate, ambulation, perambulator, ambulance, funambulist

2. It may be interesting as well as beneficial for some students to attempt to discover as many different meanings as they can for the word *band.*

VIII. OTHER SELECTIONS ON A SIMILAR THEME: A SELECTED BIBLIOGRAPHY

Daugherty, Sonia. *Ten Brave Women.* Philadelphia: Lippincott, 1953.

Judson, Clara. *City Neighbor, the Story of Jane Addams.* N.Y.: Scribner's, 1951.

Meigs, Cornelia. *Invincible Louisa.* Boston: Little, Brown, 1933.

Pace, Mildred. *Clara Barton,* N.Y.: Scribner's, 1941.

Sickels, E.M. *In Calico and Crinoline.* N.Y.: Viking, 1935.

Poetry

"A Lady Comes to an Inn" by Elizabeth Coatsworth, from *The Creaking Stair,* N.Y.: Coward-McCann, 1949.

"Nancy Hanks 1784-1818" by Rosemary Carr and Stephen Vincent Benét, from *A Book of Americans,* N.Y.: Holt, Rinehart, 1933.

HELEN KELLER

by STEWART and POLLY ANNE GRAFF

Illustrated by Paul Frame

A Discovery Book in the Yearling Biography Series

I. THE STORY

When Helen Keller was six years old she behaved like a wild, frightened animal. She could not see or hear or speak, and in her own silent, dark world she understood only that, to get what she wanted, she had to strike out for it. Then Anne Sullivan came to stay. She traced first letters, then words, in Helen's hand, until it was clear that this was how Helen would "talk" to other people and ask questions and learn. With her devoted "Teacher," Helen grew up a strong, fun-loving, intelligent girl, dedicating herself to teaching what she learned from Anne Sullivan.

II. PREREADING DISCUSSION QUESTIONS

The questions which follow are illustrative of the kinds which teachers can prepare for the purpose of releasing children to reveal how *they feel* about some of the same larger ideas and bigger meanings contained in the book *before* it is read.

About Helping the Sick or Injured

1. Try to remember a time when you were very ill (or injured) and had to stay in bed and/or remain at home for a long time. What things would have made you the happiest during this time? What things could you have had? What things could you have done? What things did you appreciate most that were done for you by other people—either things that you couldn't do for yourself or things that were "just nice" because you were sick or hurt? Who were these people? What things *didn't*

you want? What didn't you like to have people do for you at this time which, ordinarily, you would have liked? What bothered you the most?

2. Sometimes when a person is sick or injured and has to be cared for for a long time, people say that he's "being spoiled." What could they mean by this? What might some examples be?

About Being Pampered

3. When a person is sick or injured, people tend to feel sorry for him. They do things, buy things, get and bring things he wants and needs. They spend more time with him. They try to make such a person happy by giving him everything they can within reason. People do such things because they know that *happiness* is one of the best "medicines" for recovering from sickness or injury. They also do it because it takes away some of *their own* sad feelings they have for someone sick or injured who is very close to them. Sometimes people also behave this way toward very old people or toward very young children (or toward the youngest child in a family). Some people call this "pampering" and feel that it's a bad thing to do. How do you feel about the statements below:

   a. "Do too much for a person and he will do nothing for himself."
   b. "The Lord helps those who help themselves."
   c. "Do unto others as you would have them do unto you."

About Self-Pity

4. For one reason or another, some people feel sorry for themselves. Usually we are told that self-pity is a bad thing. How do you feel about it? Is self-pity ever justified? What are some of the reasons that people tend to say that self-pity is bad, harmful, or disgusting? What examples can you give?

III. PREREADING ACTIVITIES

1. When a person sprains an ankle, he limps when he walks because he's trying to make his uninjured leg take over most of

the work for both. When a person is deaf, he tends to make up for his loss by developing his other senses (especially *sight*) to new dimensions, which he otherwise might not have done. Similarly, when a person is blind, his senses of smell, taste, touch, and hearing all combine to try to *compensate* for the deficiency. Thus, such people seem to find happiness because they've learned how to "live with" their handicaps as well as with their gifts. In doing so, they have discovered that they can live "almost normal" lives, doing most of the same kinds of everyday jobs that other people do.

Try one or more of the following experiments. Then write your reactions. Tell how you felt, what things you would need in order to do a better job, what other senses you think you would need to develop more fully, and why you think you could or could not be happy if you had to live the rest of your life this way. What things (hopes, aspirations, jobs) do you think would be impossible for you?

a. Tie your right arm (if you are left-handed, tie your left arm) to your side. Try to dress yourself, wash yourself, eat, do homework, do household chores, play, etc. (A simple way, instead of tying your arm, would be to put it in a *sling* for a day, for this experiment.)

b. Using rubber earplugs (for swimming/diving) or a *large* piece of cotton, plug your ears in order to stop all sounds from entering. Then, read aloud to yourself for five or ten minutes. Watch your *favorite* TV program. Ask someone a question and "listen" (pay attention) to the response, trying seriously to understand. (You may have to repeat your question—or others—several times.)

c. In a large shopping bag, put about 15 or 20 common, ordinary, everyday objects. Then, in the same bag, (without your knowledge) ask *someone else* to put about the same number of objects and seal the bag. Before you begin, you will need a ball-point pen, paper, and a blindfold. (Eye patches may be purchased in a drugstore, an old pair of sunglasses may be *covered* to *shut out all sight,* even around the edges, or you may find it satisfactory to use a clean cloth or towel. The important thing is to make sure you *can't see anything,* even shadows.) Sit yourself at a large table or in the middle of the floor with the bag of objects handy. Also make sure the pen and paper are within reach. After you are blindfolded, open the bag and withdraw one object at a time. Examine it in any way you like. When you think you recognize it, write the name of it on the paper you have at hand. Put the object near you and reach into the bag for another, and another, etc. You may, if you wish, reexamine any object (if *without help,* you, can find it again) as many times as you want. When you have finished, remove the blindfold and write your reactions, etc., as outlined above. Another "experiment" would be to adjust your TV set so that you are able only to hear the sounds. Listen to it for a half hour and write your reactions.

2. Very often, when people are very ill, they need or ask for very strange and unusual things. Sometimes the things they want are very difficult, if not impossible, to get.
Put an "X" on the blanks in front of those statements below which *you* feel would be *very* difficult, if not impossible, *for you* to have if you were quite ill for a long period of time. Add any others you care to at the end.

___ very rare, expensive medicine
___ a person to be with you all the time
___ a room and a bed all your own
___ visits from your friends
___ your favorite toy, game, or hobby
___ your favorite food or dessert
___ a television set in your room
___ new clothes to wear after you get well
___ your pet
___ the moon
___ a special doctor
___ a private nurse
___ some books to read
___ a radio in your room

248

_____ some nice gifts or presents
_____ a stereo phonograph

_____ _____
_____ _____
_____ _____
_____ _____

IV. POSTREADING DISCUSSION QUESTIONS

1. The subtitle for this story is "Toward the Light." What different meanings might various people have for this?
2. Why would or wouldn't you consider young Helen Keller a "spoiled" child? Why do you think she acted like a wild, frightened animal? Could she have behaved any differently? How?
3. Why would a person such as Helen Keller feel different about books from the way most of us feel?
4. If there were a deaf-blind person sitting next to you in school, what problems do you think he or she would have? How would such a person's school life be different from yours? How would it be the same? How would your life, as you sat near him or her, be different? How would the teacher's teaching be different? How would the schooling of the rest of the students in the class be affected?

HELPING CHILDREN TO REVEAL THEIR
COMPREHENSION

1. Make a time and place map of Helen Keller's life, starting with June 27, 1886, in Tuscumbia, Alabama.
2. Write an "Occupational Biography" of what you feel to be the most outstanding jobs or activities Helen Keller learned to do successfully—things, perhaps, which people who are *not* blind and deaf find difficult to do.
3. Refer to the thoughts, feelings, and ideas which you had about any of the "Prereading Discussion Questions" or "Prereading Activities." How would you modify or change your responses

249

(would they be any ⌐ ⌐ ⌐ ⌐ ⌐ ⌐ ⌐ ⌐ nad had Helen Keller in mind *before* Anne Sulliva. ⌐ red her life?

4. Although the story is about Helen Keller, it is also a story of "Teacher" Anne Sullivan. What are some of the qualities you feel Anne Sullivan had that proved to be necessary to her success with Helen?

5. What if Anne Sullivan kept a diary of her work with Helen. Write a brief paragraph which summarizes her feelings and accomplishments with Helen for each of the first five years of their association.

VI. RELATED-TO-READING EXPERIENCES

1. Find out as much as you can about the life and work of Louis Braille.

2. Invite a trainer of seeing-eye dogs to come to talk with you and, perhaps, demonstrate how he trains these animals.

3. Find out as much as you can about the various charitable organizations that help the blind, the deaf, and the deaf *and* blind.

4. Visit a home or school for the blind. Notice the things blind children do and the things they say; how they are taught, etc. How would you compare their activities and interests with yours?

5. See "Learning Experience through Biographical Comparisons," pp. 213-21.

VII. VOCABULARY THAT MAY NEED DEVELOPING

1. Some students may find it possible to increase their vocabularies by examining the various meanings of the following words and using them in contexts which reveal their meanings to others.

infirmity	*handicap*	*a crippling effect*
maimed	*disability*	*mutilation*

deprivation   malfunction   ailment
a disorder   abnormality   mute, mutation

VIII. OTHER SELECTIONS ON A SIMILAR THEME: A SELECTED BIBLIOGRAPHY

DeGering, Etta. *Seeing Fingers.* N.Y.: David McKay, 1962.

Malvern, Gladys. *Dancing Star: The Story of Anna Pavlova.* N.Y.: Julian Messner, 1942.

Speare, Elizabeth George. *Calico Captive.* Boston: Houghton Mifflin, 1957.

Wheeler, Opal. *Ludwig Beethoven, and the Chiming Tower Bells.* N.Y.: Dutton, 1942.

Wilder, Laura Ingalls. *Little House in the Big Woods.* N.Y.: Harper, 1953.

Poetry

"Behind the Waterfall" by Winifred Welles, from *Skipping Along Alone,* N.Y.: Macmillan, 1931.

"The Coin" by Sara Teasdale, from *Flame and Shadow,* N.Y.: Macmillan, 1948.

"The Fog" by William Henry Davies, from *The Collected Poems of W. H. Davies,* London: Jonathan Cape, 1929.

"The Man Who Hid His Own Front Door" by Elizabeth MacKinstry, from *Gaily We Parade,* N.Y.: Macmillan, 1940.

"The Noise of the Waters" by James Joyce, from *Collected Poems,* N.Y.: Viking, 1937.

"Someone" by Walter de la Mare, from *Piping Down the Valleys Wild,* selected by Nancy Larrick, N.Y.: Delacorte, 1968.

"A Song of Greatness" by Mary Austin, from *The Children Sing in the Far West,* Boston: Houghton Mifflin, 1928.

"Who Hath a Book?" by Wilbur D. Nesbit, from *Time for Poetry,* Chicago: Scott, Foresman, 1961.

JOHN F. KENNEDY

by CHARLES P. GRAVES

Illustrated by Paul Frame

A Discovery Book in the Yearling Biography Series

I. THE STORY

When John F. Kennedy was a United States Senator, he wrote a book called *Profiles in Courage*. This book is about several great Americans who had the determination to do what they thought was right. John Kennedy admired this kind of bravery. In many ways, he was courageous himself. As a boy, he fought to win in sports. As a Navy lieutenant, he swam miles to save his shipwrecked crew. As a politician, he stood fast for the things in which he believed: freedom, equality, peace. Kennedy's presidency was called the New Frontier because he wanted America to push ahead to a better way of life for all. He was full of fun and zest, and he loved to romp with his children in the White House. Kennedy's greatest hope was that children everywhere would never know a world war. His work did much to make this vision possible.

II. PREREADING DISCUSSION QUESTIONS

The questions which follow are illustrative of the kinds which teachers can prepare for the purpose of releasing children to reveal how *they feel* about some of the same larger ideas and bigger meanings contained in the book *before* it is read.

About Frontiers
1. It is possible for a person to become a pioneer in many ways—on many different kinds of *frontiers*. Today, in fact, it is next to impossible to pick up a daily newspaper and not find an article about a *new frontier* that's been opened, or a modern

pioneer-hero—a new frontiersman of our own time. Today's *frontiers,* it seems, can be almost anything—new ideas, new places, new causes, new ways of thinking or doing things, new inventions, new organizational ways, and so forth. What examples of these "new fronts" or *frontiers* can you think of? How can you explain why they are referred to as *frontiers?* Are they really?

2. What modern-day pioneers—frontiersmen—do you know about? How famous or important does a person have to be to be given such a title?

About Reminiscences

3. What things do people (such as teachers, neighbors, employers) notice and remember about others when, after not having seen them for five or ten years, they are asked "to describe what they remember best about them?"

4. Try to think about someone you haven't seen for several years—perhaps someone who was in one of your classes at school, but who has since moved away. Make a list of the qualities which you remember that you think describes such a person best.

About Handicaps

5. A very common statement that many of us hear numerous times is "But the *odds* are all against you!" Generally this "advice" is given by someone who cares about us—cares enough to try to keep us from being disappointed. Usually, when such a person says something like this to us, he's trying to be *realistic, practical, logical,* and is basing his judgment on his past experiences or an analysis of what appears to him to be an impossible situation.

With the people mentioned below, tell what the *impossible situations* could be and who it is who is making the statement: "But the *odds* are all against you!"

a. an athlete
b. a person who wants to be elected to an office
c. a person who has an injured back (or arm or leg)

d. a person who is trying to win an art or music contest
e. a wounded soldier who is trying to rescue someone else
f. a person who is trying to go to college
g. a person who is trying to get the best mark on a test

6. Many of the world's greatest achievements have been made by men and women who were told that "they couldn't possibly succeed." What is it that makes a person try over and over again? Is it a special "something" that only a few people have, or is it something we all have? Why do so many of us give up (or feel like giving up) so easily? Which of the following statements do you hear most often and why?

a. "I might just as well give up. What's the use in trying?"
b. "If at first you don't succeed, try, try again."

III. PREREADING ACTIVITIES

1. People, animals, places, and things have been given *nicknames* for one reason or another. Some of these nicknames have been creative, some funny, and some uninteresting or with little "sense" behind them. Do some research and try to find out all you can about the reasons that we give nicknames to people and things. Make a list of famous people and their nicknames; another list of famous places with nicknames; another of things; and still another of animals. Some starters might include: Chevrolet—"Chevvy"; Thomas Jackson—"Stonewall Jackson"; Richard—"Dick"; Very Important Person—"V.I.P."; Metropolitan Opera—"The Met"; Pennsylvania—"Pa."; a ship—"Old Ironsides"; District of Columbia—"D.C."; a tiger—"a cat," and so forth.
2. Some families name certain things after their children—things such as horses, cabins, boats, cars, trees, etc., possessions of all kinds. Make a collection of as many of these as you can.

IV. POSTREADING DISCUSSION QUESTIONS

1. Tell how you feel about the statements below. What do you think they mean? What kind of a person in what kind of a situation is likely to express himself in this way?

   a. "It's nothing more than political talk, that's all!"
   b. "Hrumph! Not on your life! What's in it for me, anyway?"
   c. "When things get tough, the tough get going!"
   d. "In a *democracy*, people cannot be ignorant *and* free!"

2. On page 68, President Kennedy said, "It really does not matter as far as you and I are concerned." (He was talking about a nuclear war's killing millions of people.) "What really matters is all the children." What do you think he meant by this? Didn't he care about adults? Was he in favor of a nuclear war as long as the children wouldn't be harmed?

V. HELPING CHILDREN TO REVEAL THEIR COMPREHENSION

1. Make and display models of U.S. warships 1800-1950.
2. Draw or make a relief map of the South Pacific depicting an enlarged area surrounding the Solomon Islands and revealing, particularly, Plum Pudding Island and Ferguson Passage.
3. Beginning with the year 1926, make a "Time-Line Career Map" of John F. Kennedy's interests, experiences, accomplishments.
4. John F. Kennedy's campaign slogan "The New Frontier" was not a *place* but a way of life he dreamed of for all Americans. It was an idea he had which he felt to be more important than any battlefront. He wanted everyone to become "pioneers" on many different fronts in this New Frontier—in education, science, employment, civil rights, and so forth. How were these ideas new and different? Why did he think changes would bring a better life for more people? Suppose you were going on television to explain one or more of these and invite the American people to become pioneers. What would you say?

5. John F. Kennedy *inju*
twenty-five years *he wa*
learned to live *with eve*
and numerous *operations*
one of his most *courage*
most painfully. *Perhaps it*
back he was able to *win a*
age he was Senator *from*
prevent him from *playing*
from playing with his *young*
Kennedy's back was a *help*
have made any difference *to*
made the Harvard varsity *swim*
to make some guesses and *write*
biographies of JFK. You *migh*
Back."

6. Interview several people *you kno*
parties or coffee klatches. (1) *Write*
day tea party. (2) Read *Chapter*
found in the book *Alice's Adventure*
Carroll. After you finish, write a *brie*
remember about that particular *tea pa*
and read several accounts of the *"Bos*
then write a brief description of *what*
that particular tea party. (4) Try to *im*
type Boston Tea Parties" were like *as th*
Kennedy for her son John, who *was*
Senator.

Compare your four tea-party *descriptio*
for? Who attended? How were they *alike*
What resulted?

VI. RELATED-TO-READING EXPERIE

See "Learning Experiences through Biographical *Com*
213-221.

IV. POSTREADING DISCUSSION QUESTIONS

1. Tell how you feel about the statements below. What do you think they mean? What kind of a person in what kind of a situation is likely to express himself in this way?

   a. "It's nothing more than political talk, that's all!"
   b. "Hrumph! Not on your life! What's in it for me, anyway?"
   c. "When things get tough, the tough get going!"
   d. "In a *democracy,* people cannot be ignorant *and* free!"

2. On page 68, President Kennedy said, "It really does not matter as far as you and I are concerned." (He was talking about a nuclear war's killing millions of people.) "What really matters is all the children." What do you think he meant by this? Didn't he care about adults? Was he in favor of a nuclear war as long as the children wouldn't be harmed?

V. HELPING CHILDREN TO REVEAL THEIR COMPREHENSION

1. Make and display models of U.S. warships 1800-1950.
2. Draw or make a relief map of the South Pacific depicting an enlarged area surrounding the Solomon Islands and revealing, particularly, Plum Pudding Island and Ferguson Passage.
3. Beginning with the year 1926, make a "Time-Line Career Map" of John F. Kennedy's interests, experiences, accomplishments.
4. John F. Kennedy's campaign slogan "The New Frontier" was not a *place* but a way of life he dreamed of for all Americans. It was an idea he had which he felt to be more important than any battlefront. He wanted everyone to become "pioneers" on many different fronts in this New Frontier—in education, science, employment, civil rights, and so forth. How were these ideas new and different? Why did he think changes would bring a better life for more people? Suppose you were going on television to explain one or more of these and invite the American people to become pioneers. What would you say?

5. John F. Kennedy injured his back in 1936, and for the next twenty-five years he was reminded of it. It was a *handicap* he learned to live with even though it caused him frequent pain and numerous operations. Perhaps it could be said that during one of his most courageous moments, his back bothered him most painfully. Perhaps it could be said that as a result of his back he was able to win a Pulitzer prize. At thirty-six years of age he was Senator from Massachusetts but his back didn't prevent him from playing football; neither did it keep him from playing with his young children. Do you think John F. Kennedy's back was a *help* or a *handicap* to him? Would it have made any difference to his future—and ours—if he had made the Harvard varsity swimming team? Suppose you were to make some guesses and write another chapter to the many biographies of JFK. You might call it "A View from the Back."

6. Interview several people you know who frequently give tea parties or coffee klatches. (1) Write a description of a modern-day tea party. (2) Read Chapter VII, "A Mad Tea-Party," found in the book *Alice's Adventures in Wonderland* by Lewis Carroll. After you finish, write a brief description of what you remember about that particular tea party. (3) Go to the library and read several accounts of the "Boston Tea Party" of 1773, then write a brief description of what you found out about that particular tea party. (4) Try to imagine what the "New-type Boston Tea Parties" were like as they were given by Mrs. Kennedy for her son John, who was trying to be elected Senator.

Compare your four tea-party descriptions. What were they for? Who attended? How were they alike? How different? What resulted?

VI. RELATED-TO-READING EXPERIENCES

See "Learning Experiences through Biographical Comparisons," pp. 213-221.

VII. VOCABULARY THAT MAY NEED DEVELOPING

Word Techni-codes: Almost every profession, occupation, or specialized area of work or play has a particular *technical* vocabulary which people use in order to communicate quickly, clearly, and accurately. But to an "outsider," frequently these technical words seem as hard to understand as a secret code. Using the following words as a starting place, some children may find it exciting and valuable to break these "Techni-codes":

Nautical Techni-codes		Political Techni-codes	
port	*starboard*	*6th precinct*	*primary*
aft	*forward*	*8th district*	*campaign*
topside	*rigging*	*polls*	*page boy*
galley	*bulkhead*	*inaugural*	*candidate*
hatch	*campaign*	*platform*	*opponent*

VIII. OTHER SELECTIONS ON A SIMILAR THEME: A SELECTED BIBLIOGRAPHY

Beard, Charles Austin. *The Presidents in American History.* N.Y.: Julian Messner, 1961.

Dalgliesh, Alice. *Ride on the Wind.* N.Y.: Scribner's, 1956.

Daugherty, Sonia. *Ten Brave Men.* Philadelphia: Lippincott, 1951.

Dooley, Thomas A. *Doctor Tom Dooley: My Story.* N.Y.: Farrar, Straus, 1962.

Graham, Shirley. *Booker T. Washington: Educator of Hand, Head, and Heart.* N.Y.: Julian Messner, 1955.

———. and George Lipscomb. *Dr. George Washington Carver: Scientist.* N.Y.: Julian Messner, 1949.

McNeer, May, and Lynd Ward. *Armed with Courage.* Nashville, Tenn.: Abingdon, 1957.

Manton, Jo. *The Story of Albert Schweitzer.* N.Y.: Abelard-Schuman, 1955.

Peare, Catherine Owens. *The FDR Story.* N.Y.: Crowell, 1962.

Poetry

"The Charge of the Light Brigade" by Alfred, Lord Tennyson, available in many editions.

"Heartbeat of Democracy" by Virginia Brasier, from *The Saturday Evening Post*, January 23, 1943.

"O Captain! My Captain!" by Walt Whitman, from *Leaves of Grass*, available in many editions.

"Paul Revere's Ride" by Henry Wadsworth Longfellow, available in many editions.

"The Pioneer" by Arthur Guiterman, from *I Sing the Pioneer*, N.Y.: Dutton, 1926.

"A Song of Greatness" by Mary Austin, from *The Children Sing in the Far West*, Boston: Houghton Mifflin, 1928.